Nigeria's Book of Firsts

A Handbook of Pioneer Nigerian Citizens, Institutions and Events

by

N. Nik Onyechi

First UK edition, published in Great Britain in 2020 by Regents Court Press

An imprint of Regents Court Press Ltd, St Albans, Hertfordshire, UK

ISBN: 978 1 9163084 3 5

British Library Cataloguing-in-Publication Data

A catalogue record for this book is available from the British Library

First published in 1989 by Nigeriana Publications, 52 Christ Church Road, PO Box 691, Owerri, Nigeria

Typeset by Regents Court Press Ltd

Cover by Hello Lovely Design

I dedicate this book to:

THE NIGERIAN LIBRARIAN.....whose invaluable contributions to the growth and dissemination of knowledge and information have remained largely unacknowledged.

CONTENTS

LIST OF ILLUSTRATIONS

FOREWORD

My generation may not have fought for Nigeria's independence. We are, however, living witnesses of, and participants in, the nation's ever unfolding history and drama. It is therefore apt that this book should appear now to capture and document (especially for posterity) these events as they occur.

Nigeria's Book of Firsts is unique in more ways than one. It not only chronicles our nation's pace-setting, trail-blazing achievers, but also provides cognate biographical/background information on subjects covered. Coverage is primarily individuals, institutions and events which are epoch-making in the context of pre- and post-colonial Nigeria. This is a completely updated edition of the first, which was published over thirty years ago. Understandably, it incorporates a lot more in content, flair and currency.

I am personally quite excited that this ready-reference work was packaged by a professional colleague: Sir N. Nik Onyechi, retired Head of the Department of Information Science and Dean of the School of Industrial Sciences, Federal Polytechnic, Nekede, Owerri, an eminently qualified, experienced and exposed library science practitioner, educator and administrator.

I am quite confident that millions of information-conscious Nigerians (and non-Nigerians alike): students, researchers, business executives, communication practitioners, diplomatic/foreign missions as well as libraries, schools/colleges, and many individuals, will derive huge excitement and satisfaction from this book. I unequivocally recommend it to all!

Prof. L. O. Aina
National Librarian
National Library of Nigeria
Abuja
Nigeria

April 23, 2020

ACKNOWLEDGEMENTS

In assembling the copious mass of data associated with a work of this magnitude, one undoubtedly relied on the goodwill and support of individuals, organisations and sources too numerous to individually acknowledge. The under-mentioned are thus only a representative few.

Dr Mark Freeman, my publishing consultant, and his team for their abiding faith in the merit of this work, for unrelentingly 'pushing', guiding, directing me all the way, as well as for technical, even financial support freely given.

I am equally grateful to my colleagues in the library and information field, notably the National Librarian Prof. L. O. Aina, the heads of libraries and staff of national, university/polytechnic and public libraries in Owerri; and the National Archives (in Enugu, Owerri and Ibadan). Similarly, the following bibliographical and biographical sources were of great value: Ralph Uwechue's: *Africa Who's Who*; *Makers of Modern Africa*; and the *Daily Times* group of newspapers, especially *Headlines* and *Newswatch* magazine.

I am equally indebted to my ICT crew of Umez Okereke, Felix Ekeh and Benlyn Benjamin for so dexterously complementing my tedious, manual 'analogue' information/data-gathering techniques with modern 'digital' online methods, thus bridging the generation gap.

Special thanks also go to my editorial/desktop team at Daystar Prints: Jude, Favour and Esther for their pains and patience in typing and retyping the manuscript in response to my seemingly unending corrections.

Last and certainly not the least my adorable wife, Nkolika (Ngalaba), and children Ijay (Adaora), Ginika (Adaudo), Muchy (Omena-Nwayoo), Njideka (Afu-obiesieike) and Obiora (Obata-Ozua) for all their moral support and encouragement. God bless!

PREFACE

Nigeria's Book of Firsts is at once a ready-reference guide and a general reading text on notable individuals, organisations and events connected, one way or the other, with Nigeria that have the distinction of being 'firsts', i.e. pioneers, trail-blazers and pace-setters in their various fields of endeavour. 'Firsts' are usually revered, celebrated or even idolised the world over. At the present level of our nation's evolution, this *Book of Firsts* has become compelling not only for posterity but for our present individual knowledge and information. Herein lies the justification for this book.

Nigeria's Book of Firsts is also a biographical source, albeit of an uncommon kind. Whereas virtually every other biographical publication highlights principally, if not exclusively, the high and mighty in politics, governance or business, leaving out other 'successful' achievers, here, the coverage spans the entire spectrum of human achievement: the arts, professions, sport, religion, etc.

This second edition has not only substantially enhanced the scope, quality and currency of the earlier edition published thirty years ago, but has added extra flair and sophistication through the inclusion of a sample photo gallery of these 'greats'. As with the earlier edition, over 1,000 entries are covered over virtually all subject fields including politics and government, sports, armed forces, mass media and assorted professions.

The special chapter focusing on women was retained to spotlight the giant strides which Nigerian women have continued to make in the polity.

Entries are grouped into broad subject headings (as in the contents) with sub-divisions where appropriate, e.g. in education, politics and government and sport. Within each subject grouping, entries are then presented in as logical a sequence as is possible.

To facilitate access to entries and thus enhance the book's usability, an index has been provided. The information content of *Nigeria's Book of Firsts* is derived from usually reliable sources following extensive literature searches and returns from questionnaires. A notable feature of this edition is the huge input of online (Internet) information into the book's data bank. Notwithstanding the foregoing, *Nigeria's Book of Firsts* cannot claim infallibility or absolute authoritativeness, especially given bureaucratic and other obstacles associated with information/data-gathering in developing societies such as Nigeria.

We therefore must see this epoch-making publication, even in its second edition, as still work-in-progress: a process rather than a destination, towards whose ultimate perfection every patriotic citizen is here enjoined to key in.

Nigeria's Book of Firsts as it originally appeared in 1989.

COPY IN THE POSSESSION OF REGENTS COURT PRESS LTD.

1 ARMED FORCES

NIGERIA'S 1ST (MILITARY) COUP D'ETAT

Occurred on January 15, 1966 under the leadership of Major Chukwuma Kaduna Nzeogwu. Generally referred to as 'the Major's Coup'. Several civilian and military leaders died in the coup, including the then *Sardauna* of Sokoto, Ahmadu Bello; Prime Minister Abubakar Tafawa Balewa; Chief S. L. Akintola, then Premier of (defunct) Western Nigeria; and Chief Okotie-Eboh, Federal Minister of Finance.

Africa's 1st military coup occurred in 1952 when Colonel Abdel Nasser seized power in Egypt and sent King Faruk into exile.

From Okpanam, Delta State, Major Nzeogwu was born in Kaduna in 1937; attended St John's College, Kaduna, 1950-55; joined the Nigerian Army as Cadet in 1959, and rose to Major/Senior Instructor, Military Academy, Kaduna. Was killed in action on the Nsukka war front early August 1967 while fighting on the Biafran side in the Nigerian Civil War, 1967-70.

NIGERIA'S 1ST MILITARY HEAD OF STATE

Major-General Johnson Thomas Umunakwe Augiyi-Ironsi, from January 17, 1966 to July 29, 1966.

For biodata, see: *1st Nigerian Army Major-General.*

1ST NIGERIAN ARMY MAJOR-GENERAL

Major-General Johnson Thomas Umunakwe Aguiyi-Ironsi, appointed February 16, 1965. Also appointed General Officer Commanding (GOC), Nigeria Army, taking over from Major-General Christopher E. Welby-Everard, the retired expatriate GOC, Nigeria Army. Nigeria Army was a child of the West African Frontier Force which ceased to exist in 1957 when Ghana pulled out to form her own army.

From Umuahia-Ibeku, Abia State, Ironsi was born in March 1924. He joined the army in 1942, was commissioned in 1949 after undergoing military training in England. Appointed Equerry to Queen Elizabeth II of England on her visit to Nigeria in 1956. After further military training at Imperial Defence College, England, he acted for a while in 1961 as Major-General, commanding the UN Peace-Keeping Force in the Congo, after which he became military attaché to the Nigerian High Commission in London.

Following Nigeria's 1st coup on January 15, 1966, Ironsi took over as Nigeria's 1st Military Head of State and Supreme Commander of Nigeria's Armed Forces. Unfortunately, he was soon killed in a military mutiny at Ibadan on July 30, 1966 while a guest of Lt-Col. Adekunle Fajuyi, then military governor of then Western Region.

See also: *1st Nigerian to head the Nigerian Army; 1st Military Head of State of Nigeria.*

1ST ARMY GENERAL

General Yukubu Gowon, in October 1971.

Born in Lur, Pankshin, Plateau State, on October 19, 1934, he attended St Barth's School, Wusasa, Zaria, 1939-49; Government College, Zaria, 1950-53; Officer Cadet Training School, Teshie, Ghana, 1954; Eaton Hall, Chester, England, 1955; Royal Military Academy, Sandhurst, England, 1955-56; Young Officers' College, Hythe, Westminster, England, 1957; Staff College, Camberley, England, 1962; Joint Services Colleges, Latimer, England, 1965.

Enlisted in the Army in May 1954; appointed Adjutant, 4th Battalion, 1960-61; promoted to Major, 1962, Lt-Col., 1963, Major-General, June 1967; Chief of Staff, 1966; Head of the Federal Government and Commander-in-Chief, 1966-75. Retired in 1975. Later read for and obtained a Doctorate degree in Political Science from Warwick University, England.

NIGERIA'S 1ST MILITARY UNIVERSITY

Nigerian Defence Academy, converted to a military university with effect from September 1985.

See also entry under: EDUCATION – GENERAL.

1ST NIGERIAN ARMY MEDICAL DOCTOR

Dr Henry Edmund Olufemi Adefope, who, after qualifying as a medical doctor from the University of Glasgow, Scotland, in 1952, enlisted in the Nigerian Army (professional corps) in 1963, as Captain. Born on March 15, 1926 in Kaduna, Kaduna State; attended St Michael's School, Kaduna, 1931-32; Government School, Kaduna, 1933-35; St Peter's School, Faji, Lagos, 1935-37; CMS Grammar School, Lagos, 1938-44; University of Glasgow, Scotland, 1947-52. Served as Medical Officer in the (defunct) Western Nigeria government prior to enlisting in the Army in 1963. Promoted to Lt-Col., 1965; Director of Medical Services, Nigeria Army, 1967-75; promoted to Colonel, 1967; Brigadier, 1973. Was appointed Federal Commissioner (Minister) of Labour, 1975-78; External Affairs, 1978-79.

1ST NIGERIAN REAR-ADMIRAL

Joseph Edet Akinwale Wey, promoted to Rear-Admiral on August 1, 1967, by virtue of which he took charge of the entire Nigerian navy.

A sailor and marine engineer, he was born on March 7, 1918 in Calabar, Cross River State. Attended Holy Cross School, Lagos; Methodist School, Ikot Ekpene; St Patrick's College, Calabar. Joined the Nigerian Navy (then Nigerian Marines) in 1939 as engineer and cadet-in-intraining. Was one of the first to be enlisted and commissioned Sub-Lieutenant and Engineer, Nigerian Navy, 1956-59. He rose rapidly, becoming Captain, Chief of Naval Staff in 1963; Commodore, 1964; Rear-Admiral, 1967-71; Vice-Admiral, 1971. Other posts held include Federal Commissioner (Minister) of Establishments and Service Matters, 1967; Chief of Staff, Supreme Headquarters, 1973-75. Retired in 1975.

Also: *1st Nigerian to attain the rank of Vice-Admiral (the Navy's equivalent of Army Lieutenant-General), in 1973; 1st Indigenous Officer to attain the rank of Commander in the Royal Nigerian Navy, March 23, 1962.*

NIGERIA'S 1ST WARSHIP

NNS Obuma, formerly *NNS Nigeria*, built in 1965 by a Dutch firm, valued at N100m, it is used for training naval personnel and showing the flag of Nigeria in West African and European countries. The ship has been commanded by Vice-Admirals Aduwo and Augustus Aikhomu, and Navy Commander Andrew Kaja.

NIGERIA'S 1ST INSPECTOR-GENERAL OF POLICE

Mr C. W. Duncan CBE, a Briton, appointed on April 1, 1930 and served until 1935. Despite the amalgamation of Northern and Southern Nigeria in 1914, the Northern and Southern Police Forces continued to operate separately until April 1, 1930, when both were merged to form the present Nigeria Police Force (NPF) commanded by an Inspector-General. The title of Inspector-General was replaced with Commissioner in 1937, but the original title was reverted to in 1951 after the introduction of a new Constitution. The designation Commissioner was thenceforth assigned to officers in charge of the Regions, and later, States. In 1968 the Nigeria Police became a unified Force, leading to the absorption of the Local Government and Native Authority Police Forces in the country into the Force.

1ST NIGERIAN INSPECTOR-GENERAL OF POLICE

Mr Louis Orok Edet, appointed April 1, 1964, taking over from the last expatriate Inspector-General, Mr J. E. Hodge. Retired in August 1966.

Born on August 29, 1913 in Duketown Calabar, Cross River State, Edet attended Sacred Heart School, Calabar, and Bonny Grammar School, Rivers State. Joined the Nigeria Police Force (NPF) as Clerk in 1931; promoted to Sub-Inspector, August 1945; Assistant Superintendent of Police (ASP), 1949. Attended training courses at Ryton-on-Dunsmore in England in 1953, 1957 and 1960. Promoted to Assistant Comissioner and

Deputy Comissioner in 1960. From December 1960 to 1961 he commanded the 1st Contigent, NPF, to serve under the United Nations in the Congo. In 1961 he became Commissioner; promoted to Deputy Inspector General, 1962; appointed Inspector-General, March 1964. On retirement, he was appointed recruitment attaché in the Nigerian High Commission in London, 1966-68; Commissioner for Home Affairs and Information in then South-Eastern State, 1968-72. Conferred CFR, Queen's Police Medal (QPM) and CBE. Died January 17, 1979.

1ST UNDERGRADUATE VICTIM OF POLICE SHOOTING

Mr Adekunle Adepeju, a second-year Agriculture undergraduate, who was shot dead by the police on Monday February 1, 1971, during a police/student riot at the University of Ibadan. Some others were wounded. Students were protesting the de-humanising feeding and welfare conditions of Zik's Hall in particular, and the entire campus in general. The Vice-Chancellor had invited the police to help contain the students' action, begun on Saturday January 30, 1971, when a major confrontation ensued. February 1 is now observed every year as a lecture-free day among Nigerian universities nation-wide in commemoration.

1ST POLICE GOVERNOR(S)

Police Commissioner Joseph Deshi Gomwalk, Governor of (defunct) Benue-Plateau state; Police Commissioner Alhaji Audu Bako, Governor of Kano State; and Police Superintendent Usman Faruk of North-Western State, appointed May 27, 1967 following the creation of these states. Served until their retirement in July 1975.

See also entry under: POLITICS AND GOVERNMENT – *GOVERNORS/ PREMIERS.*

NIGERIA'S 1ST PRISON

Broad Street Prison, Lagos, established in 1872 to accommodate 300 prisoners. However, the Prison Ordinance providing for the establishment of prisons was passed along with the Supreme Court Ordinance in 1875. Broad Street Prison is no longer in use.

NIGERIA'S 1ST DIRECTOR (HEAD) OF PRISONS

Mr C. W. Duncan, October 29, 1920 to November 1, 1921.

See also: *Nigeria's 1st Inspector-General of Police.*

1ST NIGERIAN DIRECTOR OF PRISONS

Chief Frank Sunmola Giwa-Osagie, October 3, 1961 to April 30, 1972. From Benin, Bendel State, he was born on March 14, 1917 and attended King's College, Lagos and Prison's Staff Colleges in Wakefield and Balmoral (UK). He joined the Nigeria Prisons immediately on leaving college. Was conferred the chieftaincy title of *Obabaifo* of Benin. Died on June 21, 1987.

The title of the head of Nigeria Prisons has changed from Director to Controller General.

2 ARTS AND CULTURE

1ST INTERNATIONAL FESTIVAL OF THE ARTS AND CULTURE HOSTED BY NIGERIA

The 2nd World Black and African Festival of Arts and Culture (Festac) which was held simultaneously in Lagos and Kaduna from January 15 to February 12, 1977, with Ethiopia as the *Star* country.

The Festival is an effort by Black and African peoples all over the world to come together and unleash a new cultural awakening among African and Black people. The 1st Black (International) Arts Festival was held in Dakar, Senegal, March/April 1966 at which Nigeria was declared *Star* country and requested to host the 2nd session of the Festival in 1970.

However, because of Nigeria's Civil War the festival had to be postponed to 1975, and as a result of the change of Gowon's government in July 1975, to 1977. Watched by seven other Heads of State, it was declared open by then Head of State, General Obasanjo. Festac Village, Badagry, was built for the Festival, and meant to house over 14,000 people; so also was Durbar Hotel, Kaduna.

1ST NIGERIAN FESTIVAL OF THE ARTS AND CULTURE

Held in 1970 in Lagos. The well-known *Nkpokiti* acrobatic dance group from Umunze, Anambra State, won the 1st Prize (gold gong).

1ST NIGERIAN RECIPIENT OF A NOBEL PRIZE

Prof. Akinwande Oluwole Soyinka (Wole Soyinka), who won the 1986 Nobel Prize for literature (also the 1st Black winner).

See entry under: AWARDS.

1ST AHIAJOKU LECTURE

Entitled 'A Matter of Identity: *Aha me fula*', delivered by Prof. Michael Joseph Chukwudalu Echeruo on Friday November 30, 1979 at the Imo State government-owned Multi-Purpose Hall, Owerri. The Ahiajoku Lecture series has become an annual event marked by scholarly lectures on aspects of Igbo history, tradition and culture, delivered by Igbo intellectuals. It is usually held on the first Friday in November every year. Ahiajoku itself is the 'god' of Harvest in Igbo-land.

For biodata see: *1st Vice-Chancellor, Abia State University, Uturu*, **entry *under:*** EDUCATION – UNIVERSITIES.

NIGERIA'S 1ST DURBAR

Held in 1911. It is an annual event celebrated in several cities of Nothern Nigeria, e.g. Kano, Katsina, Sokoto, Zaria and Bida, to mark the end of Ramadan and is also shared with Eid al-Fitr Muslim holidays. The Durbar itself begins with prayers, followed by a parade of the Emir and his entourage on horses accompanied by musicians and ending at the Emir's palace. Durbar was introduced into Nigeria by Colonial administrators with political objectives in mind to mark the proclamation of Queen Victoria the Empress of colonial India in 1877. Today it has only cultural entertainment and ceremonial value. The word 'Durbar' is of Persian origin.

1ST ARGUNGU FISHING FESTIVAL

The festival commenced in 1934 as mark of the centuries-old hostility between the Sokoto caliphate and the Kebbi kingdom. Basically, it is annual 4-day festival in the state of Kebbi, commemorated by the citizens going fishing, with prizes awarded to those who catch the largest. Kebbi, in the North-Western part of Nigeria, is blessed with fertile land and the citizens are reputed fishermen and farmers.

The festival has grown into a global tourist attraction encompassing cultural activities, e.g. dancing, singing and other traditional arts displays.

Grand durbar in Kaduna, 1977, staged as part of the 2nd World Black and African Festival of Arts and Culture (Festac). See page 7.

PHOTOGRAPH: HELINÄ RAUTAVAARA (CC-A 2.0 GENERIC).

1ST EYO (LAGOS) CULTURAL FESTIVAL

The first procession in Lagos, Nigeria, of the Eyo Cultural Festival (Aka Adamu Orisha Play) was on February 20, 1854, to commemorate the life of Oba Akintoye of Lagos. The festival itself comprises dancers, known as 'masquerades', who 'escort the soul of a departed Lagos king or chief as well as to usher in a new one'.

The word 'Eyo' also refers to the masquerades who come out during the festival. Its origin is found in the inner workings of the secret societies of Lagos. The white-clad Eyo masquerades, who are believed to represent the spirits of the dead, accompanied by huge throngs of followers, process from Idumota to the Iga Idunga-ran palace. Eyo (Lagos) festival is widely believed to be the forerunner of the now much celebrated Brazil Carnival.

1ST NIGERIAN FEMALE TO WIN THE 'DISTINGUISHED AUTHORS AWARD'

Dr Mrs Tess Onwueme, who along with two males, Profesor M. J. C. Echeruo and Chief Arthur Nwankwo, won the award for 1987. The presentation ceremony took place at the National Theatre, Lagos on February 2, 1988. The award, Nigeria's highest literary prize, was for her total contribution to the development of literature in the country.

A playwright and lecturer, Mrs Onwueme was born on September 8, 1955 in Ogwashi-Uku, Delta state, and holds Bachelors and Masters degrees in English and literature from Obafemi Awolowo University (1979 and 1982) and a PhD degree in literature from the University of Benin, 1987. She is a prolific writer with over twelve plays to her credit.

See also: *WOMEN.*

NIGERIA'S 1ST PROFESSIONAL ACTOR

Orlando Martins, pioneer Nigerian film and stage actor and movie star in the late 1940s, when he was acclaimed one of Britain's most prominent and Top 15 favorite actors.

Born on December 8, 1899 in Lagos. He left Nigeria for the USA as a young lad in 1917 having dropped out of Eko Boys' High School, Lagos. In the US from playing 'extras' ('Nubian slaves' or 'dummies' in the film industry), he rose to proper film roles and repertory theatre. Films he acted in include 'Sanders of the River' (1935); 'Simba' (1953); 'Safari' (1956); 'Tarzan and the Lost Safari' (1957); and 'Mr Moses' (1965). He had the distinction of having co-starred with American ex-president, Ronald Reagan.

Martins married (and later, divorced) his wife, Doris, who was part-Nigerian and part-English, on November 18, 1928. On his return to Nigeria, the then Lagos state Governor Mobolaji Johnson appointed him cultural Adviser to the State government, a position he held until his death on September 25, 1985. He was conferred Member of the Order of the Niger (MON).

1ST NIGERIAN SONG PLAYED AT A NOBEL PRIZE AWARD CEREMONY

'Akinla', composed by the late Fela Sowande. Played to introduce and mark the award presentation to Prof. Wole Soyinka of Nigeria, the 1986 Nobel Prize Award winner for Literature on December 17, 1986 in Stockholm, Sweden.

NIGERIA'S 1ST MUSEUM

The Jos Museum, established in 1952. Also Nigeria's largest museum.

NIGERIA'S 1ST NATIONAL STAMPS EXHIBITION

Opened in Lagos on April 11, 1969, organised by the Federal Ministry of Communications.

INDEPENDENT NIGERIA'S 1ST 'MADE-IN-NIGERIA' EXHIBITION

Held October 1 to 22, 1960 as one of a series of activities to mark Nigeria's attainment of independence. The exhibition was declared open by Prime Minister Alhaji Sir Abubakar Tafawa Balewa on Victoria Island, Lagos, soon after being sworn in as Prime Minister.

Each of the (then) three regions had a pavilion in which its own achievements and plans, as well as various aspects of its life and culture, were displayed.

1ST NATION-WIDE 'MISS NIGERIA' BEAUTY QUEEN

Grace Tinuke Oyelude, crowned 'Miss Nigeria' for 1957 in the grand finale contest held in Island Club, Lagos on Friday, April 5, 1957. The Miss Nigeria beauty pageant was launched by the *Daily Times* in 1957; it became a yearly event until the seventies when further contests were temporarily suspended. For that year (1957) there were 600 contestants nation-wide with eight at the grand finale.

From Isanlu-Makuta in Kabba Province of Kogi State, Tinuke was born on 16 November, 1931. At the time of winning, she was 24 years old and worked for then Kingsway Stores, Kano. Her award package included a cheque for £200 and a modeling contract with West African Publicity Ltd, a return air ticket to London and an electric refrigerator. After winning, she travelled to the UK to study nursing.

NIGERIA'S 1ST MISS WORLD CONTESTANT

Miss Yemisi Rosalind Balogun, now Mrs Idowu, who as an undergraduate won the crown in 1967 to represent Nigeria in Miss World.

1ST WINNER OF THE 'MR. NIGERIA' BEAUTY CONTEST

Kio Vincent Wokoma on April 12, 1987, in what should have been the 1986 edition of the contest. The contest, introduced in 1986, was organised by IAAMI – Kingsley Promotions (Nig.) Ltd. The final of the contest, staged at the National Theatre, Iganmu, Lagos, was preceded by zonal competitions in six venues: Port Harcourt, Enugu, Benin City, Kaduna, Jos and Ibadan. Prizes: a Santana GX saloon car; a return ticket to New York (USA) to represent Nigeria at the Mr Universe Competition; a monthly stipend of N500 during the reigning year.

Wokoma, from Rivers State, was born in 1961 and is 1.93m (6′4″) tall. He was a produce officer with Rivers State Ministry of Commerce and Industry at time of winning the award.

NIGERIA'S 1ST 'BEST-DRESSED-MAN' COMPETITION

Organised in 1961 by the *Daily Times* of Nigeria to conincide with the Miss Nigeria contest of same year.

1st place was won by Mr Felix Ijeh, then a member of staff of the Nigerian Broadcasting Corporation (NBC), by a unanimous verdict of the judges. He received the *Daily Times*-donated silver cup. Former member of staff of the British Transport Commission in Manchester, England, Ijeh graduated in sociology. He was also a graduate of the Institute of Transport, and an Associate Member, London Academy of Music and Dramatic Art.

Also: *1st Nigerian (African) to win the Best-Dressed Man in Britain Award* – in 1959, in a final contest held in Liverpool City Hall and involving thirteen finalists, the 2nd and 3rd place winners being a Frenchman and a Londoner respectively.

NIGERIA'S 1ST TELEVISION LOCAL DRAMA SERIES

Village Headmaster, created by Segun Olusola, directed by Dejumo Lewis and first aired in 1956 – it ran to 1968 (audio). Starring Ted Mukoro, Femi Robinson, Justus Esiri, etc.

See also entry under: MASS MEDIA – BROADCASTING.

NIGERIA'S 1ST NOVEL IN THE ENGLISH LANGUAGE

The Palm Wine Drinkard, written by Amos Tutuola whose first volume was ready in 1949 and published in 1952 by Faber and Faber, a UK publishing firm.

From Abeokuta, Ogun State, Tutuola was born on October 21, 1923. He had very brief schooling at Salvation Army School, Ijemo-Abeokuta, before enlisting in the Royal Air Force as a coppersmith in 1944. He later served

Radio Nigeria, from where he retired in 1976. Since then he has engaged in farming and writing. His major works include *My Life in the Bush of Ghosts* (1954), *Simbi and the Satyr of the Dark Jungle* (1955); *Ajayi and His Inherited Poverty* (1967), *Feather Woman of the Jungle* (1962), *The Witch Herbalist of the Remote Town* (1981) and *Pauper, Brawler and Slanderer* (1987).

1ST NOVEL IN THE YORUBA LANGUAGE

Igbesi Aiye Emi Segilola, written by Isaac B. Thomas and published in 1929.

1ST NOVEL IN THE IGBO LANGUAGE

Omenuko, written by Pita Nwana and published in 1937.

Omenuko, by Pita Nwana, the first novel in the Igbo language, in this edition translated into English by Ernest Emenyonu.

ITEM IN THE POSSESSION OF REGENTS COURT PRESS LTD.

3 AWARDS

1ST NIGERIAN RECIPIENT OF A NOBEL PRIZE

Prof. Akinwande Oluwole Soyinka (popularly called Wole Soyinka) who won the 1986 Nobel Prize for Literature. Also the 1st African and Black man to win the prestigious award, Prof. Soyinka was described by the 200-year old Royal Swedish Academy (donors of the Nobel Prizes) as 'one of the finest dramatists/poets in the English Literature'.

The award was announced Thursday October 16, 1986 and ceremonially presented in Stockholm, Sweden on December 17, 1986. Its worth was about US $200,000.

From Abeokuta, Ogun State, Soyinka was born on January 13, 1934; attended Govenrment College, Ibadan; University College, Ibadan; University of Leeds, England. Joined the Theatre Arts Department, University of Ibadan, as Head, 1969-71. Appointed Professor of Dramatic Literature, University of Ife (now Obademi Awolowo University), Ile-Ife, in 1972, and resigned in 1986. Held several visiting professorships in African, European and Amerian universities. Authored numerous publications including *The Interpreters*, *Trials of Brother Jero*, *The Man Died*, *Prison Notes* and *Ake.* Conferred Commander of the Federal Republic (CFR) by President Babangida in October 1986; Honorary DLitt, University of Leeds. Pioneer Chairman, Federal Road Safety Corps (FRSC), in 1979.

1ST NIGERIAN RECIPIENT OF THE KING FAISAL MEMORIAL AWARD

Sheikh Abubakar Mahmud Gumi, who was one of three recipients of the award, announced on January 14, 1987. The award, which carried a cash price of US $93,000, a gold medal and a certificate, was formally presented by King Fahd of Saudi Arabia on March 8, 1987. The other two recipients were a Briton and a New Zealander. The award was in recognition of Gumi's academic excellence and contribution to Islam, which included his translation of the Holy Quran into the Hausa language in 1974. The King

Wole Soyinka (see page 16), pictured in 2019.

PHOTOGRAPH: LEV RADIN, COURTESY OF SHUTTERSTOCK.

Faisal award, in honour of late King Faisal Abdul-Aziz, was established in 1977. Gumi was also the 1st African to win the award.

Born in Gumi village, Zamfara State, in 1922, Gumi attended Sokoto Provincial Middle School, 1940; Central Middle School, Jatau; Kano School of Arabic Studies; Sharia Law School, Kano, where he read Sharia Law, before proceeding to the Institute of Education, Bahtur, Ruddah, Sudan, for postgraduate studies.

Became Deputy Grand Khadi, Northern Nigeria, October 1960; later Grand Khadi. Established the Nigerian Embassy in Saudi Arabia. Was 1st Chairman, Nigeria Pilgrims Welfare Board, 1973; Chairman, Nigerian Teachers Institute, Kaduna. Bagged two honorary doctorate degrees in law in 1965 (University of Ibadan and ABU).

1ST NIGERIAN RECIPIENT OF THE INTERNATIONAL EDITOR-OF-THE-YEAR AWARD

Raymond Amos Ekpu, voted the International Editor-of-the-Year 1987, by the *World Press Review*, a US-based magazine. The award was announced in December 1987 and formally presented on Tuesday May 10, 1988 at the Overseas Press Club, New York, USA. Ekpu was the 15th recipient of the prestigious award as well as the 1st African. The honour was for his commitment to work in the 'public interest'.

The yearly award commenced in 1975, for outstanding editors outside the United States of America for 'courage, enterprise and leadership on an international level in advancing press freedom and responsibility, defending human rights, and fostering journalistic excellence'.

A mass communications graduate from the University of Lagos, Ekpu has at various times edited the *Chronicle* and *Sunday Times*, and has also been Chairman, Editorial Board, Concord Newspapers. Born on August 6,1948 in Abak, Cross Rivers State; attended Ibibio State College, Ikot-Ekpene; Holy Family College, Abak; University of Lagos; Indiana State University, Bloomington, Indiana, USA.

1ST NIGERIAN CONFERRED THE TITLE OF 'QUEEN'S PRIVY COUNCILLOR' (P.C.)

Rt Hon. Dr Nnamdi Azikiwe, on November 16, 1960 (his birthday), had the prestigious title of Member of Her Majesty's Privy Council conferred on him by Queen Elizabeth II. The swearing-in ceremony was performed on August 2, 1961.

For biodata see: *Nigeria's 1st President,* ***entry under*** POLITICS AND GOVERNMENT – HEADS OF STATE/GOVERNMENT.

1ST NIGERIAN 'GRAMMY' MUSIC AWARD RECIPIENT

Helen Folasade Adu (known as Sade), the celebrated London-based Nigerian musician who won the award in 1986 under the 'Best New Artist' category. The coveted Grammy Music Award was inaugurated by the National Academy of Arts and Science (USA) in 1958, covering about twenty different genres of music in America. The award represents the highest international musical recognition and honour.

From Ikere-Ekiti; attended Martinus School of Arts. Lead singer for Epongan group. She is best known for her popular 'Sweetest Taboo'.

Also the first African recipient, Sade Adu was born in 1959 of Nigerian father and expatriate (white) mother. Her record albums include *When Am I Going To Make A Living?*, *Diamond Life*, *Promise* and *Stronger than Pride*. She featured on the cover of *Ebony* and *Time* magazines.

1ST NIGERIAN AWARDED THE FRANKLIN MINT PEACE MEDAL

Chief Samuel Olasebikan Adebo on January 18, 1967, while serving as Nigeria's Ambassador and Permanent Representative at the United Nations in New York, USA, in recognition of his contribution 'in pursuit of world peace and understanding in the preceding year' (1966). He won the medal again the next year, 1968.

A lawyer, administrator and diplomat, Adebo was born on October 5, 1913 in Abeokuta, Ogun State; educated at St Peter's Day School, Abeokuta;

Abeokuta Grammar School, 1927-28; King's College, Lagos, 1929-32. Called to the Bar (Gray's Inn), London, 1948. Joined the Civil Service, and rose to Chief Secretary to the Western Nigeria Government and Head of the Civil Service, 1957-62. Appointed Nigeria's Ambassador and Permanent Representative to the UN, New York, USA, 1962-67; Under-Secretary-General, UN, and Executive Director, UN Institute of Training and Research, 1968-72; Chairman, National Universities Commission, 1975.

1ST NIGERIAN RECIPIENT OF THE 'INTERNATIONAL RECOGNITION AWARD'

Mrs Maryam Babangida, who bagged the prestigious award for the year 1988. The award was instituted in 1969 by the US-based New Future Foundation, and conferred annually to black women in Africa, United States and the Caribbean for fostering understanding, peace and progress among black women.

Given in recognition of her efforts/achievements and endeavours to eradicate drug abuse in Nigerian society.The award was received on her behalf by Mrs Amina Ahmadu, wife of Nigeria's Ambassador to the USA on April 15, 1988. Celebrated for her 'Better Life for Rural Women' programme.

1ST NIGERIAN (NON-AMERICAN) CONFERRED LIFE MEMBERSHIP OF THE U.S.-BASED NATIONAL ASSOCIATION FOR THE ADVANCEMENT OF COLORED PEOPLE (N.A.A.C.P.)

Bashorun Moshood Kashimawo Olawale Abiola, on Wednesday July 15, 1987, at the organisation's 78th annual convention held in New York, USA. It is America's biggest civil rights organisation.

An accountant, publisher, business tycoon, sports enthusiast, entrepreneur, and philanthropist, Abiola was born on August 24, 1937 in Abeokuta, Ogun State; attended Baptist Boys' High School, Abeokuta, 1951-56; University of Glasgow, Scotland, 1961-63. Had been Deputy Chief Accountant, Lagos University Teaching Hospital (LUTH), 1965-67; Controller, Pfizer Products Ltd, 1967-69; Controller, ITT (Nig.) Ltd, 1971;

Proprietor, Concord Press (Nig.) Ltd, (publisher of *Concord* papers). Conferred the traditional title *Aare Onakanfo* of Yoruba-land.

1ST NIGERIAN CONFERRED THE LEGION OF MERIT AWARD

Navy Captain Allison Madueke, Fleet Commander of Western Naval Command, Tuesday, May 5, 1987, by US President Ronald Reagan, for his exceptional meritorious conduct in the performance of his duties as Deputy Adviser at the Nigerian Embassy in Washington DC, USA, 1982-84.

Navy Captain Madueke hails from Inyi, Enugu State, and was one-time Governor, Anambra State, January 1984 to August 1985; Governor, Imo State, August 1985 to September 1986.

1ST NIGERIAN AWARDED 'HENRY DUNANT MEDAL'

Mr Justice Joseph Adetunji Adefarasin, who was conferred with the award at the 6th General Assembly of the World Red Cross and Red Crescent Societies held in Rio de Janeiro, Brazil, in 1987.

The award, the highest in the World Red Cross Movement, was in recognition of Adefarasin's contribution to the work of the Red Cross all over the world when he was President of the World Federation of the Red Cross Movement, 1977 to 1981.

For biodata see: *1st Nigerian (African) President of the World Federation of the Red Cross Movement,* ***entry under:*** MISCELLANEOUS.

1ST NIGERIAN RECIPIENT OF THE W.H.O. 'LEON BERNARD FOUNDATION AWARD'

Prof. Olikoye Ransome-Kuti in May 1986 for his outstanding accomplishments in the field of social medicine. The award was formally presented in Geneva, Switzerland. Also 1st African and 4th recipient of the award in the world.

The award was valued at 3,000 Swiss francs, and was donated by Prof. Ransome-Kuti to the Institute of Child Health and Primary Care of the College of Medicine, University of Lagos.

A paediatrician, Prof. Ransome-Kuti was appointed Nigeria's Minister of Health in September 1985. Before then he was Professor and Head of Paediatrics, College of Medicine, University of Lagos. Was also, for several years, Director of the Institute of Child Health of the institution. From Ijebu-Ode, Ogun State, Kuti was born on December 30, 1927; attended Abeokuta Grammar School, 1936-44; Higher College, Yaba, Lagos, 1946-47; University College, Ibadan; Trinity College, University of Dublin, Eire, 1948-54; Postgraduate Medical School, London, 1960-62.

On return to Nigeria, he was appoined Senior Registrar (Paediatrics), University of Ibadan, 1962-63. Later joined University of Lagos as lecturer in Paediatrics, 1963, and rose to Professor and Head, 1970-77. Fellow of the Royal College of Physicians, Edinburgh; Fellow, Nigerian Medical College of Paediatricians, 1972.

1ST NIGERIAN RECIPIENTS OF THE FRENCH NATIONAL MERIT AWARD

Dr S. O. Aje of the Department of Languages and Linguistics, University of Jos and Prof. Abiola Francis Irele of the University of Ibadan.
The award: *Chevaller dans' l'Ordre Des Palmes Academiques* (Knight of the Order of Academic Excellence) was made on July 17, 1986.

Prof. Irele, a linguist, was born on May 22, 1936 in Ora, Benin, Edo State; attended St Gregory's College, Lagos, 1949-54; Nigerian College of Arts, Science and Technology, Ibadan, 1955-57; University College, Ibadan, 1957-60; University of Paris, France, 1960-66. After a brief career in teaching and publishing, he joined University of Ibadan as Senior Lecturer, Department of Modern Languages in 1973 rising to Professor and Head of Department in 1977.

From Owo, Ondo State, Dr Aje was born on March 5, 1950; attended Universities of Caen and Paris (both in France), and obtained Diplome d'Etudes Superieures, 1973; BA, 1974, MA, 1977, and PhD, 1979, all in

French. A prolific writer, Dr Aje has been Head, Department of Languages and Linguistics, University of Jos, 1983-86, and a member of many learned societies including the African Literature Association (USA) and the African Literary Society of Nigeria.

1ST NIGERIAN RECIPIENT OF 'OSCAR D'ITALIA' AWARD

Isiaka Adams Osunde, a sculptor, in 1985; in recognition of his contributions and activities as a world-class artist.

From Benin, Edo State, Isiaka Osunde was lecturer and Head, Department of Fine Arts, Yaba College of Technology. His works were set in wood, stone, bronze and clay, and adorn many public buildings throughout the country including State House, Marina, Lagos. He possesses Fine Arts degrees from Ahmadu Bello University, Zaria, and the University of Kiev, a Diploma from the Academy of Fine Arts, and a postgraduate diploma in Design Education from Middlesex Polytechnic, London.

1ST NIGERIAN 'GRAND COMMANDER OF THE FEDERAL REPUBLIC OF NIGERIA' (GCFR)

General (retired) Olusegun Obasanjo. President Shehu Shagari performed the investiture on September 23, 1981. It is Nigeria's highest honour on its most distinguished citizens.

The other beneficiary on the same occasion, Rt Hon. Dr Nnamdi Azikiwe, Nigeria's 1st President and *Owelle* of Onitsha, could not attend in person on grounds of ill health.

For biodata on Obasanjo, see: *1st Nigerian Head of State to relinquish power voluntarily,* ***entry under:*** POLITICS AND GOVERNRMENT – HEADS OF STATE/GOVERNMENT.

1ST RECIPIENT(S) OF NIGERIA'S 'NATIONAL MERIT AWARD'

Prof. Chinua Achebe, Prof. Taslim Olawole Elias, Dr Abubakar Imam and Prof. Thomas Adeoye Lambo. These four jointly won the award for 1979, the same year it was instituted. The award, Nigeria's highest honour for academic excellence and notable contribution to national development, carried a N20,000 cash prize plus a certificate of authentic recognition. The annual award is usually made on October 1, the country's independence anniversary.

Chinua Achebe. A novelist and academician from Ogidi, Anambra State, he was born on November 16, 1930; educated at Government College, Umuahia, 1944-48; University College, Ibadan, 1949-53. A renowned broadcaster, Achebe was Head, Voice of Nigeria, Lagos, 1961-66. Also Professor of English, University of Massachusetts, Amherst, Mass., USA, 1972-75; University of Connecticut, USA; University of Nigeria. A literary giant, author of several novels including the classics *Things Fall Apart*, *No Longer at Ease* and *There Was a Country*.

Also: *1st Pro-Chancellor, Anambra State University of Technology, Enugu.*

T.O. Elias. ***For biodata see:*** *1st Nigerian Federal Attorney-General Minister of Justice,* ***entry under:*** POLITICS & GOVERNMENT – MINISTERS. ***Also:*** *Nigeria's 1st Attorney-General/Minister of Justice.*

Dr Abubakar Imam. An obstetrician and gynaecogist from Kano, he was born on July 13, 1931; attended Kaduna College, 1944-47; University College, Ibadan, 1948-53; University of Aberdeen, Scotland, 1953-56 and 1961-63. Appointed Chief Medical Officer, Kano State, on October 14, 1968. Member, Royal College of Obstetricians and Gynaecologists.

Prof. Adeoye Lambo. See: *1st Nigerian Deputy Director-General, World Health Organization (WHO),* ***entry under:*** MEDICINE.

1ST RECIPIENT OF THE ALL-AFRICA 'OKIGBO PRIZE' FOR POETRY

J. B. Tati Lontard, Congolese poet. The award was presented to him on Saturday, November 21, 1987, at the National Theatre, Iganmu, Lagos. The award was the highlight of the 7th annual conference of the Association of Nigerian Authors held in Lagos, November 18-21, 1987. Worth US $1,500 (N6,000), the prize, an annual event, was endowed by 1986 Nobel Laureate Prof. Wole Soyinka, in commemoration of one of Nigeria's foremost poets, the late Christopher Okigbo, slain during the 1967-70 Nigerian Civil War. Lontard, currently Congolese Minister of Culture, won the Okigbo prize with his collection *In Tradition du Songe*, published by Presence Africaine.

Christopher Okigbo was born on August 16, 1932 in Ojoto, Anambra State; attended Government College, Umuahia; University College, Ibadan, 1951-56, where he obtained an honours degree in Classics. Thereafter he went into teaching, publishing and librarianship, and writing poetry, winning 1st prize for Poetry at the 1st Festival of Negro Arts held in Dakar, Senegal, in 1966. On the outbreak of Nigeria's Civil War in 1966, he joined the Biafran side and was killed in action in October 1967

1ST RECIPIENT OF THE 'JOSE AWARD' FOR JOURNALISM

Isaac Akinkunmi in 1984. The *Jose* award was instituted by the *Daily Times of Nigeria (DTN)* newspaper, in honour of one of Nigeria's 'Fathers of Modern Journalism' (Alhaji (Dr) Babatunde Jose), for promoting the profession and practice of journalism in Nigeria.

Akinkunmi graduated in mass communication from the University of Lagos in 1981.

1ST WINNER OF THE U.A.C. 'MERIT AWARD' FOR JOURNALISTS

Mr Oluwaseun Oladapo Ogunseitan, on June 30, 1987, with his entry entitled 'Gas Leakage: Onne Faces Air Pollution Threat', an article published in the *Guardian,* Sunday December 1, 1985. The annual award, which carries a prize of a 10-week postgraduate course at the Thompson Foundation Institute, London, was instituted in January 1987 by United Africa Company (UAC) Nig. PLC, in association with UAC International, London, and the Nigerian Union of Journalists (NUJ), to promote the development of the profession and practice of journalism in Nigeria. Born on March 31, 1960, Ogunseitan attended Birch Freeman High School, Surulere-Lagos, 1972-77; The Polytechnic, Ibadan, 1977-79; University of Ibadan, 1979-84, graduating BSc (Zoology). Joined Guardian Newspapers on July 1, 1985 where he served as science and agriculture correspondent.

1ST NIGERIAN RECIPIENT OF THE U.S. SOCIETY FOR EDUCATION THROUGH ARTS (U.S.S.E.A.) AWARD

Prof. Solomon Wangboje, who won the coveted award for 1988 in recognition of his immense contributions in the field of creative arts and design at both national and International levels. Also known as the International Ziesfeld Award, it was bestowed on Prof. Wangboje.

Wangboje, a Professor of Arts at the University of Benin, was born in Ivbiaro-Owan in Edo State in 1933; attended Edo College, Benin-City; Nigerian College of Arts, Science and Technology, Zaria; Cranbrook Academy of Art, Michigan, USA (bagging the Master of Fine Art (MFA) degree in 1963); New York University, USA (bagging a PhD in June 1968). One-time Africa's Representative on the World Council of the International Society for Education through Art (INSEA).

4 BUILDING SCIENCES

1ST NIGERIAN SURVEYOR

Herbert Samuel Macaulay, who read Land Surveying and Civil Engineering in Plymouth, England from 1890 to 1893. On his return to Nigeria in 1893, he joined the colonial Civil Service as government surveyor in charge of Crown Agents.

See also: *1st Nigerian sponsored oveseas on scholarship for a professional course,* ***entry under:*** *EDUCATION – ACADEMIC DISTINCTIONS/HONOURS; Nigeria's 1st Political Party Leader,* ***entry under:*** *POLITICS AND GOVERNMENT – GENERAL.*

1ST NIGERIAN ARCHITECT

Arc. Michael Olatusen Onafowokan, who so qualified in 1952.

Also: *1st President, Nigerian Institute of Architects.*

1ST NIGERIAN FEMALE ARCHITECT

Arc. (Mrs) Duoton Nwosu (née Spiff).

1ST NIGERIAN PROFESSOR OF ARCHITECTURE

Prof. Yinka Adeyemi, appointed Professor of Architecture by Ahmadu Bello University, Zaria, in 1977.

1ST NIGERIAN QUANTITY SURVEYOR

Emmanuel Osigwe Nwogu, who obtained the professional registration qualification of Associateship of the Royal Institute of Chartered Surveyors (ARICS) (UK) in 1963. Also obtained the Associateship of the Nigerian Institute of Quantity Surveyors, (ANIQS) in 1972.

From Nkwerre, Imo State, he was born on November 26, 1932, and attended St Augustine's Grammar School, Nkwerre, 1947-52; South-East Essex Technical College, Walthamstow, London, 1957-59; The Polytechnic, Regent Street, London, 1960-63. Managed a large company with a large network all over the country. Later conferred the Prestigious Fellowship of the Nigerian Institute of Quantity Surveyors (FNIQS); Fellowship of the Royal Institute of Chartered Surveyors (FRICS); and the PPNIQS.

1ST NIGERIAN FEMALE QUANTITY SURVEYOR

Margaret O. Olatunde, who obtained the professional registration qualification of Associateship of the Nigerian Institute of Quantity Surveyors (ANIQS) in 1982.

From Lagos State, she was born on October 1, 1959; attended Queen's College, Yaba, Lagos, 1971-75; Ahmadu Bello University, Zaria, 1975- 79, obtaining a BSc (Quantity Surveying) degree in 1979.

1ST PRESIDENT, NIGERIAN INSTITUTE OF QUANTITY SURVEYORS

Chief Gabriel Adetona Balogun, from 1972 to 1973. The Institute started to function in 1968 but was not registered until November 1969.

From Ikoto-Ekiti in Ondo State, he was born on June 23, 1934; attended Christ's School, Ado Ekiti, 1948-53; Regent Polytechnic, London, 1964-67. Later Fellow, Nigerian Institute of Quantity Surveyors (FNIQS) and Royal Institute of Chartered Surveyors (FRICS).

5 EDUCATION

5.1 *GENERAL*

NIGERIA'S 1ST EDUCATION BUDGET

Prepared in 1918: 1% of the nation's total budget expenditure was devoted to education.

1ST PRESIDENT, NIGERIAN UNION OF TEACHERS (N.U.T.)

Rev. Israel Ransome-Kuti, President from July 1931 to January 1955. The NUT was formed in 1931.

***See also entry under*:** LABOUR.

NIGERIA'S 1ST FREE PRIMARY EDUCATION SCHEME

The Free Universal Primary Education Scheme took off on Monday January 17, 1955, in the Former Western Region (present Oyo, Ondo, Ogun, Lagos, Edo and Delta States), then under the premiership of Chief Obafemi Awolowo.

NIGERIA'S 1ST NATION-WIDE (UNIVERSAL) PRIMARY EDUCATION (U.P.E.) SCHEME

Launched on Monday September 6, 1976, by General Olusegun Obasanjo, then Head of State. The scheme was first announced in 1974. Total enrolment in all primary schools was 8.2 million pupils (as opposed to the projected 7.4m), out of which Primary One pupils alone accounted for 3 million.

1ST PRIMARY SCHOOL IN NIGERIA

Methodist Primary School, Lagos, established in 1842 by the Methodist missionaries when they first set foot in Nigeria.

1ST MUSLIM PRIMARY SCHOOL IN LAGOS

Talim-Ul-Islam Ahmadiyyat School, established at Elegbata Street, Lagos Island, on Monday, September 4, 1922.

1ST ROMAN CATHOLIC PRIMARY SCHOOL IN EASTERN NIGERIA

Holy Trinity School, Onitsha, Anambra State, established in 1893.

See also entry under: *RELIGION.*

NIGERIA'S 1ST SECONDARY SCHOOL

CMS Grammar School, Lagos, established in June 1859. Its 1st Principal was Rev. Thomas Babington Macaulay, who graduated BA from Fourah Bay College, Sierra Leone. First recruited as Curate of the Anglican Church, Owu, Abokuta, and later became Principal.

1ST SECONDARY SCHOOL IN EASTERN NIGERIA

Hope Waddell Training Institution, Calabar, Cross River State, founded in 1893 by the Church of Scotland Mission. Its 1st African Principal was Dr Akanu Ibiam, 1st Governor of (defunct) Eastern Nigeria.

1ST ROMAN CATHOLIC SECONDARY SCHOOL IN EASTERN NIGERIA

Christ the King College (CKC), Onitsha, founded in 1933.

NIGERIA'S 1ST CO-EDUCATIONAL SECONDARY SCHOOL

Aggrey Memorial College, Arochukwu, Imo State. Started in 1932 as a teacher training institution and converted in 1935 into a secondary

Hope Waddell Training Institution, Calabar (see page 30): entrance photographed in 2012.

PHOTOGRAPH: UMOHDUKE (2012, CC-BY-SA 3.0).

grammar school. Has remained co-educational since inception in 1932. Established by Dr Alvan Ikoku, the renowned pioneer Nigerian educationist, who was not only the school's proprietor and founder but also its principal for thirty-five years from its inception (1932).

1ST NIGERIAN TEACHER AT KING'S COLLEGE LAGOS

Mr Ernest Sesei Ikoli, assistant maths master from 1913 to 1919, when he resigned from the school over an incident involving European racial arrogance at the College. A European master and colleague had addressed Ikoli rather harshly, which he considered an insult to his person and colour. Was himself a pioneer student of King's and 1st student from east of the River Niger to study there.

See also: *1st editor of* Daily Times *newspaper,* ***entry under:*** *MASS MEDIA – NEWSPAPERS.*

1ST NIGERIAN PRINCIPAL OF QUEEN'S COLLEGE, YABA, LAGOS

Mrs Iphigenia Efunjoke Coker (née Soluade); appointed Principal of the high-brow institution in 1963, serving until 1977 when she retired.

From Lagos state, born on September 29, 1924. She attended St Theresa's High School; St Agnes Teacher and Training College; Queen's College, Yaba, Lagos; before proceeding to University College, Dublin, Ireland, where she bagged Bachelor's degrees in Mathematics and English and a Masters degree in English 1952-56.

On return to Nigeria, she taught at Queen's School, Ede; Government College, Ibadan; from where she was appointed Vice-Principal of Queen's College, Yaba (1962), and next year (1963) elevated to Principal (the first Nigerian and youngest thus far). Conferred the prestigious honour of Member of the Order of the Federal Republic (MFR) in 1977 by President Obasanjo for being 'a dedicated teacher, moral tutor and pacesetter in the emancipation of Nigerian womanhood'.

One-time member, Advisory Council, University of Ibadan; President, Lagos State Red Cross Society. Member, Directorate of the National Youth

Service Corps (NYSC); President, Zonta Int'l Club, Lagos. Died late 2019, buried January 17, 2020.

1ST NIGERIAN REGISTRAR/C.E.O., WEST AFRICAN EXAMINATIONS COUNCIL (W.A.E.C.)

Prof. Vincent Chukwuemeka Ike, appointed Registrar/Chief Executive of WAEC with head office in Accra, Ghana, from 1971 to 1979.

Born on April, 28, 1931, in Ndikelionwu, Anambra State; attended Government College, Umuahia, 1945-50; University College, Ibadan, 1951-55; Stanford University, USA, 1966. Served as Assistant Registrar, University College, Ibadan; Deputy Registrar, University of Nigeria, Nsukka, 1960-63; Registrar, University of Nigeria, Nsukka, 1963-71. Was also Visiting Professor, University of Jos.

A renowned novelist, Ike authored several works including *Toads for Supper* (1965), *The Naked Gods* (1970), *Expo 77*, *University Development in Africa*, *The Nigerian Experience*, *Potters Wheels* (1973) and *The Chicken Chasers* (1981).

Married to Mrs Bimpe Ike, one-time University Librarian, Abubakar Tafawa Balewa Federal University of Technology, Bauchi; Visiting Prof., Nnamdi Azikiwe University, Awka; was crowned *Igwe* (*Eze*) of Ndikelionwu. Died January 2020.

NIGERIA'S 1ST TERTIARY EDUCATION INSTITUTION.

Yaba Higher College, founded in 1932, but formally opened January 1934. Its first phase of existence came to an end with a name change to Yaba College of Technology in September 1963, from when it reverted to a regular Polytechnic.

NIGERIA'S 1ST UNIVERSITY INSTITUTION

University of Ibadan, established in 1948 as University College, Ibadan, as an affiliate of the University of London until 1962, when it became

Yaba College of Technology, founded in 1932 as Yaba Higher College (see page 33).

PHOTOGRAPH: TOPEOMOKUNGBE (2018; CC-BY-SA 4.0).

independent while remaining a legal successor to the University College before it.

NIGERIA'S 1ST (FULL-FLEDGED) INDIGENOUS UNIVERSITY

University of Nigeria, Nsukka (UNN), founded in October 1960 but had its Statute of Incorporation in May 1955. Its Provisional Council was inaugurated in 1959 with Rt Hon. Dr Nnamdi Azikiwe as 1st Chancellor/Chairman of Council. Princess Alexandria of Kent laid the foundation stone of the University on October 7, 1960.

1st batch of 220 students and 13 academic staff commenced classes on October 17, 1960. In 1961, former College of Arts, Science and Technology, Enugu, was incorporated to form an Enugu Campus of the University. Another campus was established in Calabar (Cross River State) in October 1973 with 153 students. This developed into a full University of Calabar in September 1976.

UNN, originally owned by the Eastern Nigeria Government, was taken over by the Federal government on April 1, 1973.

NIGERIA'S 1ST UNIVERSITY OF TECHNOLOGY

Anambra State University of Technology (ASUTECH), Enugu, (then) Anambra State. The Act establishing it was enacted on July 30, 1980 (only one month before that establishing Rivers State University of Science and Technology, Port Harcourt) by the Anambra State Legislature under Governor Jim Nwobodo. Its Act provided for campuses at Enugu, Awka, Abakaliki and Onitsha.

The first batch of 300 students commenced classes in October, 1980 at the Enugu and Awka campuses. 1st President (V-C) was Prof. Kenneth Onwuka Dike.

Also: *1st Nigerian University Vice-Chancellor.*

NIGERIA'S 1ST NON-RESIDENTIAL UNIVERSITY

Ondo State university, Ado-Ekiti, Ondo State (formerly Obafemi Awolowo University), established as a totally non-residential university, i.e. not at all involved in housing and feeding and other municipal services for its students. Established in 1982 but commenced classes on January 10, 1983, with 136 students.

NIGERIA'S 1ST MILITARY UNIVERSITY

The Nigerian Defence Academy (NDA), Kaduna, which was upgraded to university status in September 1985. NDA was founded in 1964 with the technical assistance of the Indian Armed Forces and has since its inception been the premier training institution for the Armed Forces, training officer cadets of the Army, Navy and Air Forces.

Unlike the previous three-year course which led to the NDA Certificate of Education (NDACE) which is equivalent to GCE 'A' levels, the new degree programme is of five-year duration (post-'O' levels). Initially the military university started with two faculties – Science and Liberal Studies – and later added on Faculties of Engineering and Technology.

The University convocated its first set of 142 Army, Navy and Air Force cadets at a graduation ceremony held on Saturday, September 24, 1988 at which General Yakubu Gowon (Retired), Former Military Head of State, represented President Ibrahim Babangida.

NIGERIA'S 1ST PRIVATE UNIVERSITY

Imo Technical University, Imerienwe Owerri, Imo State, established in 1983 under the auspices of the Technological and Economic Development Mission (TEDEM), a body with Dr Basil Nnanna Ukegbu, a renowned educationist, as its Co-ordinator. The University's first batch of 200 undergraduates began their orientation programme on December 2, 1983, and formal classes on December 7, 1983.

It was shut down following a federal government order proscribing private universities, announced on February 10, 1984 by then Chief of Staff,

Supreme Headquarters, Brigadier Tunde Idiagbon. Several other private universities, however, sprang up later (and have been flourishing) since the late 1990s.

NIGERIA'S 1ST UNIVERSITY TEACHING HOSPITAL

University College Hospital (UCH), Ibadan, Oyo State, established and declared open by the Princess Royal in November 1957 as the teaching hospital arm of the medical school of the University of Ibadan (former University College, Ibadan).

See also entry under: *MEDICINE.*

1ST NIGERIAN UNIVERSITY VICE-CHANCELLOR

Prof. Kenneth Onwuka Dike, Vice-Chancellor, University of Ibadan, from 1962 to January 27, 1967. Had earlier (in 1960) suceeded expatriate Principal Dr J. H. Parry to become the 1st African Principal of the institution when it was yet a College of the University of London.

A renowned historian and educational administrator, Dike was born in 1917 in Awka, Anambra State. At various times he was Head, Department of History; Dean, Faculty of Arts; and Vice-Chancellor, all in the University of Ibadan. Also 1st general editor of the Ibadan History Series.

Among his numerous published works are *Trade and Politics in the Niger Delta* (1956), *Origins of the Niger Mission 1841-91* and *The Aro and Their Neighbours*. He co-founded the Nigerian Institute of International Affairs (NIIA), Lagos, 1964, and was founder and 1st Director, Institute of African Studies, University of Ibadan, 1962-67. Later 1st University President (V-C)/Chairman, Governing Council, Anambra State University of Science and Technology, Enugu. He was awarded over fifteen honorary doctorate degrees. Died October 26, 1983.

NIGERIA'S 1ST FEMALE VICE-CHANCELLOR

Prof. (Mrs) Grace Awani Alele-Williams, appointed Vice-Chancellor, University of Benin, Edo State, on October 4, 1985.

Born in Warri, Delta State, December 16, 1932; educated at Queen's College, Lagos, University of Ibadan, and University of Chicago, USA. A professor of mathematics, Mrs Alele-Williams was Director, Institute of Education, University of Lagos, prior to her appointment as Vice-Chancellor.

NIGERIA'S 1ST FEMALE POLYTECHNIC RECTOR

Dr (Mrs) Humulhairi O. Anjorin, appointed Rector of Lagos State Polytechnic, Ikorodu, on October 2, 1985.

The Polytechnic was established in 1977 with initially five academic schools (agriculture, engineering, environmental studies, management and business studies, and technology) in four campuses located in Isolo, Surulere, Ikosi and Ikorodo. Mrs Anjorin obtained a doctorate degree in Agriculture.

1ST NIGERIAN UNIVERSITY REGISTRAR

Mr Saburi Oladeni Biobaku, appointed Registrar, University College, Ibadan (later University of Ibadan), from August 1, 1953 to September 1957. Biobaku replaced expatriate Registrar Mr F. F. G. Hunter, and was himself replaced by another expatriate – Mr J. D. Irwin.

1ST NIGERIAN FEMALE UNIVERSITY REGISTRAR

Mrs E. A. Bamgbose, appointed Registrar, Lagos State University, Badagry, on May 14, 1985.

1ST CHAIRMAN, COMMITTEE OF VICE-CHANCELLORS (C.V.C.) OF NIGERIAN UNIVERSITIES

Prof. Kenneth Onwuka Dike, appointed from the body's inception in December 1962 with the five universities existing then as members, (University of Ife, University of Ibadan, University of Nigeria, Nsukka, University of Lagos and Ahmadu Bello University, Zaria). The CVC today comprises all Federal Government-owned universities.

1ST SECRETARY, NATIONAL UNIVERSITIES COMMISSION (N.U.C.)

Dr Okoi Arikpo, from October 1962 to September 1968.

A lawyer, Okoi Arikpo was born in 1913 in Obubra, Cross River State. A Senior Advocate of Nigeria (SAN), he was subsequently appointed Federal Commissioner (Minister) of External Affairs, September 1968 to July 1975, under Gowon's administration.

1ST EXECUTIVE SECRETRY, NATIONAL UNIVERSITIES COMMISSION (N.U.C.)

Dr (later Prof.) Jubril Aminu, from 1975 to 1980. Although the NUC was established in October 1962 with Dr Okoi Arikpo as its 1st Secretary, the post title of Executive Secretary first came into being in 1975 following the promulgation of the NUC decree and the transformation of the NUC into an autonomous body from its erstwhile department in the Federal Cabinet Office, Lagos.

Born 1939 in Song, Adamawa State, Prof. Aminu attended Barewa College, Zaria, 1952-57; Nigerian College of Arts, Science and Technology, Zaria, 1958-60; University College, Ibadan, 1960; University of London, 1969-72. Taught at the University of Ibadan, rising to Senior Lecturer in 1975 at time of his appointment as Executive Secretary. Subsequently Visiting Prof. to Harvard University, USA, from 1980; Vice-Chancellor, University of Maiduguri, July 1980 to September 1985; Federal Minister of Education, September 1985. Later entered the political arena, and was elected Senator of the Federal Republic of Nigeria.

1ST NIGERIAN VICE-CHANCELLOR OF A NON-NIGERIAN UNIVERSITY

Prof. Adamu David Baikie, appointed Vice-Chancellor, National University of Lesotho, in January 1988. Prior to that, Prof. Baikie had served as Vice-Chancellor, University of Benin (Uniben) from 1978 to 1985.

An educationist, he was born on October 2, 1931; educated at CMS Middle School, Wusasa, Zaria, 1946-48; St Peter's College, Zaria, 1949-50, 1953-54;

Nigerian College of Arts, Science and Technology, Zaria, 1957-62; Indiana University, Bloomington, Indiana, USA, 1962-64, 1967-69. Prior to his appointment as Vice-Chancellor, Uniben, Prof. Baikie lectured at Ahmadu Bello University, Zaria, where he rose from Assistant Lecturer in 1964 to Professor, 1971-78.

1ST NIGERIAN VICE-CHANCELLOR APPOINTED CHAIRMAN, NATIONAL UNIVERSITIES COMMISSION (N.U.C.)

Prof. E. U. Essien-Udom who, having been Vice-Chancellor of the University of Maiduguri from October 1975 to September 1979, was on September 10, 1986 sworn in as the (5th) chairman, Board of NUC.
NUC superintends over the affairs of universities in the country and serves as liaison between government and the people. In addition to the Basic Act, Decree 1 of 1974, Decree 16 vests in the NUC the power to advise the President, Head of State through the Minister, on the recognition or derecognition of any academic programme or qualification in universities, after appropriate investigation: in other words, the power of accreditation.

See also: *1st Vice-Chancellor, University of Maiduguri (Unimaid).*

1ST EXECUTIVE SECRETARY, NATIONAL BOARD FOR TECHNICAL EDUCATION (N.B.T.E.)

Engr Isaac I. Inwang, appointed from the Board's inception in 1977 to his retirement in March 1986.

The NBTE, established by Decree 9 of January 11, 1977, has the primary function of coordinating all aspects of technical and vocational education falling outside the universities, i.e. polytechnics, colleges of technology and technical colleges.

Inwang, from Cross River State, had, prior to his appointment as Executive Secretary, served as Acting Principal, Yaba College of Technology, and Federal Government Adviser on Technical Education.

1ST CHIEF EXECUTIVE OF JOINT ADMISSIONS AND MATRICULATION BOARD (J.A.M.B.)

Mr Michael Saidu Angulu, appointed Registrar and Secretary from 1977 to October 1986.

JAMB was set up by Act 2 of 1978 to co-ordinate the entrance examinations which Nigerian universities used to conduct individually. Thus, instead of the prospective student entrant/applicant filing to all institutions of his choice, he files only once covering his choices.

An educationist, from Bida, Niger State, Angulu was born on December 26, 1933; attended St John's School, Bida, 1941-46; CMS Middle School, Wusasa, Zaria, 1947-49; St John's College, Owo, 1950-51, 1954-55; University College, Ibadan, 1957-62. He taught briefly before joining the Registry Division of Ahmadu Bello University, Zaria in 1962, rising to Registrar, 1973-75. Before his appointment as JAMB Registrar he had been Permanent Secretary, North-Western State, 1976; Permanent Secretary, Niger State, 1977.

1ST NIGERIAN (INTERNATIONAL) STUDENT TO SERVE ON THE U.S.-BASED INDIANA UNIVERSITY OF PENNSYLVANIA COUNCIL OF TRUSTEES

Mr Daniel Dogo-Esekie, a US-based Nigerian student, who was so appointed in July 1987. The Council of Trustees is the University's highest governing body.

1ST FEMALE NIGERIAN UNIVERSITY LECTURER

Mrs Bolanle Alake Awe (née Fajamibola), appointed lecturer in the Department of History, University College, Ibadan (University of Ibadan) in 1960.

Born on January 28, 1933, educated at University of St Andrews (Scotland) and Somerville College, University of Oxford (England). Married to Prof. Olumuyiwa Awe, a physicist, also of the University of Ibadan. Had served as Director in the University's Institute of African Studies. Had at various periods been Commissioner for Education, Trade, Industries and Cooperatives in (defunct) Western State government.

1ST MAJOR (VIOLENT) STUDENT RIOT IN A NIGERIAN UNIVERSITY

That by students of the University of Nigeria, Nsukka (UNN) who on Wednesday, October 31, 1962 staged a violent riot over 'objectionable' hostel regulations (not being allowed to visit their female counterparts in their rooms). On November 6, 1962, all the 1,200 students of the institution were 'summarily expelled' for the strike action. The university was, however, re-opened on Thursday, November 26, 1962, but 16 students identified as ring-leaders were rusticated. The Vice-Chancellor at the time was Prof. George Johnson.

1ST BATCH OF STUDENTS TO GRADUATE FROM AN INDIGENOUS NIGERIAN UNIVERSITY

A batch of 149 graduates who successfully completed their Bachelors degree courses in the 1962-63 academic session from the University of Nigeria, Nsukka, and convocated on June 15, 1963. In the week-long series of activities to mark the convocation, some eminent Nigerians were honoured with doctorate degrees.

1ST SET OF POSTGRADUATE STUDENTS IN A NIGERIAN UNIVERSITY

Five students – Emmanuel Emovon (Chemistry), J.O. Ezeilo (Mathematics), C. Olaniyan (Zoology), A. Onwumechili (Physics) and C. Ifemesia (History) – who on graduation in June 1955 were selected to poineer postgraduate study programmes at the University of Ibadan (formerly University College, Ibadan). They were, however, registered for degrees of the University of London. All five later became professors and held important public positions, including as Vice-Chancellors (Emovon, Onwumechili, Ezeilo) and a Federal Cabinet Minister (Emovon).

1ST NIGERIAN UNIVERSITY TO MOUNT A DEGREE COURSE IN ARCHITECTURE

Ahmadu Bello University, Zaria, which started its degree programme in Architecture in 1962.

1ST NIGERIAN UNIVERSITY TO MOUNT A DEGREE COURSE IN FOOD SCIENCE AND TECHNOLOGY

University of Ife (Obafemi Awolowo University), Ile-Ife, whose four-year BSc degree programme commenced in 1971, graduating its 1st batch of students in June 1975.

1ST NIGERIAN UNIVERSITY TO MOUNT A LIBRARY SCIENCE PROGRAMME

University of Ibadan (former University College, Ibadan) in 1959.

For further details see entry under: *LIBRARY SCIENCE.*

1ST NIGERIAN UNIVERSITY TO ESTABLISH A FORMAL PUBLIC RELATIONS (P.R.) DEPARTMENT

University of Nigeria, Nsukka, in 1975. One of the University's products of journalism, Mr Dike Ogu, was charged with the task of setting up a new Public Relations unit.

1ST NIGERIAN UNIVERSITY TO OFFER A COURSE IN MEDICINE

University of Ibadan (formerly University College, Ibadan), which introduced training facilities for Medicine right from the institution's inception in October 1948. However only pre-clinical courses were available until the opening of the 500-bed University College (Teaching) Hospital in November 1957.

The 1st batch of 13 medical doctors, wholly trained in Ibadan, graduated MBBS (London) in 1960. Later (June 1967), the 1st set of medical doctors to receive Ibadan degrees graduated with the MBBS (Ibadan) degree.

1ST NIGERIAN UNIVERSITY TO MOUNT A DEGREE PROGRAMME IN PHARMACY

University of Ife (now Obafemi Awolowo University), Ile-Ife, from the institution's inception in 1961.

1ST NIGERIAN UNIVERSITY GAMES ASSOCIATION (N.U.G.A.) MEET

March 22 to 29, 1966 at the University of Ibadan.

See also entry under: *SPORTS – GENERAL/ATHLETICS.*

5.2 ACADEMIC DISTINCTIONS/ HONOURS

1ST NIGERIAN GRADUATE TEACHER

Alvan Ikoku, who bagged a University of London degree in philosophy (as external candidate) in 1928 while already engaged in teaching. Later, in May 1951, he was awarded an MA degree in Moral Philosophy by the same University (London).

A renowned educationist, labour leader and politician, Ikoku was born in Amanagwu, Arochukwu, Abia State on August 1, 1900; educated at Government School, Calabar; Hope Waddell Training Institution, Calabar. Taught at St Paul's Teacher Training College, Awka, Anambra State.

Was elected National Vice-President, Nigerian Union of Teachers (NUT), 1940-55; President, NUT, 1955. Nominated into (old) Eastern House of Assembly and appointed Regional Minister of Education in 1946. Also Member of Council, University College, Ibadan; West African Examinations Council (WAEC); Chairman, Civil Aviation Training Centre. Conferred honorary Doctor of Laws (LLD) degree, University of Ibadan, in 1965. Died November 18, 1971.

1ST NIGERIAN CHEMISTRY GRADUATE

Stephen Oluwole Awokoya.

Born on July 9, 1913 in Awa, Ijebu-Ode, Ogun State; attended St Andrew's College, Oyo; Higher College, Yaba; University of London. Positions held include: Education Officer, Ministry of Education, Western Region, 1952-56; Principal, Federal Emergency Science School, Lagos, 1958-61; Permanent Secretary and Chief Federal Adviser on Education, Lagos, 1962-67; Director, Department of Application of Science to Development, UNESCO, 1967- 68; Member, Board of Trustees, International Foundation for Science, 1975.

1ST NIGERIAN FEMALE PROFESSOR

Prof. (Mrs) Felicia Adetoun Ogunsheye (née Banjo), appointed Professor of Library Studies, University of Ibadan, with effect from October 1, 1973.

Born in Benin, she hails from Ijebu-Ode, Ogun State; attended Queen's College, Lagos; Yaba Higher College, bagging a Bachelor of Arts degree and a Diploma in Stenography. One of pioneer 102 students of the University College, Ibadan (UCI). Later joined UCI as librarian in 1960. Obtained a postgraduate degree in Library Science from Simmons College, Boston, Mass., USA, 1962. Posts held include Head, Department of Library Studies, Ibadan. Retired in September 1987. Later conferred the chieftaincy title of *Iyalaje* of Ile-Oluji.

Also: *1st Female President, Nigerian Library Association (NLA).*

1ST NIGERIAN PROFESSOR OF MATHEMATICS

Prof. Chike Obi, appointed Associate Professor of Mathematics, University of Lagos (Unilag) 1970, and next year (1971) full Professor.

Born on April 7, 1921 in Onitsha, Anambra State, Prof. Chike Obi retired from Unilag and active teaching in 1986.

1ST NIGERIAN TO RECEIVE A D.SC. DEGREE IN MATHEMATICS

Prof. Sunday Osarumwense Iyahen of the University of Benin, who bagged the DSc degree in Mathematics from University of Keele, England, in July 1987.

Born on October 3, 1937 in Benin-City, Edo State; attended St Matthew's CMS School, Benin-City, 1944-45; St Peter's CMS School, Benin-City, 1946-51; Edo College, Benin-City, 1952-56; Government College, Ibadan, 1959-64; University of Glasgow, Scotland, 1964-65; University of Keele, England, 1965-67. Bagged BSc and PhD degrees, both in Mathematics. Has been lecturing at University of Benin since 1971 when it was yet the Institute of Technology, Benin-City.

1ST NIGERIAN PROFESSOR OF MUSIC

Prof. Lazarus Edward Nnanyelu Ekwueme, appointed Professor of Music in 1978 by the University of Lagos (Unilag).

Born on January 28, 1936 in Oko, Anambra State; attended Government College, Umuahia; Royal College of Music, London; University of Munich, Germany; Yale University, New Haven, Connecticut, USA. Taught music at the University of Nigeria, Yale University and State University of New York. Later Associate Professor, then Professor and Head, Department of Music, Unilag.

1ST NIGERIAN GRADUATE IN METALLURGY

Dr Edward Ugo Chukukere, who bagged the BSc (Glasgow) degree in Metallurgy in 1961.

Born in Owerre-Nkwoji, Imo State, in 1934; attended Government College, Umuahia; Technical Institute, Yaba, 1953-54; University College, Ibadan, 1954-56; Kumasi College of Technology, Ghana, 1956-57; University of Glasgow, 1957-61; Royal College of Science and Technology, Glasgow, 1957-61; University of Toronto, Canada, 1962-66. Qualifications obtained include BSc (Glasgow) ARCST (BSc), Strathclyde, in Metallurgy and

Metallurgical Engineering, 1961; MASc, PhD (Toronto) in Metallurgical Engineering and Materials Science, 1963, 1966 respectively.

Positions held include: Consultant, Nigerian Institute for Social and Economic Research (NISER), Ibadan, 1970-72; General Manager, Nigersteel Company Ltd, Emene-Enugu, 1972-77; Chairman, Clay Products Ltd, Okigwe, 1979; member of the Federal Government team that planned the establishment of the Ajaokuta Steel Complex.

Also: *1st Fellow, Nigerian Metallurgical Society (November 1988).*

1ST NIGERIAN PROFESSOR OF METALLURGY AND MATERIALS ENGINEERING

Prof. Vincent Okenwa Nwoko, so appointed by the Federal University of Technology, Owerri (FUTO), in September 1981. Prior to the appointment, Prof. Nwoko was Senior Lecturer and, later, Associate Professor (1974-81) in the Department of Chemical and Petroleum Engineering, University of Benin.

Born on July 7, 1933, in Umuahia, Abia State; attended Methodist Secondary School, Uzuakoli, 1947-52; Dennis Memorial Grammar School, Onitsha, 1953; University College, Gold Coast (Ghana), 1954-56; University of Manchester, England, 1957-60, 1962-63; Massachusetts Instittute of Technology, Cambridge, Mass., USA, 1963-64: University of London, 1964-68. Prof. Nwoko holds BSc Tech, MSc Tech, Master of Science in Metallurgy (SM) and PhD (1968) degrees.

His work experience includes Lecturer in Chemical Technology, University of Science and Technology, Kumasi, Ghana, 1968-74, before he joined the University of Benin. One-time General Manager/Chief Executive, International Glass Industries Ltd, Aba, Abia State, 1987-90.

1ST NIGERIAN PROFESSOR OF OPTOMETRY

Prof. Paul Olekamma Ogbuehi, so appointed on August 16, 1976 by the University of Benin, Edo State. He pioneered the Optometry programme there and served until retirement following a ghastly motor accident.

Born on September 5, 1936 in Umuahia, Abia State; attended University College, Ibadan, 1954 to June 1959 (obtaining a BSc degree in Physics); University College, Ibadan, 1960-64 (bagging a PhD in Physics); New England College of Optometry, Boston, USA, 1972-June 1974, (bagging a Doctor of Optometry (OD) degree). Posts held include: Lecturer in Physics, University of Ibadan, 1964-66; Lecturer in Physics, University of Nigeria, Nsukka, 1966-70; Senior Lecturer, University of Benin, September to December 1970; Professor of Optometry, 1976 to retirement. Has spent over fifteen years as Head of Department and Dean of Faculty. Elected fellow, American Academy of Optometry, 1981; President, Nigerian Optometric Association, June 1988.

1ST NIGERIAN PROFESSOR OF PHARMACEUTICS

Professor Ebenezer Olanrewaju Ogunlana, appointed Professor of Pharmaceutics by the University of Ife (now Obafemi Awolowo University), Ile-Ife, in 1976.

Born in 1936; educated at Methodist Boys' High School, Lagos; College of Technology, Birmingham, England; University of Nottingham, England; and Purdue University, USA. Prof. Ogunlana joined the then University of Ife as Demonstrator in 1963 and rose to Professor in 1976. Served as Chairman, Committee of Deans of the University, and Deputy Vice-Chancellor. Was, for seven years, member of the Executive Board of West African Health Community. Also Consultant to UNIDO and OAU/STRC, and later Chairman, National Universities Commission Panel on Minimum Standards for Pharmacy. Professor Ogunlana, who holds the chieftaincy title of *Fiwajoye* of Ile-Ife, retired from service in September 1988.

1ST NIGERIAN PROFESSOR OF STATISTICS

James Nwoye Adichie, so appointed in 1976 by the University of Nigeria, Nsukka (UNN).

Born on March 1, 1932; from Abba, Anambra State. Prof. Adichie obtained a BA in Mathematics (London) from University College, Ibadan (now University of Ibadan), 1960, before proceeding to the University of California, USA, where he bagged a PhD degree in statistics in 1966.

Thereafter, he returned to University of Nigeria (UNN) as a lecturer prior to his appointment as professor.

Professor Adichie is father to the budding global literary giant Chimamanda Ngozi Adichie.

1ST NIGERIAN UNIVERSITY TO CONFER HONORARY DOCTORATE DEGREE ON ITS VICE-CHANCELLOR (V-C)

University of Lagos (Unilag), which, in 1973, conferred the honorary Doctor of Science (DSc) degree on its pioneer Vice-Chancellor, Prof. Eni Njoku. Prof. Njoku was V-C, Unilag, from May 27, 1962 to 1965.

For biodata, see: *1st Vice-Chancellor, University of Lagos.*

1ST ALUMNUS OF A NIGERIAN UNIVERSITY CONFERRED HONORARY DOCTORATE DEGREE

Chief Engr (Dr) Emmanuel Chukwuemeka Iwuanyanwu, conferred Doctor of Business Administration degree (*honoris causa*), by his alma mater, University of Nigeria, Nsukka, in December 1986.

Born on September 4, 1942 in Atta, Ikeduru, Imo State, Chief Iwuanyanwu is an engineer, renowned businessman, sports proprietor, newspaper publisher and philanthropist. Attended New Bethel College, Onitsha, 1953-59; Federal School of Science, Lagos, 1961-63; University of Nigeria, Nsukka, 1963-71, where he graduated BSc (Civil Engineering), 1971.

He set up the Hardel and Enic Group of Companies; also Iwuanyanwu Nationale Football Club (now Heartland FC, Owerri); Champion Group of newspapers.

Conferred LLD degree of Shaw University, North Carolina, USA; DSc (Engineering), Morgan State University, Baltimore, Maryland, USA, 1986; Fellowship, Nigerian Society of Engineers (NSE), 1987; 'Most Distinguished Alumnus of University of Nigeria, Nsukka'; Member of the Federal Republic of Nigeria (MFR), October 1981; bestowed the Igbo traditional title of *Aha-eji ejemba.*

1ST RECIPIENT OF A NIGERIAN UNIVERSITY DOCTOR OF SCIENCE (D.Sc.) DEGREE

Dr Jerome O. Nriagu, by the University of Ibadan on November 17, 1987.

Dr Nriagu, an environmental geochemist, hails from Aguata in Anambra State.

1ST NIGERIAN FELLOW, TEXTILE INSTITUTE (U.K.) (F.T.I.)

Prof. Samuel Chukwunweike Okafor Ugbolue, who became the Institute's Fellow in 1981. A professor of polymer science and textile technology, Ugbolue was born on July 6, 1945 in Issele-Uku, Delta State, attended College of Technology and Design, Blackburn, England, 1965-68; University of Strathclyde, Glasgow, Scotland, 1967-74. From lecturer, Ahmadu Bello University, Zaria, in 1976, he joined Federal University of Technology, Owerri, rising to Professor and Dean of the University's School of Earth, Mineral and Natural Sciences in 1987.

Also: *1st Nigerian (African) to bag a PhD degree in Fibre Science from a British University, 1974.*

1ST NIGERIAN SPONSORED OVERSEAS (ON SCHOLARSHIP) FOR A PROFESSIONAL COURSE

Herbert Samuel Heelas Macaulay, granted a scholarship on July 1, 1890 by the colonial governor of Lagos, Sir Alfred Moloney, to study Land Surveying and Civil Engineering at Plymouth, England. Returned to Lagos (Nigeria) in 1893 and joined the colonial Civil Service as Government Surveyor in charge of Crown Agents for five years. He later became known as the 'father' of Nigerian nationalism.

Born in Lagos, November 14, 1864, he died on May 7, 1946 after taking ill in Kano in the course of leading his political party, NNDP, on a campaign tour. Was grandson of the 1st African Bishop in West Africa, and son of the 1st Principal of the 1st Secondary Grammar School in Nigeria.

Also: *1st Nigerian to qualify as a Surveyor.*

1ST NIGERIAN RECIPIENT OF THE UNITED AFRICAN COMPANY (U.A.C.) SCHOLARSHIP

Alhaji Adegoke Oduola Akande Adelabu, who won the scholarship in 1935, with which he embarked on his studies following his admission into Yaba Higher College (now Yaba College of Technology), then the nation's highest educational institution. He had, however, a very brief stay there, abandoning his studies in June of same year to become Secretary to the Regional Manager, UAC, Ibadan.

A politician, Adelabu was born on September 3, 1915 in Ibadan, Oyo State. Was NCNC's Assistant Secretary for Western Nigeria; National Vice-President; Leader of NCNC Opposition in Western House, 1951-54; Federal Minister of Natural Resources and Social Services, 1954-56. Died March 23, 1958 in a car accident.

1ST BLIND STUDENT TO BAG A DEGREE FROM A NIGERIAN UNIVERSITY

Mr Christopher Chike Aniegbuna who on June 20, 1966 received a combined BSc honours degree in Mathematics and Economics from the University of Nigeria, Nsukka.

Adegoke Adelabu, first recipient of the UAC scholarship, in 1935 (see above). Adelabu was later, briefly, a government minister, and opposition leader in the Western Regional Assembly

PHOTOGRAPH: *DAILY TIMES* OF NIGERIA, IN THE PUBLIC DOMAIN

5.3 UNIVERSITIES

ABIA STATE UNIVERSITY, UTURU (ABSU) FORMERLY IMO STATE UNIVERSITY, ETITI

1ST CHANCELLOR

Eze (Dr) Akanu Ibiam, *Eze-Ogo Isiala* I of Unwana, installed on January 1986. The University is one of seven state universities that came into being on February 8, 1981, when Governor Sam Mbakwe, of Imo State, approved setting up Imo State University at Madonna High School, Etiti.

Born on November 29, 1906, in Unwana, Dr Ibiam attended Hope Waddell Training Institution, Calabar, Cross River State, and King's College, Lagos, before proceeding to St Andrews University, Scotland, where he studied medicine with specialisation in tropical medicine.

After engaging in private medical practice for a while on his return, he abandoned medical practice in 1967 to become the Principal of Hope Waddell, Calabar, until 1960 when he was appointed the 1st Indigenous Governor of (defunct) Eastern Nigeria. He was Chairman of Council, University College, Ibadan, 1958-61. Became traditional ruler of Unwana in 1978; Chairman of former Imo State Council of Chiefs and Traditional Rulers.

For biodata, see also: *1st indigenous Governor, (defunct) Eastern Nigeria.*

1ST PRO-CHANCELLOR

Dr Dick Waobianyi Emuchay, from June 25, 1981, when the university's governing council was inaugurated, to 1987. A medical practitioner, born on August 5, 1919 in Azumini, Abia State; attended King's College, Lagos, 1936-37; Yaba Higher College, Lagos, 1938-43; University of St Andrews, Scotland; Liverpool School of Tropical Medicine. Served as medical officer in government hospitals in Aba and Degema before establishing his in Azumini. Was Chairman, Public Service Commission, (defunct) East

Central State, 1972-76; Imo State, 1976-1981; after which he was appointed Pro-Chancellor.

1ST VICE-CHANCELLOR

Prof. Michael Joseph Chukwudalu Echeruo, from 1981 to February 1988.

Born on March 14, 1937 in Umunumu-Mbano, Imo State; attended Stella Maris College, Port Harcourt, 1950-54; University College, Ibadan, 1955-60; Cornell University, Ithaca, New York, USA, 1962-65. Taught at Nigerian College of Arts, Science and Technology before joining University of Nigeria, Nsukka, in 1961, where he rose to Professor of English in 1973. Joined University of Ibadan as Professor in August 1974, and later became Dean, Postgraduate School, a position he held until his appointment as Vice-Chancellor.

Also: *1st Ahiajoku Lecturer.*

1ST UNIVERSITY LIBRARIAN

Kalu K. Oyeoku, appointed January 1, 1982.

Born on April 9, 1936 at Ebem-Ohafia, Abia State; attended Hope Waddell Training Institution, Calabar, 1948-55; University College, Ibadan, 1958-63. Served as librarian, University of Nigeria, Nsukka, from 1963 until his appointment as University Librarian.

AHMADU BELLO UNIVERSITY (A.B.U.), ZARIA

1ST CHANCELLOR

Alhaji Sir Ahmadu Bello, *Sardauna* of Sokoto, installed Chancellor on November 23, 1963. The university was established in October 1962.

For biodata, see: *1st Premier, Northern Nigeria.*

1ST PRO-CHANCELLOR

Alhaji Umaru Ibn Suleiman, Emir of Bedde, appointed from the university's formal establishment in 1962, serving to 1972. The 1st Chairman of the institution's Provisional Council (1960-62) was, however, Sir Kashim Shettima Ibrahim.

1ST VICE-CHANCELLOR

Prof. (later Sir) Norman Stanley Alexander, from 1961 to 1966. A New Zealander by birth, Alexander had served as Professor of Physics in the University of Malaya, at University College, Ibadan, and at Middle-East Technical University, prior to his appointment as Vice-Chancellor.

1ST NIGERIAN VICE-CHANCELLOR

Prof. Ishaya Sha'aibu Audu, appointed March 10, 1966, taking over from expatriate V-C, Prof. Alexander. Served until 1975. Was in Lagos University Medical School prior to his appointment.

Born in Zaria on March 1, 1927. Was a pioneer student of University College, Ibadan, in 1948. Left Ibadan for the University of London, 1951-1954, then proceeded to the University of Liverpool, England, 1954-60, and Ohio University, Athens, USA, 1964.

Was House-Officer, 1955-58; Personal Physican to Sir Ahmadu Bello, (late) Premier, (defunct) Northern Region, 1960-62; Lecturer (later, Professor of Paediatrics), University of Lagos, 1962-66; Visiting Research Professor of Paediatrics, School of Medicine and Dentistry, University of Rochester, New York, USA. Later became Nigeria's External Affairs Minister, 1979-82.

1ST INAUGURAL LECTURE

Titled: 'Political Legitimacy in New States', delivered by Prof. J. O'Connell on November 6, 1969. Professor O'Connell was the University's Head, Department of Government and Dean, Faculty of the Arts and Social Sciences.

AMBROSE ALLI STATE UNIVERSITY, EKPOMA

1ST CHANCELLOR

Dr Fom Bot Gbong Gworn Jos, appointed February 1985. The traditional ruler of Jos, Plateau State, born 1935 in Ropp; attended South Devon College, Torquay, England, 1962-63, where he obtained a Diploma in Local Government Administration. Was appointed District Head of Jos in 1970.

1ST PRO-CHANCELLOR

Dr Abel Kprogidi Ubeku, from the institution's inception in 1981 to 1983.

Born on February 24, 1936, in Araya, Isoko Local Government Area of Edo State; attended Nigerian College of Arts, Science and Technology, Ibadan; London School of Economics; University of Sussex, England. Qualifications include LLM, PhD (Industrial Relations) and Certificate in Management.

Positions held include Executive Secretary, Industrial Training Fund (ITF), 1972. Later joined Guinness (Nig.) Ltd, as Personnel Manager, in 1975, rising to Deputy Managing Director, March 1979, and Managing Director/Chief Executive, 1982. Fellow, Institute of Personnel Management of Nigeria; Member, Governing Council, Centre for Management Development (CMD), Lagos; Chairman, Former Bendel State School Take-over/Compensation Panel.

1ST VICE-CHANCELLOR

Prof. Michael Ihimekpen Ogbeide, appointed from the institution's inception in 1981 but served for only a few months.

A physician and educational administrator, born on September 16, 1925 in Ekpoma, Edo State; attended Government College, Ibadan, 1940-44; Technical College, Yaba, 1945- 46; University College, Ibadan, 1949-51; University of London, St Thomas's Hospital Medical School, 1951-54. Prior to his appointment as Vice-Chancellor he had served as Provost (1975-78) and, later, Professor of Child Health, University of Benin Teaching Hospital, and Deputy Vice-Chancellor, University of Benin, 1978.

1ST UNIVERSITY LIBRARIAN

Dr Sam. E. Ifidon, appointed 1983. Prior to this appointment, he held an identical post in the University of Maiduguri, 1979-83.

From Ora in Owan LGA, Edo State; attended University of Ibadan and University of Western Ontario, Canada, obtaining BA (classics), Diploma in Librarianship, Master of Library Science and PhD (Library Science).

See also: *1st University Librarian, University of Maiduguri.*

1ST INAUGURAL LECTURE

Titled 'The Hound of Heaven and the Children of Men', delivered by Prof. S. U. Erivwo, the institution's Head of Deptartment of Religious Studies and Philosophy, on Friday December 11, 1987.

FEDERAL UNIVERSITY OF TECHNOLOGY, AKURE (F.U.T.A.)

1ST CHANCELLOR

HRH Alhaji Zulkarnaini Gambari Mohammed CFR, Emir of Ilorin, appointed Chancellor in August 1981 and formally installed on November 7, 1987.

Born into the ruling family of Abdul Salam, the first Emir of Ilorin, June 1914; attended Institute of Administration, Nigerian College of Arts, Science and Technology. Worked as Court Registrar and, later, Chief Court Registrar and Inspector of Native Courts in then Northern Region of Nigeria, 1956; installed Emir of Ilorin, 1959; appointed Northern Regional Minister (without portfolio), 1960; Chairman, Kwara State Council of Chiefs, 1967; conferred Commander of the Federal Republic (CFR), 1979, and honorary Doctor of Laws (LLD) degree (Federal University of Technology, Akure) on November 7, 1987.

1ST PRO-CHANCELLOR

High Chief (Dr) Gabriel Akin-Deko, appointed Pro-Chancellor and Chairman, Governing Council, October 1981 to January 31, 1983.

Born on October 30, 1913 in Lagos, attended Higher College, Yaba, and Brixton School of Building, England. Member, old Western Nigeria House of Assembly; later Western Nigeria's Minister of Agriculture, 1950-61; Chairman, Western Nigeria Development Corporation (WNDC); Regional Representative for Africa, Food and Agriculture Organisation (FAO), 1962; Chairman, National Sports Council. Formerly Pro-Chancellor, Federal University of Technology (now Federal University of Agriculture), Abeokuta. Died November 10, 1987.

1ST VICE-CHANCELLOR

Prof. Theodore Idibiye Francis, appointed Vice-Chancellor on November 19, 1981 and assumed duties in Akure on January 1, 1982, Served until November 1988.

A physician and educationist, Prof. Francis was born on August 9, 1933, at Nembe, Rivers State; educated at St Cyprian's School, Port Harcourt, 1939-46; Government College, Umuahia, 1947-52; University College, Ibadan, 1952-56; Guy's Hospital, London, 1956-59; Thorndike Memorial Laboratory, Boston, Mass., USA, 1966-68. Practised medicine in Britain from 1955 to 1963 before returning to take up appointment with the University College Hospital, Ibadan, 1963-64. Other posts held prior to his appointment as Vice-Chancellor are Senior Lecturer and later, Professor and Head, Department of Medicine, University of Ibadan. Member, Royal College of Surgeons; Fellow, Royal College of Physicians, Edinburgh and London.

1ST DEPUTY VICE-CHANCELLOR

Prof. Albert Adeoye Ilemobade, appointed the university's first Deputy Vice-Chancellor on May 21, 1987.

Born on April 12, 1914 in Ondo, educated at Ahmadu Bello University, Zaria; University of Ibadan; University of Oklahoma, USA, obtaining DVM, 1969; MS; PhD, 1976. He became a Professor of Veterinary Parasitology and Entomology, Ahmadu Bello University, Zaria, 1980; Assistant Dean, Postgraduate and Research, 1979; Professor and Head, Department of Animal Production and Health, Federal University of Technology, Akure (FUTA), 1983; Dean, School of Agriculture and Agricultural Technology, 1984.

1ST UNIVERSITY LIBRARIAN

Mr Festus Adetunji Akinyotu, so appointed on August 1, 1982.

Born on July 7, 1939 in Ondo, Ondo State; attended University of Ibadan and Kent State University, Ohio, USA; University of London, 1964; PGD Library Science (Ibadan), 1967; Cert. Adv. Studies in Lib. Sc. (Kent State), 1974. Served as Assistant Librarian, Senior Librarian and Deputy University Librarian, University of Ibadan Library, from 1967 until his appointment as University Librarian in 1982.

1ST INAUGURAL LECTURE

Delivered by Prof. L. K. Opeke on April 17, 1984, with the title 'Daily Bread Equations'. Prof. Opeke was Head, Department of Crop Production of the University.

1ST CONVOCATION

Held for the installation of the first Chancellor and conferment of the first honorary degree, first and higher degrees on Saturday, November 7, 1987. During the ceremony, the first Chancellor, His Royal Highness, Alhaji Zulkarnaini Gambari Mohammed, CFR, was conferred with the degree of Doctor of Laws (LLD) (*honoris causa*).

The first graduates of the University were conferred the degree of Bachelor of Technology (BTech) in their various disciplines and the first postgraduate degree of Master of Technology (MTech). was awarded to Dr Olugbenga O. Ogunyemi. In all, 99 graduate and one postgraduate degrees were awarded that day. Two of the first graduates had first-class honours.

FEDERAL UNIVERSITY OF TECHNOLOGY, MINNA

1ST PRO-CHANCELLOR

Chief Edwin Kiagbodo Clark, appointed in 1983. Was also, 1st Pro-Chancellor/Chairman of Council, University of Benin, 1971-74.

For biodata, see: *1st Pro-Chancellor/Chairman of Council, University of Benin.*

1ST VICE-CHANCELLOR

Prof. Jonathan Osman Ndagi, in 1983.

Born on November 1, 1950 in Katcha, Sokoto State; attended Christ's Church School, Gusau, 1940-44; Nigerian College of Arts, Science and Technology, Zaria, 1952-57; University College, Ibadan, 1959-63; University of Wisconsin, USA, 1968-69.

FEDERAL UNIVERSITY OF TECHNOLOGY, OWERRI (F.U.T.O.)

1ST CHANCELLOR

Dr Frederick Oritseatseghan Esiri, from October 1981 to March 1985. FUTO, one of three federal universities of technology, was officially established in October 1980 and commenced classes in October 1981.

For biodata, see: *1st Nigerian oto-laryngologst,* **entry under:** *MEDICINE.*

1ST PRO-CHANCELLOR

HRH Chukumela Nnam-Obi II, *Eze-Ogba* of Ogbaland, from October 1980 to 1984.

A first-class traditional ruler in Rivers State; born on November 20, 1942 in Omoku, Egbema Division, Rivers State; attended St Michael's School, Omoku, 1952-56; Santa Maria High School, Omoku, 1962-66. Installed *Eze-Ogba* of Ogbaland on December 19, 1970.

1ST VICE-CHANCELLOR

Prof. Umaru Dechi Gomwalk, from October 1980 to September 1987.

A Professor of Chemistry, born on March 27, 1938, in Amper, Plateau State; educated at Gindiri Secondary School; Nigerian College of Arts, Science and Technology, Zaria; University College, Ibadan; University of Strathclyde, Scotland. Bagged BSc (Chem.), 1964; PhD (Chem.), 1968. Taught at Ahmadu Bello University, Zaria, rising to Professor and Head, Deptartment of Chemistry, 1977-79, and Dean, Faculty of Science, 1979-80, prior to his appointment as Vice-Chancellor. Later appointed Sole Administrator VC, University of Nigeria, Nsukka; died 2019.

1ST UNIVERSITY LIBRARIAN

Joseph Chike Anafulu, appointed in April 1981; served to 1996.

Born on September 3, 1939 in Awkuzu, Anambra State; attended St John's College, Kaduna, 1954-58; University of Ibadan, 1963-64; University of Pittsburgh, USA, 1974-75, acquiring Diploma in Librarianship (DipLib) and Master of Library Science (MIS).

Prior to the appointment he had served as Assistant Librarian, Librarian, Senior Librarian and Deputy University Librarian, all in the University of Nigeria, Nsukka, 1966-79; Chief Librarian (head), Institute of Management and Technology (IMT), Enugu, 1979-81. Died 2014.

1ST INAUGURAL LECTURE

Titled 'Food Processing and Preservation: Paths to Self-Sufficiency', delivered by Prof. Edward Opuada Iwo-Nte Banigo on Saturday, January 18, 1986. Prof. Banigo was later appointed Vice-Chancellor, Rivers State University of Science and Technology, Port Harcourt.

OBAFEMI AWOLOWO UNIVERSITY (O.A.U.), ILE-IFE (FORMERLY, UNIVERSITY OF IFE)

1ST CHANCELLOR

Chief Obafemi Awolowo, appointed November 1960 and served until 1964. The university was established on June 26, 1961 with an initial student enrolment of 244. Commenced with five faculties: Agriculture, Arts, Social Sciences, Law and Science. Its original name, University of Ife, was changed to Obafemi Awolowo University in 1987 in honour of its founding father and first Chancellor, who died on May 9, 1987.

For biodata, see: *1st Premier, (defunct) Western Nigeria.*

1ST PRO-CHANCELLOR

Chief Frederick Rotimi Alade Williams.

1ST VICE-CHANCELLOR

Prof. Oladele Adebayo Ajose, from 1961 to 1966.

A Professor of Preventive and Social Health, Ajose had served as Head of Department from the inception of the University College, Ibadan, in the 1948-49 session. Died July 3, 1978 at the age of 70.

1ST ALUMNUS APPOINTED VICE-CHANCELLOR

Prof. Eyo Okon, an alumnus of OAU from 1962 to 1966, who was appointed 2nd Vice-Chancellor of the state-owned University of Cross River State, Uyo, with effect from September 22, 1987.

A zoologist, Prof. Okon was born on June 10, 1944 in Ibiono, Akwa Ibom State; attended University of Ife (Obafemi Awolowo University), Ife, 1962-66, graduating BSc in Zoology. Proceeded to King's College, University of London, 1968-71, for his PhD. Prior to his appointment as Vice-Chancellor, he was Lecturer, University of Ife, 1971-1979; Professor, University of Ife, from 1979.

OGUN STATE UNIVERSITY, AGO-IWOYE

1ST VICE-CHANCELLOR

Prof. John Olubi Sodipo, in September 1982 (when the university was established).

Born on October 15, 1935, in Illishan-Remo, Ogun State; was educated at Remo Secondary School, Sagamu, 1948-53; Nigerian College of Arts, Science and Technology, 1954-56; University College, Ibadan, 1956-60; University of Durham, England, 1961-64, bagging a PhD degree in Philosophy. Before appointment as Vice-Chancellor, he had been Dean of Arts, 1973-76. Was foundation President of Nigerian Philosophical Association.

1ST UNIVERSITY LIBRARIAN

Mrs 'Laide O. Soyinka, appointed substantively in 1987 after serving in an acting capacity since 1983. Prior to the appointment, Mrs Soyinka was Deputy University Librarian, University of Ibadan.

1ST INAUGURAL LECTURE

Titled 'Nigeria's Social Formation and Health Planning', delivered by Prof. O. A. Erinosho, on Tuesday March 29, 1988, under the chairmanship of the Vice-Chancellor, Prof. J. Olubi Sodipo.

ONDO STATE UNIVERSITY, ADO-EKITI

1ST PRO-CHANCELLOR

Chief B. A. Ajayi, in February 1982. The university was established by the Ondo State government under former Governor Chief Michael Ajasin in 1982.

1ST VICE-CHANCELLOR

Prof. Ifedayo Olawole Oladapo, from February 1982 to 1989. An engineer and educationist, from Ondo, Ondo State; born on May 18, 1934; attended Government College, Ibadan, 1954-56; University of St Andrews, Scotland, 1956-59; University of Cambridge, England, 1959-62.

Taught briefly (1963-64) at Ahamdu Bello University, Zaria, before joining the University of Lagos as Lecturer in 1964, rising to Professor of Civil Engineering in 1970 and later Deputy Vice-Chancellor in 1977, a position he held at the time of his appointment as Vice-Chancellor. Fellow, Nigerian Society of Engineers, and Fellow, Nigerian Academy of Science.

RIVERS STATE UNIVERSITY OF SCIENCE & TECH. (R.U.S.T.), PORT HARCOURT

1ST CHANCELLOR

HRH (Dr) James Orchivirigh Akperan Orshi, *Tor Tiv* III, from 1980 to 1984. Prior to August 6, 1980 the institution was known as the Rivers State College of Technology, Port Harcourt.

Born on March 12, 1925, in Tse Kur Baka, Benue State, he was educated at the Institute of Education, University of London, England, 1956-57; Institute of Admin. ABU, Zaria, 1958-60. Called to the Bar (Middle Temple), London, 1963; Nigerian Law School, Lagos, 1963. Posts held include: Magistrate, rising to Solicitor-General and Perm. Secretary, Benue-Plateau State, 1974; Secretary to the Military Government and Head of Service, Benue State, February to June 1976; Chairman, Nigeria Airways. Was *Tor Tiv* III from April 1979 to date. Awarded Order of the Niger (OON).

1ST PRO-CHANCELLOR

Prof. Tekena Nitonye Tamuno, from September 1, 1980 to May 31, 1988. A renowned historian and educator from Okrika, Rivers State, he was born on January 28, 1932; educated at Okrika Grammar School, 1947-51; University College, Ibadan, 1953-58; University of London, England, 1960-62; Columbia University, New York, USA, 1965-66. Has been at the University of Ibadan since, rising to Professor of History, Dean of Arts, and Vice-Chancellor, 1975-79. He has also held the following positions: 1st Principal, University College, Ilorin (1975); Chairman of Board, New Nigerian Newspapers Ltd.

1ST VICE-CHANCELLOR

Prof. Turner Timinipre Isoun, from September 1, 1980 to April 30, 1984. A veterinary pathologist, Isoun was born on September 2, 1938, in Odi, Rivers State; attended Okrika Grammar School; Hope Waddell Secondary Grammar School, Calabar; Michigan State University, East Lansing, USA, 1960-65, 1968-70. Posts held include Professor and Head, Department of Veterinary Pathology, University of Ibadan.

1ST UNIVERSITY LIBRARIAN

Mr Jigekuma Ayebabari Ombu, appointed from the university's inception in August 1980. Prior to the appointment he was Librarian-in-charge of the College of Science and Technology, Port Harcourt, nucleus of the new university.

From Okpoma, Rivers State, Ombu was born on May 4, 1938, and attended University of Ibadan, 1963-64. Positions held include Assistant Librarian, later, Sub-Librarian, University of Ibadan; Librarian, College of Science and Technology, Port Harcourt.

1ST INAUGURAL LECTURE

Titled 'Soils and Man in a Changing World', delivered by Prof. A. G. Ojanuga on April 2, 1986.

UNIVERSITY OF BENIN (UNIBEN), BENIN-CITY

1ST CHANCELLOR

Sir Adetokunbo Adegboyega Ademola, from 1972 to December 1975. Uniben first came into being in November 1970 as the Institute of Technology, Benin City.

For biodata, see: *1st indigenous Chief Justice of the Federation,* ***entry under:*** *LAW.*

1ST PRO-CHANCELLOR

Chief Edwin Kiagbodo Clark, from July 1971, when the university (formerly Institute of Technology, Benin-City) was established, to 1975.

From Western Ijaw, Clerk State, he was born on May 25, 1932, and educated at Government Teacher Training College, Abraka, 1949-53; Holborn College of Law, London, 1961-64. Posts held include Commissioner for Information, January to July 1975, and Chairman, Mid-West Lines, 1973-74.

Also: *1st Pro-Chancellor and Chairman of Council, Federal University of Technology, Minna.*

1ST VICE-CHANCELLOR

Prof. Glyn Phillips, from November 1970 to July 1971. However, the first person to be officially designated Vice-Chancellor was expatriate Prof. Kenneth Hill, from July 1972 to January 1973.

1ST NIGERIAN VICE-CHANCELLOR

Prof. Tikani Momodu Yesufu, from October 1974 to October 1978. Although the institution started in November 1970 as the Institute of Technology, Benin-City, its substantive chief executives prior to Prof. Yesufu were all expatriates.

An economist and educationist, Prof. Yesufu was born on June 21, 1926, in Agbede, Etsako Division of Edo State, and educated at Edo College, Benin-City, 1940-43; Government College, Ibadan, 1944-46; University of Exeter, England, 1952-55; London School of Economics and Political Science, University of London, 1960.

He was Labour Officer with the Department of Labour, 1955-57; with the International Labour Office (ILO), Geneva, 1958-60; Federal Ministry of Labour, 1960-65. Appointed Professor and Head of Applied Economics, University of Lagos, from 1965 to the time of his appointment as Vice-Chancellor, University of Benin, in 1973. Later appointed Director of Human Resources, University of Lagos, 1976-79; Executive Director, Lagos Chamber of Commerce and Industry, 1979; Fellow of the Nigerian Institute of Management (NIM).

1ST NIGERIAN FEMALE VICE-CHANCELLOR

Prof. (Mrs) Grace Awnai Alele-Williams, from October 4, 1985.

For further details, see: *Nigeria's 1st Female Vice-Chancellor.*

UNIVERSITY OF CALABAR (UNICAL), CALABAR

1ST CHANCELLOR

HRH Dr Haruna Rashid, Emir of Gwandu, from 1980 to July 1984. Unical was established in September 1976.

A traditional ruler, he was born in 1913 in Gwandu, Sokoto State; attended Birnin-Kebbi Elementary School; Sokoto Middle School; Katsina Teachers' College. He was Chancellor of the Exchequer (*Ma'aji*) of Gwandu Emirate in January 1954. Positions held include: Vice-President, Northern House of Chiefs, 1956-58; President, Northern House of Chiefs, 1958-66; Acting Governor of Northern Nigeria, 1965. Also, one-time Chairman, Board of Governors, Sokoto College of Education. Conferred Commander, Order of the Federal Republic (OFR), and awarded honorary LLD degree, 1980.

1ST PRO-CHANCELLOR

Alhaji Shettima Ali Monguno, so appointed from June 1976 to September 1980.

A politician, born in Monguno, Borno State, in 1926. Alhaji Shettima attended Bauchi Teacher Training College, 1944-47; Katsina Higher College, 1949-51; Nigerian College of Arts, Science and Technology, Zaria, 1954-56; University of Edinburgh, Scotland. Was one-time Federal Minister of Internal Affairs, 1965-66; Federal Commissioner (Minister) for Mines and Power, 1971-75; Member, Constituent Assembly, 1977-78.

1ST VICE-CHANCELLOR

Prof. Emmanuel Ayakanmi Ayandele, from June 1976 to September 1981. Prior to the appointment, Ayandele was Provost of the institution, then a campus of the University of Nigeria, Nsukka, from October 1973 to September 1976.

A Professor of History, Ayandele was born on October 12, 1936 and atended Baptist Boys' High School, Oyo; Nigerian College of Arts, Science and Technology, Ibadan; University College, Ibadan; and University of

London, England. He joined the University of Ibadan as a history lecturer and rose to Professor of History before he moved to the Jos Campus of the University of Ibadan as Acting Principal, from where he moved on to Unical, first as Provost, then Vice-Chancellor.

1ST UNIVERSITY LIBRARIAN

Mr Nduntuei Otu Ita, from 1977. A librarian/lawyer from Oron, Akwa Ibom State, he was born on November 22, 1936; attended Urhobo College, Warri, 1951-56; University of Ibadan, 1960-61; University of London, England. Prior to his appointment as University Librarian, he had served in various senior library positions in (defunct) Eastern Nigeria Library Board, Enugu, and (defunct) North-East College of Arts and Science, Maiduguri.

1ST INAUGURAL LECTURE

Titled 'Natural Resources of the Cross River State of Nigeria', by Prof. S. W. Petters.

UNIVERSITY OF CROSS RIVER, UYO

1ST CHANCELLOR

Oba Okunade Adele Sijuade, *Ooni* of Ife, appointed in 1983 but installed at the first convocation of the university held at Uyo, capital of Akwa Ibom State, on Saturday March 5, 1988. An honorary Doctor of Letters (DLitt) degree was also conferred on him on the occasion. The University, statutorily established by Chief (Dr) Clement Isong, then governor, Cross River State, in 1980, commenced in 1983 with an initial intake of 232 students.

Born on January 1, 1930 in Ile-Ife, Oyo State, Oba Sijuade attended St John's School, Igbesin, Abeokuta; Oduduwa College, Ile-Ife; British Institute of Management, Holborn, England. Work career included Managing Director, National Motors. Was crowned *Ooni* of Ife, Olubuse II, in November 1980.

1ST VICE-CHANCELLOR

Prof. Donald U. Ekong, from the University's inception in 1982 to February 1987.

For biodata, see: *1st Vice-Chancellor, University of Port Harcourt.*

UNIVERSITY OF IBADAN (U.I.), FORMERLY UNIVERSITY COLLEGE, IBADAN

1ST CHANCELLOR

Alhaji Sir Abubakar Tafawa Balewa, appointed in 1962 (when the institution, formerly, University College, Ibadan, became a full-fledged independent university) and installed on November 18, 1963. Served until killed in Nigeria's military coup on January 15, 1966.

Although the office of Chancellor was created by Ordinance in 1954, it was not until 1962 that the 1st appointment was made.

For biodata, see: *Nigeria's 1st (only) Prime Minister,* ***entry under:*** *POLITICS AND GOVERNMENT – HEADS OF STATE/GOVERNMENT.*

1ST PRO-CHANCELLOR

Dr Okechukwu Ikejiani, from 1961 to 1965. Was already Chairman of Council at the point when the institution (formerly University College) became the University of Ibadan in 1962. However, Sir Francis Akanu Ibiam was 1st Chairman of the institution's Council from 1958 to 1961 when it was yet a College.

For biodata, see: *1st Nigerian Chairman, Nigerian Railway Corporation,* ***entry under:*** *TRANSPORT AND COMMUNICATIONS.*

1ST VICE-CHANCELLOR

Prof. Kenneth Onwuka Dike, from the university's inception in 1962 to 1967. Was Principal prior to 1962 when the university was yet a College of the University of London.

For biodata, see: *1st Nigerian University Vice-Chancellor,* **entry under:** *EDUCATION – GENERAL.*

1ST ALUMNUS APPOINTED ITS VICE-CHANCELLOR

Prof. Tekena N. Tamuno, who had graduated BA (History) from the University of Ibadan (formerly University College, Ibadan). Appointed the university's Vice-Chancellor from December 1975 to December 1979.

For biodata, see: *1st Pro-Chancellor and Chairman of Council, Rivers State University of Science and Technology, Port Harcourt.*

1ST PRINCIPAL, UNIVERSITY COLLEGE, IBADAN (U.C.I.)

Dr Kenneth Mellanby, from 1947 to 1953. An entomologist, Mellanby had a PhD degree from London University and ScD from Cambridge University. Rose to Reader (Medical Entomology) at the London School of Hygiene and Tropical Medicine, from where he assumed the Principalship of University College, Ibadan, at the age of 39.

1ST NIGERIAN PRINCIPAL OF THE UNIVERSITY COLLEGE, IBADAN (U.C.I.)

Dr Kenneth Onwuka Dike, appointed on October 1, 1960 and served until 1962 when the College was elevated to the status of a full (autonomous) university.

For biodata, see: *1st Nigerian Vice-Chancellor,* **entry under:** *EDUCATION – GENERAL.*

1ST NIGERIAN FEMALE UNIVERSITY OF IBADAN LECTURER

Mrs Bolanle Alake Awe (née Fajemibola), appointed lecturer in the Department of History in 1960, when the institution was yet University College, Ibadan.

See also: *1st Nigerian female lecturer in a Nigerian university,* ***entry under:*** *EDUCATION – ACADEMIC DISTINCTIONS/HONOURS.*

1ST MATRICULATION AS A FULL UNIVERSITY

On November 3, 1962, the first set of students, numbering over 600, were admitted and matriculated in Trenchard Hall, University of Ibadan.

1ST INAUGURAL LECTURE

Entitled 'Bilingualism', delivered by Dr Paul Christophersen on Foundation Day, November 17, 1948.

UNIVERSITY OF ILORIN (UNILORIN)

1ST CHANCELLOR

HRH Alhaji Umar Sulaiman, from 1978 to 1981. University of Ilorin came into being in October 1977.

1ST PRO-CHANCELLOR

HRH Justice Ambrose Ezeolisa Allagoa, *Mingi* XI, *Amanyanabo* of Nembe, from 1978 to 1982.

Born on August 24, 1914 in Onitsha, Anambra State, but hails from Nembe, Rivers State. Justice Allagoa attended Government School, Owerri, 1927; St Mary's School, Onitsha, 1932-36; Council of Legal Education, London. Posts held include Mayor of Port Harcourt, 1948-61; Judge, High Court, of Eastern Region, 1962-67; Judge, High Court. River State, 1976. Awarded: Commander, Order of the Niger (OON), 1977. One-time Chancellor, Federal University of Technology, Owerri (FUTO), 1985 to 1990.

1ST VICE-CHANCELLOR

Prof. Oladipo Olujimi Akinkugbe, from the university's inception in October 1977 to October 1978. Earlier he had headed the same institution as Principal, December 1975 to September 1977, when it was a College of the University of Ibadan.

A physician from Ondo State, he was born on July 17, 1933 and educated at Government College, Ibadan, 1946-51; University College Ibadan, 1951-55; The London Hospital, University of London, England, 1955-58; University of Liverpool, England 1960; University of Oxford, England, 1962-64.

Practised medicine in England for a while before joining University of Ibadan as lecturer, rising to Professor of Medicine (1968) and Dean, Medical School (1970-74). Member, Royal College of Surgeons, England.

1ST UNIVERSITY LIBRARIAN

Babatunde Abayomi Oni-Orisan, from August 1976. Born in Lagos on June 4, 1932, he attended Eko Boys' High School, Lagos, 1946-51; University of Ibadan, 1955-59, 1961-62, 1965-66.

Appointed Assistant Librarian, Ibadan University Library, October 1964, and rose to the position of Senior Sub-Librarian in 1972. Joined University of Ife Library as Deputy University Librarian in November 1972 and served in that capacity until his appointment as University Librarian.

1ST INAUGURAL LECTURE

Delivered by Prof. Oladele Awobuluyi on 15 February, 1979 titled 'The New National Policy on Education in Linguistic Perspective'. Prof. Awobuluyi was also the 1st Dean of the Faculty of Arts of the University from September 1976 to July 1980.

UNIVERSITY OF JOS (UNIJOS)

1ST VICE-CHANCELLOR

Prof. Gilbert Obidifo Onuaguluchi, from the university's inception in October 1975 to September 1978.

A physician and educationist, Prof. Onuaguluchi was born on January 1, 1927, in Augu, Enugu State. He attended Dennis Memorial Grammar School, Onitsha, 1941-44; Higher College, Yaba, 1945-46; Medical School, Yaba, 1947-48; University College, Ibadan, 1949-51; West London Hospital Medical School, England, 1955; Institute of Chest Diseases, University of London, 1956; University of Glasgow, Scotland, 1959-61.

After some medical practice, he joined the University of Ibadan as Senior Lecturer in 1962, rising to Professor of Clinical Pharmacology and Therapeutics in 1965. Transferred to University of Nigeria, Nsukka, as Professor/Head of Pharmacology and Therapeutics in 1967 as a result of civil disturbances, a position he held at time of his appointment as Vice-Chancellor in 1975.

Member, Royal College of Physicians, Glasgow; Member, Royal College of Surgeons; Honorary President, West African Society for Pharmacology, 1971.

1ST UNIVERSITY LIBRARIAN

Bartholomew U. Nwafor, from August 1976. Prior to his appointment he had been Deputy Librarian in charge of Calabar Campus, University of Nigeria, Nsukka, 1973-75, and College Librarian, Alvan Ikoku College of Education, Owerri, 1975-76.

Born in Abba, Anambra State, Nwafor attended College of Immaculate Conception (CIC), Enugu, 1955-59; Ealing Technical College, England; University of Pittsburgh, Pittsburgh, Pennsylvania, USA, 1973, bagging the Associateship of the Library Association (UK) (ALA), June 1963, and Master of Library Science (MLS) degree, 1973.

UNIVERSITY OF LAGOS (UNILAG)

1ST VICE-CHANCELLOR

Prof. Eni Njoku, appointed on May 27, 1962 (following the university's inception in April 1962), and resigned in 1965 over a crisis about his re-appointment for another term.

Born at Ebem-Ohafia, Abia State, on November 6, 1917; educated at Hope Waddell Training Institution, Calabar, 1933-36; Yaba Higher College, Lagos; University of Manchester, England; University of London, England. Obtained a BSc degree in Botany with 1st-class Honours, 1947, MA, 1948 and PhD, 1954.

Taught at the University of Ibadan, rising to Professor and Dean of Science, 1959-62. Appointed Chairman, National Electric Power Authority (NEPA), 1956; Vice-Chancellor, University of Nigeria, Nsukka, 1966-67, when the Civil War broke out. Was also a parliamentarian and politician: Federal Minister of Mines and Power, 1952-53; Senator, Federal Republic of Nigeria, 1960-61. Honorary degrees conferred on him include DSc (UNN), 1964 and DSc (Unilag), 1973. Died in London on December 22, 1974.

Also: *1st Nigerian Vice-Chancellor, University of Nigeria, Nsukka.*

1ST VICE-CHANCELLOR, UNILAG, TO BE CONFERRED THE INSTITUTION'S HONORARY DOCTORATE DEGREE

Prof. Eni Njoku, Vice-Chancellor, Unilag, from May 27, 1962 to 1965 who was conferred the honorary Doctor of Science (DSc) degree by the University of Lagos in 1973.

See also: *1st Nigerian University to confer honorary doctorate) degree on its former Vice-Chancellor,* ***entry under:*** *EDUCATION – ACADEMIC DISTINCTIONS/HONOURS.*

UNIVERSITY OF MAIDUGURI (UNIMAID)

1ST CHANCELLOR

HRH Oba Daniel Aladesanmi II, *Ewi* of Ado-Ekiti, from December 1979 to January 1983, when he died. Unimaid was established in 1975.

1ST PRO-CHANCELLOR

Chief Abdu Eke, born on September 7, 1923; educated at Yaba Higher College; University College, Ibadan; Sidney Sussex College, Cambridge, England. Posts held include Registrar, University of Ife (Obafemi Awolowo University), 1961-62 (June); Commissioner for Information, Western Region, June to July 1962; Registrar (1st), University of Lagos, 1962-71; Federal Commissioner (Minister) for Education, 1971-74.

1ST VICE-CHANCELLOR

Prof. E. U. Essien-Udom, from October 1975 (when the institution was established) to September 1979.

For biodata, see: *1st Nigerian Vice-Chancellor appointed chairman, National Universities Commission (NUC),* ***entry under*****:** EDUCATION – GENERAL.

1ST Ph.D. GRADUATE

Mrs Hauwa Ali, who bagged the institution's PhD degree in Education at the University's 9th Convocation ceremony held on Saturday February 6, 1988. Unimaid was established in 1975.

Mrs Ali was at the time a mother of four.

1ST UNIVERSITY LIBRARIAN

Dr Samuel E. Ifidon, appointed in 1979 and served in that capacity until 1983 when he took up an identical post at Bendel State University (BENSU).

For biodata, see: *1st University Librarian, Ambrose Alli State University.*

UNIVERSITY OF NIGERIA, NSUKKA (U.N.N.)

1ST CHANCELLOR

Rt Hon. Dr Nnamdi Azikiwe, from 1961 to 1966. Also the first Chairman of its Governing Council.

Born on November 16, 1904, in Zungeru, Niger State, Dr Azikiwe attended Hope Waddell Training Institution, Calabar; Methodist Boys' High School, Lagos; Storer College, West Virginia, USA; Howard University, Washington DC, USA; Lincoln University, Pennsylvania, USA; Columbia University, Morningside Heights, New York, USA. Dr Azikiwe holds the MA and MSc degrees and honorary LLD, DLitt and LittD degrees from various internationally recognised universities.

A well-known Nigerian journalist and politician, Dr Azikiwe was also the founder, as well as Governing Director, of African Continental Bank Ltd, and Premier of Eastern Region of Nigeria from 1954 to 1959. He also held several top positions in Nigeria's political hierarchy: President of the Nigerian Senate, 1960; Governor-General and Commander-in-Chief of the Armed Forces of the Federation of Nigeria, 1960 to 1963; President of the Federal Republic of Nigeria, 1963 to 1966. During the Second Republic, he was the leader of the Nigerian People's Party (NPP) and the party's presidential candidate. Dr Azikiwe was honoured by his kindred with the traditional title of *Owelle* of Onitsha.

Also: *1st Premier (defunct) Eastern Nigeria; 1st Nigerian Governor-General of the Federation; 1st President of Nigeria; 1st Queen's Privy Councillor in Nigeria; 1st President of Nigeria's Senate; among 1st set of Nigerians to be awarded the Grand Commander of the Federal Republic of Nigeria.*

Statue of Dr Nnamdi Azikiwe (see page 76) in Heroes Square, Owerri, Imo State.

PHOTOGRAPH BY FARIDHASL (2020, CC-BY-SA 4.0).

1ST PRO-CHANCELLOR

Sir Francis Akanu Ibiam, from 1966 to 1967. Note that, as 1st Chancellor, Dr Nnamdi Azikiwe had the additional portfolio of Chairman of the institution's Governing Council.

Born on November 29, 1906, Dr Ibiam holds the MBChB degrees and an honorary LLD of the University of Nigeria, 1961. He was a retired physician and politician. He attended Hope Waddell Training Institution, Calabar; King's College, Lagos; University of St Andrews, Scotland; and London

School of Hygiene and Tropical Medicine, England. He founded Abiriba Hospital in 1936 and was a Medical Superintendent of the Church of Scotland Mission Hospital, Itu, Akwa Ibom State, from 1945 to 1948.

As a politician, he was a member of the Legislative Council of Nigeria from 1947 to 1952 and a member of the Executive Council of Nigeria. He also served as the Governor of (defunct) Eastern Nigeria, 1960-1966. Dr Ibiam was knighted by the Queen of England in 1951, but renounced the title later. The traditional ruler of Unwana, Ebonyi State, with the title *Eze Ogo* I.

Also: *1st Governor, (defunct) Eastern Nigeria.*

1ST VICE-CHANCELLOR

Prof. George Marion Johnson, from the institution's inception in 1960 to 1964.

Born in Albuquerque, New Mexico, USA, in 1900, Dr Johnson held AB, LLB and JSD (California) degrees, Hon. LLD (Nigeria), Hon. LLD (Michigan State University, MSU), and was Professor Emeritus (MSU). A professor of Law and Dean of Howard University's Law School, he came to Nigeria on October 6, 1960 as head of an advisory group from MSU to supervise the take-off of the University of Nigeria.

On his arrival at Nsukka, he was appointed Acting Principal by the Provisional Council of the University.

Professor Johnson was a member of the Civil Rights Commission, whose activities helped to lay the foundation for the Voting Rights Acts of 1965 in the USA. He retired as Professor of MSU and died in Hawaii on Tuesday, August 11, 1987, at the age of 87 years.

1ST NIGERIAN VICE-CHANCELLOR

Prof. Eni Njoku, appointed in 1966 in succession to expatriate Vice-Chancellor, Prof. George Johnson. His tenure was however interrupted in May 1967 with the outbreak of the Nigerian Civil War.

Also: *1st Vice-Chancellor, University of Lagos, 1962-65.* ***For biodata, see:*** *1st Vice-Chancellor, University of Lagos (Unilag).*

1ST UNIVERSITY LIBRARIAN

Mr Sam. C. Nwoye, appointed in 1963, to 1988.

For biodata, see: *1st Nigerian University Librarian,* ***entry under:*** *LIBRARY SCIENCE.*

1ST U.N.N. ALUMUNUS CONFERRED HONORARY DOCTORATE DEGREE

Chief Engr (Dr) Emmanuel Chukwuemeka Iwuanyanwu, who was conferred the honorary Doctor of Business Administration (DBA) degree at the University of Nigeria, Nsukka, in 1986.

For biodata, see: *1st Nigerian University Alumnus to be conferred honorary doctorate degree,* ***entry under:*** *EDUCATION – ACADEMIC DISTINCTIONS/HONOURS.*

1ST NIGERIAN FEMALE U.N.N. PROFESSOR

Prof. Juliet Ijeoma Okonkwo, whose elevation to Professor was announced in September 1987, though with effect from October 1, 1984.

A Professor of English, specialising in African Literature, Mrs Okonkwo, from Anambra State, was educated at Queens College, Lagos; University of Ibadan (BA English); Oxford University, England (MA); UNN (PhD). Married with four children, three boys and a girl.

UNIVERSITY OF PORT HARCOURT (UNIPORT)

1ST CHANCELLOR

Alhaji Mustapha Umar El-Kanemi, Shehu of Bornu.

1ST PRO-CHANCELLOR

Alhaji Muhammed Tukur, OFR, OBE, the *Emu* of Youni.

1ST VICE-CHANCELLOR

Prof. Donald E. U. Ekong, appointed Principal, University College of Port Harcourt in September 1973 and formally assumed duty as Vice-Chancellor in February 1976, serving to 1981.

Born in 1933, Prof. Ekong graduated with a 1st-class (Honours) degree in Chemistry from University College, Ibadan (University of Ibadan), in 1967. Also possesses the Diploma Chemiker and Dr.rer.nat. at Heidelberg University Germany, 1962. After his post-doctoral research at Cambridge University, England, 1962-63, he joined the University of Ibadan as Lecturer in 1963, rising to Professor of Chemistry in 1969. Was Member, Governing Council, University of Ibadan. Later appointed Principal, Calabar Campus of University of Nigeria, Nsukka, on its creation in 1973.

Also: *1st Vice-Chancellor, University of Cross River State, Uyo.*

1ST UNIVERSITY LIBRARIAN

Mr George B. Affiah, appointed September 1976.

From Ikot-Edet, Abak, Akwa-Ibom State, born on October 20, 1939; attended Qua-Iboe Mission Secondary School, Etinan, 1953-57; Hope Waddell Training Institution, Calabar, 1958-59; University College, Ibadan, 1960-63 and 1964-65, bagging a BA (London) degree and Postgraduate Diploma in Librarianship (Ibadan).

Prior to the appointment, he occupied various library positions at the Economic Development Institute (EDI) of University of Nigeria, Enugu Campus, 1965; University of Lagos, 1965-73; The Polytechnic, Calabar, August 1973 to September 1976.

1ST INAUGURAL LECTURE

Titled 'Beyond the Python's Eye', by Prof. E. J. Allagoa. Prof. Allagoa holds a PhD (London) degree, and was also the institution's 1st Deputy Vice-Chancellor.

1ST MATRICULATION

Held on Saturday January 28, 1978, for 330 pioneer freshmen who commenced classes on November 24, 1977. The number comprised: Humanities – 49; Social Sciences – 58; Education – 56; Biological Sciences – 72; Chemical Sciences – 37; Physical Sciences – 52.

USMAN DANFODIO UNIVERSITY, SOKOTO (FORMERLY UNIVERSITY OF SOKOTO)

1ST CHANCELLOR

HRH Oba Lamidi Olayiwola Adeyemi III, *Alaafin* of Oyo, so appointed March 1980. The university was established along with seven others in September 1975.

A traditional ruler, Oba Adeyemi was born in 1939 in Oyo, Oyo State; educated at Ake School, Abeokuta; Tinubu Methodist School, Lagos; St Gregory's College, Lagos. He was installed *Alaafin* of Oyo on November 19, 1970.

1ST PRO-CHANCELLOR

F. O. Ihenacho, appointed in June 1978.

1ST UNIVERSITY LIBRARIAN

Mr. S. O. Agidee, so appointed in 1983. Earlier he had held the position in an acting capacity. Prior to his appointment, Agidee was Deputy University llbrarian, University of Ife (Obademi Awolowo University), Ile-Ife.

6 FINANCE, BANKING AND INSURANCE

1ST NIGERIAN CHARTERED ACCOUNTANT

Akintola Williams, who obtained the qualifying professional qualification in 1949.

Also: *1st Nigerian accountant to set up private accounting practice in Nigeria (1956).*

1ST NORTHERN NIGERIAN CHARTERED ACCOUNTANT

Alhaji Aliko Mohammed, who qualified in 1964.

From Bissau in Bauchi State, born on September 15, 1934; educated at Bissau Elementary School, 1942-51; Kano School of Hygiene, 1951-53; South London College of Commerce, 1960-64. Served in various capacities in the United Africa Company (UAC), Kano; Barclays Bank (Union Bank); Gaskiya Corporation; Northern Nigeria Housing Corporation, 1966-68; New Nigerian Development Co., Kaduna, 1968-71.

1st Chairman, National Insurance Corporation of Nigeria (NICON), 1970-76; Chairman, *Daily Times* Group Ltd, 1975-80; Chairman, Bank of the North; President, Nigerian Stock Exchange (NSE), 1980-88.

1ST NIGERIAN FEMALE CHARTERED ACCOUNTANT

Chief (Mrs) Olutoye Olusola Olakunrin who qualified as chartered accountant in England in 1964.

From Lagos, born on November 4, 1937, and educated at Government Secondary School, Aba; CMS Girls' School, Lagos; St Anne's School, Ibadan; Hawthorne School, Frinton-on-Sea, England; University of Birmingham, England. On qualifying as a chartered accountant, she returned to Nigeria to join the auditing firm of Messrs Peat, Marwick, Casselton, Elliot and Co. Was appointed Assistant Manager, Nigerian Industrial Development Bank (NIDB), 1972. Member, Constitution Drafting Committee, 1977-78; Fellow, Institute of Chartered Accountants of Nigeria (FCA), and pioneer President, Society of Women Accountants of Nigeria (SWAN).

1ST PRESIDENT, ASSOCIATION OF ACCOUNTANTS IN NIGERIA

Chief Akintola Williams, OFR, from the Association's inception to September 1965. The Association is forerunner to the present Institute of Chartered Accountants of Nigeria (ICAN), which was legally established in 1965 through Act. No. 15 of September 1, 1965.

Also: *1st Nigerian Accountant to set up private accounting practice in Nigeria.*

1ST NIGERIAN VICE-PRESIDENT, INTERNATIONAL FEDERATION OF ACCOUNTANTS (I.F.A.C.)

Olusola Faleye, elected to the 2nd highest office of the World Accounting body on November 9, 1984 at the IFAC Council meeting held in Manila, Philippines.

Nigeria had remained one of the Council's 15 members of the 66-nation body since it unseated South Africa in 1977 and prevented her from representing Africa on the Council.

1ST NIGERIAN FEMALE ACCOUNTANT-GENERAL

Mrs Victoria Obianuju Eronini (née Okeke), appointed Accountant-General of (the newly created) Imo State in 1976 and served until 1981.

From Nnewi, Anambra State, but married into Mbieri, near Owerri, Imo State. She was born on August 31, 1936, and attended CMS Central School, Nnewi, 1943-48; Methodist Girls' School, Ovim, 1949-50; Archbishop Crowther Memorial Girls' School, Elelenwa, 1951-55; Balham and Tooting College of Commerce, London, 1956-59; University of London, 1982-84; Nigerian Law School, Lagos. Holds the Fellowship of the Chartered Institute of Secretaries (FCIS), LLB (London), 1984, and BL (1985). Was first appointed Accountant, former Eastern Nigeria Civil Service, in May 1959, rising to Chief Accountant, East Central State, in 1974. Later rose to Permanent Secretary, Cabinet Office, 1981, before her retirement in May 1986. Chairman, Board of Directors, Imo Concorde Hotel, Owerri; Member, Board of Trustees Imo State Airport Trust Fund.

1ST NIGERIAN FEMALE LICENSED STOCK-BROKER

Dr (Mrs) Ndi Okereke-Onyiuke, Director of Research and Information Systems and Assistant General Manager of the Nigerian Stock Exchange (NSE), Lagos; later DG (Chief Executive), NSE. Was spotted by a Federal Government delegation on the trading floor of the New York Stock Exchange in 1983 and invited home to help nurture the NSE.

Born in 1951, she holds an MBA degree in Finance and Computer Science and PhD in Business Administration from New York University, USA. The only female Director of the Co-operative and Commerce Bank (CCB), she was also Director in the National Directorate of Employment.

NIGERIA'S 1ST CURRENCY

Issued July 1, 1959, following the formal commencement of operations by the Central Bank of Nigeria. The issuance thus terminated the issue functions of the West African Currency Board in Nigeria.

NIGERIA'S (1ST) CHANGE TO DECIMAL CURRENCY

On January 1, 1973, by virtue of the Decimal Currency Decree No. 21 of May 1971, which gave legal effect to the currency change plan.

By this change the unit of currency in Nigeria became the Naira, which is divisible into 100 Kobo. Thus under the decimal system only two units are in use, Naira being the major and Kobo the minor unit, Prior to the change the country operated the three-unit colonial system of pounds (£), shillings (s.) and pence (d.).

Above: bank note for £1, depicting the Central Bank of Nigeria Building in Lagos. Nigeria used the British currency system of pounds, shillings and pence until 1973 (see page 84).

BY PRACHAYA ROEKDEETHAWEESAB, COURTESY OF SHUTTERSTOCK.

Above: 50-kobo bank note, issued from 1973 to 1978, following Nigeria's conversion to decimal currency.

ITEM IN THE POSSESSION OF REGENTS COURT PRESS LTD.

NIGERIA'S (1ST) CHANGE-OVER OF ITS FISCAL (FINANCIAL) YEAR FROM APRIL–MARCH, TO JANUARY–DECEMBER

The Bill authorising the change was passed into law by the Senate on February 12, 1980, under President Shehu Shagari. Its effective year was the 1980 financial year, meaning that the financial year spanned April 1 to December 31, 1980.

1ST STATE WHOSE ANNUAL BUDGET (APPROPRIATION) HIT THE BILLION NAIRA MARK

Lagos State, in its 1988 budget announced on January 11, 1988 by Governor Mike Akbigbe. The total budget package was N1.76 billion.

1ST NIGERIAN UNIVERSITY TO MOUNT A DEGREE PROGRAMME IN ACCOUNTANCY

University of Nigeria, Nsukka, from 1961 at its Enugu Campus.

1ST GOVERNOR OF CENTRAL BANK OF NIGERIA (C.B.N.)

Sir Ray P. Fenton, appointed in September 1958 and served until 1963. A British citizen, Fenton was invited to set up the Central Bank of Nigeria (CBN) from the Bank of England where he was serving prior to his appointment.

Although the motion for the establishment of a Central Bank for Nigeria was introduced in the House of Representatives by Hon. Kingsley Ozumba Mbadiwe on April 9, 1952, it was not until March 1958 that Chief Festus Okotie-Eboh, then Federal Minister of Finance, announced in the Federal Parliament that, come 1959, the CBN would be established.

Thus, following the passage of the Bill into law, the CBN was formally opened on July 1, 1959 in a six-storey building at Tinubu Square, Lagos. Later transferred headquarters to nation's capital Abuja.

1ST NIGERIAN GOVERNOR OF CENTRAL BANK OF NIGERIA

Alhaji Aliyu Mai-Bornu, Governor from 1963 to 1967. From Bornu State, he was born in 1919 and educated at Yola Middle School; Kaduna College; University of Bristol, England, 1954-57. Served as Administrative Officer of Northern Nigeria, 1957-59, before joining the Central Bank of Nigeria, first as Secretary, 1961-62, then Deputy Governor, 1962-63, and Governor, 1963-67. Was also Acting Governor, International Monetary Fund for Nigeria, 1963-67.

NIGERIA'S 1ST COMMERCIAL BANK

First Bank of Nigeria Ltd, established in 1894 as Bank of British West Africa. Functioned as the Government's official bank until the establishment of the Central Bank of Nigeria in 1959.

First Bank is jointly owned by the Federal Government (44.8%), the Nigerian public (17.2%) and the Standard Chartered Bank Ltd, London (38%).

Name changes are: First Bank of Nigeria Ltd, 1977-date; Standard Bank of Nigeria Ltd, 1969-77; Bank of West Africa Ltd, 1959-69; Bank of British West Africa, 1894-1959.

NIGERIA'S 1ST INDIGENOUS COMMERCIAL BANK

National Bank of Nigeria Ltd, established (incorporated) in 1933. Owned largely by Odu'a Investment Co. Ltd, (99.8%) and Nigerian citizens (0.2%).

NIGERIA'S 1ST MERCHANT BANK

NAL Merchant Bank Ltd (fomerly Nigerian Acceptances Ltd), incorporated in 1960. Shareholding: Federal Government – 20%; National Insurance Corporation of Nigeria (NICON) – 25%; New Nigerian Development Co. Ltd – 10%; NAL Staff and Nigerian citizens – 6.4%; American Express Bank Ltd – 26%; John Holt Group – 10%; Credit Lyonnais – 2.6%.

1ST NIGERIAN MANAGING DIRECTOR, WORLD BANK

Dr Ngozi Okonjo-Iweala, appointed as the first Black Managing Director (Operations) in 2007. Number 2 position in the apex global development finance institution, the 1st Nigerian to be so appointed. In 2012 she contested the Presidency of the organisation but lost.

An economist and international development professional with over thirty years' experience working in Africa, Asia, Europe and Latin America, Mrs Okonjo-Iweala hails from Ogwashi-Ukwu, Delta State. Had served twice as Nigeria's Finance Minister, 2003-06 and 2011-13, and briefly Foreign Minister, 2006, thus also becoming 1st female to occupy both positions.

Listed among: 'World's Top 50 Most Influential Women' and 'Africa's Top 10'.

See also entry under: *WOMEN.*

1ST NIGERIAN HEAD, AFRICAN DEVELOPMENT BANK (A.D.B.)

Dr Akinwumi Adesina, appointed president, African Development Bank (ADB) on September 21, 2015. ADB is a financial institution comprising 54 African and 26 non-African countries, and promotes economic and social progress in Africa through loans, equity investment and technical assistance. Was established in 1964 with headquarters in Tunisia.

Born in Ibadan, Oyo State, on February 6, 1960, he graduated BSc (1st-class) andnd MSc in Agricultural Economics, both from Obafemi Awolowo University (OAU), Ile-Ife, and later proceeded to Purdue University, Indiana, USA, bagging a PhD degree in 1988.

Subsequently worked in research centres specialising in rice. Was Nigeria's Minister of Agriculture (under president Goodluck Jonathan) at time of his appointment into ADB.

1ST M.D./C.E.O., AFRICAN CONTINENTAL BANK (A.C.B.)

Christian Adibe, appointed Managing Director/Chief Executive of the bank in March 1988. Since the bank's inception in 1947, its chief had been designated General Manager. ACB, the nation's second oldest indigenous bank, was jointly owned by the governments of old Anambra, Imo and Rivers States. Until his appointment as Managing Director, Mr Adibe was the General Manager/Project Co-ordinator of the Lagos-based Emzor Pharmaceutial Company.

Born in 1947 in Ajalli, Anambra State, he possesses a BSc degree in Economics and Social Sciences from Harvard University, USA, 1975, and a Master of Business Administration degree from Harvard Graduate School of Business, Boston, USA. One time Deputy Manager (Corporate Finance), International Merchant Bank (IMB), Lagos.

1ST CHAIRMAN, NIGERIAN INDUSTRIAL DEVELOPMENT BANK (N.I.D.B.)

Chief Mathias Nwafor Ugochukwu, appointed in 1964. The bank was established on January 22, 1964, under the original name Nigerian Industrial Bank, for the purpose of encouraging the growth of indigenous middle and large businesses through granting of loans.

A successful businessman from Umunze, Anambra State, Ugochukwu was born in 1926, attended St Augustine's School, Umunze; Government School, Jos; Southern Police College, Ikeja. He had enlisted in the Nigeria Police Force in 1946. Proprietor, Ugofoam (Nig.) Ltd. Also Chairman, Nigerian Railway Corporation; Chairman, Marketing Board; Chairman, Federal Tenders Board; Chairman, John Holt (Nig.) Ltd. Crowned the traditional titles: *Igwe* of Orumba and *Abilikete* of Umunze.

1ST NIGERIAN FEMALE BANK CHAIRMAN

Chief (Mrs) Dorcas Bolajoko Ayodele Kuforiji-Olubi (née Kuforiji), appointed Chairman, United Bank for Africa (UBA) in November 1984. UBA is one of Nigeria's largest commercial banks.

An economist, Chief (Mrs) Kuforiji-Olubi was born on September 28, 1936 in Lagos, attended St Theresa's Convent, Jos, 1944-51; St Agnes' Teachers' Training College, Ikeja, 1951-55; University of London, 1960-63. Joined Vivian, Younger and Bond (Nig.) Ltd in 1968, rising to Managing Director in the early 1970s. She has been Chairman, Ogun-Oshun River Basin Development Authority; Member, Institute of Chartered Secretaries, Institute of Directors and Institute of Chartered Accountants of Nigeria (ICAN).

Also: *1st Female Member, Institute of Chartered Accountants of Nigeria, 1970; 1st Female President, Institute of Chartered Accountants of Nigeria (ICAN), June 1989.*

NIGERIA'S 1ST INSURANCE COMPANY

Royal Exchange Assurance, a British insurance firm, whose first branch office in Nigeria was opened in Lagos in 1921. The firm dominated the Nigerian insurance scene until 1949 when three other expatriate (British) firms joined. Wholly indigenous insurance firms first appeared in Nigeria after independence (1960).

Royal Exchange was later incorporated in Nigeria in 1969 with joint foreign and indigenous equity participation.

1ST CHAIRMAN, NATIONAL INSURANCE CORPORATION OF NIGERIA (N.I.C.O.N.)

Alhaji Aliko Mohammed, from 1970 to 1976.

For biodata, see: *1st Northern Nigerian Chartered Accountant.*

NIGERIA'S 1ST-EVER AGRICULTURAL INSURANCE SCHEME

Launched by the Niger Insurance Co. Ltd on Monday May 4, 1987.

The Federal Government approved the scheme, under which poultry and livestock farmers would be indemnified against losses in their animal stock. The scheme only covered losss resulting from death due to accidents or unpreventable diseases. Losses through theft, mysterious disappearance, or other unaccountable shortage were not covered. Losses in the event of fire were also indemnified.

Niger Insurance Company Ltd, formerly Yorkshire Insurance Company, was established in 1961 and is one of Nigeria's oldest insurance underwriters.

7 INDUSTRY, SCIENCE AND TECHNOLOGY

1ST PRESIDENT, NIGERIAN ACADEMY OF SCIENCE (N.A.S.)

Prof. Victor Adenuga Oyenuga, from 1977 to 1978. NAS confers on its benefactors the authority to add the letters FAS to one's name.

Born on April 9, 1917 in Isenyin, Ijebu-Ode, Ogun State. Oyenuga attended King's College, Newcastle-upon-Tyne, 1945-48; University of Durham, England, 1958-51, obtaining BSc, PhD and DSc degrees in Agricultural Sciences. Between 1951 and 1979, he served as lecturer, Professor, Head of Department, Dean of Faculty and Deputy Vice-Chancellor in the Universities of Ibadan and Ife (Obafemi Awolowo University). Was President, Agric. Society of Nigeria, 1962-64; President, Nutrition Society of Nigeria, 1966-68; President, Science Association of Nigeria, 1967-70.

1ST NIGERIAN TO HEAD THE CENTRE FOR THE DEVELOPMENT OF INDUSTRY (C.D.I.) OF THE A.C.P.-E.E.C. LOMÉ CONVENTION

Dr Isaac Adebayo Akinrele, appointed Director of CDI on March 20, 1985. By this appointment he also became the 1st CDI Director to come from an ACP (African, Caribbean, Pacific) country. Dr Akinrele joined the CDI at its inception in January 1977 and served as Deputy Director under Lomé I and II Conventions. His appointment as Director lasted the duration of the 3rd Lomé Convention.

From Ondo State, Dr Akinrele was born in 1934 and had his university education at Cambridge, London and Ibadan, bagging a PhD in Food Biochemistry and Technology.

Before joining the CDI he was Director of Research and Managing Director of the Commercial Production Unit at the Federal Institute of Industrial Research, Oshodi (FIIRO), Lagos.

1ST NIGERIAN M.D./C.E.O., FOOD SPECIALITIES (NIG.) LTD.

Chief Olusegun Osunkeye, whose appointment was announced by the company's Chairman, Prince Ado Ibrahim and published in *National Concord* of Monday June 27, 1988. He succeeded the expatriate (Swiss) Managing Director, Mr Frei.

Prior to his appointment, Chief Osunkeye was Deputy Managing Director.

1ST NIGERIAN M.D./C.E.O., INTERNATIONAL PAINTS (WEST AFRICA) (I.P.W.A.)

Mr Claudius Omosalewa Williams, appointed with effect from August 1, 1988, in succession to Mr R.T. Temple, a Briton. IPWA was incorporated in Nigeria in 1961.

Williams was educated at Baptist Academy, Lagos, and Staffordshire College of Commerce (now West Bromwich College of Technology). An Associate Member of the Chartered Institute of Management Accountants, and a Fellow of the Institute of Chartered Accountants of Nigeria. He joined IPWA in January 1976 as Chief Accountant, rising to Deputy Managing Director before his most recent appointment.

NIGERIA'S 1ST MOTOR-CAR ASSEMBLY PLANT

The Volkswagen Assembly Plant at Ojo, Lagos State, commissioned by then Head of State, General Yakubu Gowon, on March 21, 1975.

Using completely-knocked-down (CKD) components imported mainly from Brazil, the plant manufactured the Volkswagen brands of cars and had an installed capacity of 40,000 cars per annum. Built at a cost of N423.4 million. The company's partnership arrangement comprises: Volkswagen of Germany – 40%; Federal Government of Nigeria – 35%; Lagos State Government – 4%; Nigerian Distributors – 10%; BHF Frankfurt (Private Financer) – 11%.

1ST 'MADE-IN-NIGERIA' CAR PISTONS

Developed and manufactured in December 1986 by a team of research scientists from the Department of Metallurgical and Materials Engineering, Anambra State University of Technology (ASUTECH), Enugu, led by Dr I. C. Okafor.

The project begun in 1985, and reached completion stage after a series of modifications and tests. On February 12, 1987, the pistons were tested by fixing a set of four in a university vehicle with registration number AN 4076K. The vehicle and pistons indicated perfect working condition. Compression tests also carried out at the UTC Motors, Enugu on March 17, 1987 confirmed earlier findings.

IST 'MADE-IN-NIGERIA' COMPUTER

The *ASUTECH 80* model, designed, developed and built by the Anambra State University of Technology, Enugu in 1982-83.

NIGERIA'S 1ST-EVER EXPORT OF AMMONIA PRODUCT

On July 23, 1987, when 8,000 metric tonnes of ammonia, worth about US $1m, produced by the N700m National Fertilizer Company, (NAFCON), Onne, near Port Harcourt, Rivers State, was carted away from the company's port by a ship *MV Kongsgas* bound for Spain.

NIGERIA'S 1ST CEMENT FACTORY

The Nigerian Cement Company Ltd, Nkalagu, near Enugu, incorporated on November 13, 1954 to manufacture cement. Commenced production on January 1,1958 with the brand name *Nigercem.*

Jointly owned by the Federal, old Anambra and Imo State governments, as well as Nigerian shareholders. Shares were first offered to the public on November 5, 1958. The factory closed down on August 20, 1967, on account of the Nigerian Civil War and re-opened on September 9, 1971. The company's authorised, issued and fully paid share capital was N12 million in 6.3 million ordinary shares of N2.00 each.

NIGERIA'S 1ST PHARMACEUTICAL MANUFACTURING PLANT

Built and commissioned in 1962 in Aba, Abia State, by Pfizer (Nig.) Ltd. was irreparably damaged as a result of the Nigerian Civil War, 1967 to 1970.

NIGERIA'S 1ST NEWSPRINT MANUFACTURING COMPANY

The Nigerian Newsprint Manufacturing Company (NNMC), Oku-Iboku, Akwa Ibom State, commissioned in July 1986 by President Ibrahim Babangida, although the agreement for its establishment was signed as far back as January 30, 1975 in Lagos between the Federal Commissioner (Minister) of Industries, Colonel M. I. Wushishi and a foreign construction firm. The contract value was N76 million at the time. Produced pulp and newsprint paper.

1ST TIME COAL WAS MINED IN NIGERIA

In 1916 at Udi Mines, Enugu State, although coal deposit was first discovered in large commercial quantities in the Enugu coalfield in 1909. The strategic importance of this discovery stimulated the development of coal mining during the First World War. The first colliery was thus opened in 1915.

The Mines were first administered by the Railways but later became the responsibility of a separate government department. Nigerian coal is mostly of the 'bituminous' grade, next in quality only to the 'anthracite' grade. There are, however, only four Nigerian coal mines: Onyeama and Okpara mines (both in Enugu and underground) and Okaba and Owukpa mines (both in Benue State and surface).

NIGERIA'S 1ST BEER BREWERY

Nigerian Brewery Ltd (NBL) factory at Iganmu, Lagos, which came on stream in 1949. Started off with the production of 'Star' lager beer. The company was incoporated in Nigeria on November 16, 1946.

1ST GUINNESS BREWERY OUTSIDE THE BRITISH ISLES

At Ikeja, Lagos, commissioned in 1962 but went on stream in March 1963. Initially employed 400 Nigerians and produced 400 barrels of 'stout' beer per day. Capacity doubled with expansion work in 1970.

Although Guinness (Nig.) Ltd was incorporated as limited liability company as far back as 1950, it initially engaged importation and distribution of Guiness stout from the parent stock in Dublin, Ireland and went into local production much later.

1ST NIGERIAN BREWERY TO ACHIEVE 100% LOCAL-CONTENT PRODUCTION

Guinness Nigeria Ltd, in its production of the new beer brand called 'Merit' lager beer, which was introduced into the Nigerian market in 1987. The beer is brewed with 100% maize as substitute for imported barley, whose local growing (in Nigeria) in commercial quantities has thus far proved unsuccessful.

NIGERIA'S 1ST DISCOVERY OF CRUDE OIL IN COMMERCIAL QUANTITY

At Oloibiri in the Brass Division of Bayelsa or Rivers State, in January 1956 by then Shell BP Oil Company (now Shell Petroleum Development Company).

Before the discovery Shell had sunk over N30 million in fruitless oil exploration, starting with its first well at Iho, near Owerri, Imo State. As at February 1988, no fewer than eight wells had been completed at Oloibiri, five producing oil.

Shell, the Anglo-Dutch consortium, was incorporated in Nigeria in 1936 and commenced operations in 1937, following the grant to it by Nigeria of sole concessionary rights covering the whole territory of Nigeria.

PLACE WHERE OIL (PETROLEUM) WAS 1ST PROSPECTED IN NIGERIA

Araromi area of Ondo State in 1908 by a German firm called the Nigerian Bitumen Manufacturing Corporation. Unfortunately little luck attended the exercise.

SHELL PETROLEUM DEVELOPMENT COMPANY (S.P.D.C.)'S 1ST OIL (PETROLEUM) WELL IN NIGERIA

Dug at Iho, 16 kilometres from Owerri, capital of Imo State, in 1951, Unfortunately, oil was not found in commercial quantity.

NIGERIA'S 1ST EXPORT OF CRUDE OIL

On February 17, 1958, when the Anglo-Dutch Consortium (SPDC) shipped 9,000 tonnes of Nigeria's first crude oil from Port Harcourt in an 18,000-ton oil tanker – *Hemifusus* – to the Royal Dutch Shell refineries in Holland. Sitting Prime Minister Abubakar Tafawa Balewa performed the loading ceremony, which was watched by several local and foreign dignitaries including Mr R. A. Njoku, then Federal Minister of Transport, Alhaji Muhammadu Ribadu, then Federal Minister of Lagos Affairs, Mines and Power, and Mr D. Fleming, then General Manager, Shell-BP.

NIGERIA'S 1ST PETROLEUM REFINERY

Sited at Alesa-Eleme, Port Harcourt, Rivers State, and commissioned in October 1965. Original name: Nigerian Petroleum Refining Company. Now: NNPC Refinery.

At inception the plant had a processing capacity of 60,000 barrels of crude oil per day.

When in 1954 the Federal Government granted an oil prospecting licence to then Shell-BP, the contract agreement stipulated that as soon as crude oil production reached the 500,000 barrels-per-day mark, a refinery should be built in Nigeria. This target was reached in 1958, from which time the refinery construction began, culminating in its completion and commissioning in October 1965. The contract between the Federal Government and Shell-BP Petroleum Company Ltd for the construction and operation of the refinery (Port Harcourt) was signed on July 25, 1962, while actual construction work started in 1963. The total cost then was N20 million.

Nigeria's second petroleum refinery at Warri, Delta State, was commissioned in 1978, while the third at Kaduna was commissioned in 1980.

NIGERIA'S 1ST NATIONAL OIL MUSEUM

At Oloibiri in Brass Local Government Area of Rivers or Bayelsa State. The foundation stone was laid on May 16, 1983.

1ST NIGERIAN O.P.E.C. PRESIDENT

Alhaji Yahaya Dikko, so elected on September 9, 1982. Dikko was at the time Presidential Adviser on Petroleum Resources during President Shagari's regime. He was unanimously re-elected at OPEC's 67th extra-ordinary meeting held on March 12, 1983.

A chartered engineer from Kaduna State, Dikko was born on August 12, 1932; educated at Brighton Technical College, England. Fellow of the Institute of Electrical Engineers, UK. Also foundation member, Nigerian Society of Engineers. Was 1st General Manager, National Electric Power Authority, (NEPA), 1973. Awarded national honour of Officer of the Federal Republic of Nigeria (OFR).

1ST NIGERIAN PRESIDENT OF O.P.E.C. TO BE ELECTED FOUR CONSECUTIVE TIMES

Alhaji Rilwanu Lukman, whose fourth-term re-election at the 82nd meeting of OPEC in Vienna, Austria, was announcd by the Public Affairs Department of the Nigerian National Petroleum Corporation (NNPC) in Lagos on Wednesday, December 9, 1987. Alhaji Rilwanu was first elected OPEC President on June 25, 1986; re-elected, October 6, 1986; December 13, 1986; December 9, 1987. Re-elected for a record seventh time, June 1989.

Born in Zaria in 1938, he attended Barewa College, Zaria; Nigerian College of Arts, Science and Technology, Zaria; Ahmadu Bello University, Zaria; University of London. Graduated as a mining engineer in 1962 from the Royal School of Mining of the University of London's Imperial College.

On return to Nigeria, he joined the Federal Ministry of Mines and Power, Jos, as Senior Inspector of Mines; Cement Company of Northern Nigeria, Sokoto in 1970, as General Manager, where he served until 1974 before his posting back to the Nigerian Mining Corporation, Jos, this time as General Manager/Chief Executive.

One-time Nigeria's Minister of Mines, Power and Steel, 1984-86, before his posting as Minister of Petroleum Resources. Conferred honorary doctorate degree of University of Bologna, Italy; and Knight Commander of the Order of the British Empire (KBE).

1ST NIGERIAN HEAD/C.E.O., N.N.P.C. REFINERY, ALESA-ELEME, PORT-HARCOURT

Iheakachi Tamunonenginye James Ordor. Was General Manager (Chief Executive) from 1973 to 1975. An engineer from Akwette in Ukwa LGA of Abia State.

NIGERIA'S 1ST-EVER NATIONAL 'SCIENCE & TECHNOLOGY FAIR'

A six-day fair declared open in Lagos on Monday October 10, 1988 by Chief of General Staff, Vice-Admiral Augustus Aikhomu. Over twenty-five research institutes and higher institutions exhibited inventions, productions and prototypes at the fair, whose principal objective was to provide exposure to local inventors and inventions as well as stimulate indigenous technology. Held at the Tafawa Balewa Square, Lagos, as part of a National Science and Technology Week.

8 LABOUR

NIGERIA'S 1ST TRADE UNION

The Southern Nigeria Civil Service Union, inaugurated on August 19, 1912. Later changed name to Nigerian Civil Service Union after the creation of modern Nigeria in 1914 with the amalgamation of the Northern and Southern Protectorates.

NIGERIA'S 1ST NATIONAL TRADE UNION LEADER

Comrade Michael Athokhawien Ominus Imoudu. The Railway Workers' Union, which he led, was the first Union to be registered according to the Trade Union Ordinance of Nigeria, 1938, which legalised trade unions and gave them the right to engage in collective bargaining.

Born in Sabongida-Ora, Edo State, on September 17, 1902, Imoudu attended several primary schools, finishing at Agbor Government School in 1927. He joined the Posts and Telegraphs (P&T) Department, Lagos, in 1928 as a linesman. Resigned and joined Nigerian Railways in 1929, first as labourer and later as an apprentice turner. Helped found the Railway Workers' Union in 1932, which he led in its now-historic 1st railway workers' march from Railway headquarters, Ebute Metta, to the Government House, Lagos on September 30, 1941, protesting the hourly pay system for workers. On retirement, he was conferred Life Presidency, Railway and Port Workers' Union.

NIGERIA'S 1ST RECORDED GENERAL (NATION-WIDE) WORKERS' STRIKE

Began on June 22, 1945. Led by Michael Imoudu, it lasted 37 days and involved all the technical workers of 17 labour unions, to back up their demand for a 50% pay rise, dubbed Cost-of-Living Allowance (COLA), and for a minimum daily wage of 2s. 6d. (N50,000 in modern values). Started in Lagos but soon spread nation-wide involving big cities like Ibadan, Enugu and Port Harcourt. Two frontline newspapers, the *Daily*

Comet and *West African Pilot*, were banned on July 7, 1945 as a result of their strike involvement

NIGERIA'S 1ST LABOUR MINISTER

Chief Matthew Tawo Mbu, Federal Minister of Labour from 1953 to 1954.

For biodata, see: *Nigeria's 1st Representative at the United Nations (UN),* ***entry under:*** *POLITICS AND GOVERNMENT – DIPLOMATIC/EXTERNAL AFFAIRS.*

1ST PRESIDENT OF NIGERIAN LABOUR CONGRESS (N.L.C.)

Alhaji Hassan Sunmonu, following the inauguratiuon of the reconstituted NLC on February 28, 1978 in Ibadan. Nigeria's 41 industrial unions merged into one Nigerian Labour Congress (NLC). Sunmonu was re-elected for a second term as President in 1981 and vacated in February 1984. Prior to his election as NLC President, he was President of the Civil Service Technical Workers' Union.

See also: *1st Nigerian Executive Secretary-General of the continental Organisation of African Trade Union Unity (OATUU).*

1ST PRESIDENT, NIGERIAN UNION OF TEACHERS (N.U.T.)

Rev. Israel O. Ransome-Kuti, elected President in July 1931 and served until January 1955. The NUT, generally regarded as Nigeria's first organised trade union, started in 1931 as a federation of five member unions, and was administered as a federal body until January 1941, when it was re-organised into a unitary organisation.

Prior to 1931 only teachers in Lagos and the five Yoruba towns of Lagos, Abeokuta, Agege, Ibadan and Ijebu-Ode had banded themselves together to form unions for the purpose of effecting collective bargaining.

Rev. Ransome-Kuti was born in Abeokuta, Ogun State in 1900. A renowned educationist, he was Principal, Ijebu-Ode Grammar School, 1918-32;

Principal, Abeokuta Grammar School, from 1932 to his retirement in 1954. Died April 6, 1955.

1ST CONFERENCE OF THE INTERNATIONAL LABOUR ORGANIZATION (I.L.O.) HELD IN NIGERIA

Opened in Lagos, on December 10, 1963, with 22 African countries participating.

1ST NIGERIAN (AFRICAN) CHAIRMAN OF INTERNATIONAL LABOUR ORGANIZATION (I.L.O.)

Chief Joseph Modupe Johnson, from 1963. He later resigned in protest against South Africa's presence at the ILO Conference in Geneva.

From Lagos, born on March 30, 1912, he attended St Mathias Catholic School, Lagos, 1918-24; Holy Cross School, Lagos, 1924-28; William Wilberforce Academy, Lagos, 1928-32. Worked with the British Bank for West Africa (now, First Bank), 1932-35. Enlisted in the Army in Northern Nigeria in 1938 and was discharged on March 30, 1946 as Warrant Officer II. Elected NCNC Councillor for Ibadan District Council, March 1954. Became Federal Minister of Labour, Welfare and Internal Affairs in 1957 and resigned in 1959. Was conferred the title *Apesin* of Lagos by the then *Oba* of Lagos, Sir Adeniji Adele II. Died in May 1987.

1ST NIGERIAN SECRETARY-GENERAL, ORGANISATION OF AFRICAN TRADE UNION UNITY (O.A.T.U.U.)

Alhaji Hassan Sunmonu, elected on October 24, 1986, at the 2nd Extra-ordinary Congress of the OATUU in Addis Ababa, Ethiopia, thus replacing Kenya's James Denis Akumu, the pioneer Secretary-General from 1974. OATUU'S Secretriat is in Accra, Ghana.

Prior to his appointment, Sunmonu was President, Nigerian Labour Congress (NLC) from 1978 to 1984.

See also: *1st President, Nigerian Labour Congress (NLC).*

1ST NIGERIAN PRESIDENT, WORLD CONFEDERATION OF ORGANISATIONS OF THE TEACHING PROFESSION (W.C.O.T.P.)

Dr Joseph Odidi Itotoh, August 2, 1986 to 1990, following a keen contest in Regina, Saskatchewan, Canada, at the 31st Biennial Assembly of delegates. By this appointment, Dr Itotoh became the political head of WCOTP, the largest teacher organisation in 101 countries all world-wide, the 2nd Black occupant of the post.

Dr Itotoh graduated from University of Nigeria, Nsukka, with BA (Hons), 1965. Thereafter he took Teachers Grade II exam. Enrolled with London University for a diploma in education, Master's degree and thereafter PhD degree from the University of Ibadan (in education). One-time Principal, Immaculate Conception College (ICC), Benin-City.

NIGERIA'S 1ST POST-INDEPENDENCE GENERAL WORKERS' SALARY REVIEW

The Morgan Salary Review, which was commissioned on October 10, 1963, headed by Mr Justice Adeyinka Morgan, the commission completed and submitted its report to the government on March 31, 1964. The government's acceptance of the report's recommendations was announced on May 22, 1964.

1ST WOMEN'S UPRISING (RIOT) IN NIGERIA

Aba Women's Unprising of 1929, protesting payment of taxes. Lasted from December 9 to 12, 1929.

1ST NIGERIAN TO ORGANISE A SUCCESSFUL STRIKE

Obafemi Awolowo, in 1937, when he organised an eight-day strike of motor transport owners throughout the (defunct) Western Region. Was also one of the founders of the 1st Trade Union Congress of Nigeria – the first national labour organisation in Nigeria.

For biodata, see: *1st Premier, (defunct) Western Nigeria,* ***entry under:*** *POLITICS AND GOVERNMENT – GOVERNORS/PREMIERS.*

1ST MAY DAY TO BE MARKED WITH NATION-WIDE PUBLIC HOLIDAY IN NIGERIA

May Day, i.e. May 1, 1981, under President Shehu Shagari. May 1 every year has always been declared Workers' Solidarity Day throughout the world since 1886, following the first ever workers' strike action called to protest severe, inhuman, work hours. Following the strike action, work hours were reduced to eight hours a day from as high as 18 hours previously.

Obafemi Awolowo, who organised Nigeria's first successful strike in 1937 (see page 103). He was later the first Premier of Western Nigeria (see page 154). This image shows how he is depicted on N100 bank notes.

BY PRACHAYA ROEKDEETHAWEESAB, COURTESY OF SHUTTERSTOCK.

9 LAW

1ST NIGERIAN LAWYER

Christopher Alexander Sapara-Williams, who, on completion of full legal studies at Wesley College, Sheffield, England from 1876 to 1879, was called to the Bar (Inner Temple), and enrolled as the 1st indigenous Barrister and Solicitor of the Gold Coast Colony (Ghana, to which Lagos Colony was then attached), on August 27, 1880.

Born on July 19, 1855, Sapara-Williams was one of the Sierra Leone Creole children of Yoruba 'recaptives' believed to be an Ijesha Yoruba. Attended CMS Grammar School, Lagos; Wesley College, Sheffield, England, 1875-79. Entered private legal practice, first in the Gold Coast (Ghana) then Lagos, Nigeria. Was member of the Legislative Council (Legco) from 1901 until his death on March 14, 1915.

1ST NIGERIAN ENROLLED AS LAWYER IN NIGERIA

Nash Hamilton William, enrolled (sworn in) in the colonial Supreme Court of Nigeria on February 20, 1886.

1ST IGBO LAWYER

Louis Nwachukwu Mbanefo, called to the Bar (Middle Temple), London, in 1935 after obtaining the LLB degree from the University of London in the same year. Enrolled at the Supreme Court, Lagos on August 13, 1937.

From Onitsha, Anambra State, he was born on May 13, 1911; educated at St Mary's School, Onitsha; Methodist Grammar School, Lagos; King's College, Lagos. Rather than enter legal practice he proceeded to King's College, Cambridge, and bagged the BA and MA degrees in History. Commenced private legal practice in Onitsha on return. Also engaged in politics. Was member, Eastern House of Assembly, 1950-52. Appointed Judge of the Supreme Court (1952); Judge of the High Court of Eastern Nigeria (1956); Judge of the Federal Supreme Court of Appeal (1958); ad-hoc Judge,

International Court of Justice at the Hague (1961). Pro-Chancellor, University of Ibadan; 1965-67; President, Christian Council of Nigeria; President, World Council of Churches, 1972. Awarded honorary LLD of the University of Nigeria, Nsukka (1963). Died March 28, 1977.

***Also:** 1st Igbo Magistrate, 1948; 1st indigenous Chief Justice of Eastern Nigeria, 1959.*

1ST NIGERIAN FEMALE LAWYER

Mrs A. R. O. M. Alakija, enrolled as a lawyer on May 13, 1946 and called to the Bar on July 3, 1946.

Born in 1921. Educated at University of Glasgow; London School of Economics and Political Science, University of London; University of Cambridge. Was Member, Nigeria's Delegation to the UN, 1961-65; President, International Federation of Women Lawyers (FDA). Awarded honorary LLD by Columbia University, New York, USA.

NIGERIA'S 1ST CHIEF JUSTICE

Sir Stafford Foster-Sutton, appointed in 1956, retired in February 1958, replaced by Nigeria's 1st indigenous Chief Justice of the Federation.

NIGERIA'S 1ST INDIGENOUS CHIEF JUSTICE

Sir Adetokunbo Adegboyega Ademola, appointed in 1958 and served until 1972.

Born on February 1, 1906 in Abeokuta, Ogun State; attended St Gregory's Grammar School. Lagos; King's College, Lagos; University of Cambridge, England. Called to the Bar (Middle Temple), London, 1934. Was in private practice until 1939 when he became a magistrate, High Court Judge, then Chief Judge of Western Region, before his appointment as Chief Justice of the Federation in 1958. One-time Chairman, Federal Census Board; Chancellor, University of Nigeria, 1976. A Knight Commander of the Order of the British Empire (KBE), and Member, International Commission of Jurists.

Also: *1st Chairman Governing Board, Nigerian Institute of International Affairs (NIIA), Lagos.*

1ST NORTHERN NIGERIAN CHIEF JUSTICE OF THE FEDERATION.

Hon. Justice Muhammed Bello, who was so sworn in by President Babangida as Nigeria's seventh indigenous Chief Justice on Monday, March 9, 1987 in succession to Mr Justice Ayo Irikefe.

Born 1930 in Katsina; attended Middle School, Katsina, 1945-55; University College, Ibadan, 1953-55. Called to the Bar (Lincoln's Inn), London, September 1955; served as Director of Public Prosecutions, Northern Nigeria; acted as Chief Justice, Northern Nigeria, on several occasions. Appointed Justice, Suprme Court of Nigeria, from October 1975 until his appointment as Chief Justice.

One-time Chairman of Council, Nigerian Institute of Advanced Legal Studies, 1978.

1ST NIGERIAN CHIEF JUSTICE OF A SISTER AFRICAN COUNTRY

Sir Justice Egbert Udo Udoma, appointed Chief Justice of Uganda on March 26, 1963 and served until 1969.

A distinguished jurist, born on June 21, 1917, Udoma hails from Akama Opobo, Cross River State; attended Methodist Collage, Uzuakoli; Trinity College, Dublin, Ireland; St Catherine's College, University of Oxford, England. Was called to the Bar (Gray's Inn), London, 1945. Entered legal practice, 1946-61. Member, Federal House of Representatives, Lagos, 1952-59; Judge, High Court of Lagos, 1961-63, before being appointed Chief Justice of Uganda. Later Judge, Supreme Court of Nigeria, 1969. Chancellor, Ahmadu Bello University, Zaria, 1972. Awarded the traditional title of *Obong Ikpa Isong Ibibio* as well as hononary LLDs of University of Ibadan (1967), Ahmadu Bello University, Zaria (1972), and Trinity College, Dublin (1973).

NIGERIA'S 1ST MINISTER OF JUSTICE AND ATTORNEY-GENERAL

Dr Taslim Olawole Elias, appointed from 1960 to 1966.

See also entry under: *POLITICS AND GOVERNMENT – MINISTERS.*

NIGERIA'S 1ST FEMALE ATTORNEY-GENERAL

Mrs Victoria Ayodele Uzoamaka Onejeme, sworn in as Attorney-General and Commissioner for Justice of Anambra State on February 16, 1977, in succession to Dr Augustine Nnamani following the latter's appointment into the federal service as Attorney-General of the Federation. Served until August 1977, when she retired. Prior to her appointment, Mrs Onejeme was Anambra State Commissioner for Establishments.

From Awka in Anambra State, she was enrolled as a lawyer in the Supreme Court, Lagos, on July 30, 1965. Appointed Judge of the High Court of Justice, Federal Capital Territory, Abuja. with effect from November 16, 1984.

Also: *1st Female (civil) Commissioner, Anambra State.*

1ST NON-INDIGENE TO HEAD STATE JUDICIARY

Mr Justice Obi Okoye, an Enugu High Court Judge from Anambra State, who was appointed Chief Judge of Plateau State with effect from November 18, 1979. The appointment was made under Governor Solomon Lar's administration of Plateau State.

NIGERIA'S 1ST FEMALE HIGH COURT JUDGE

Mrs Modupe Omo-Eboh, appointed on November 13, 1969.

1ST NIGERIAN FEMALE FEDERAL HIGH COURT JUDGE

Justice (Mrs) Rose Menyen Ukeje, who on November 13, 1986 was sworn in as a Federal High Court Judge by then Chief Justice of the Federation, Justice Ayo O. Irikefe. The High Court was established by Decree 13 in

1973, and comprises a Chief Judge of the Federal High Court and any number of Judges as determined by an Act of the National Assembly.

Before her appointment, Mrs Ukeje was the Deputy Legal Draughtsman of the Federal Ministry of Justice. Enrolled June 17, 1971.

1ST FEMALE JUDGE OF THE FEDERAL COURT OF APPEAL

Justice Aloma Maryama Mukhtar, of Federal Court of Appeal, Jos, so sworn in on Friday, September 25, 1987 by Chief Justice Bello, along with five other (male) Judges also appointed. The Court of Appeal was established in 1964.

Enrolled in the Supreme Court on June 26, 1967; appointed High Court Judge, Kano State, January 1, 1977.

1ST CHIEF JUDGE OF LAGOS STATE

Mr Justice John Idowu Conrad Taylor, from 1964 until his death on November 7, 1973.

From Lagos State, he was born on August 24, 1917; attended Methodist Boys' High School, Lagos, but completed his secondary education in England at Cullford Secondary School, Suffolk. Gained admission to study medicine at London University but soon changed to law at Brasenose College, Oxford University, at the instigation of his prominent lawyer father. Called to the Bar in January 1940. On return to Nigeria, he started legal practice by joining his father (the late Mr E. J. Alexander Taylor, popularly referred to as 'the cock of the Bar' and a pioneer lawyer in Nigeria). After fifteen years of legal practice, he joined the Bench in the following capacities: Judge of the High Court of Western Nigeria, 1956-60; Judge of the Spreme Court, 1960-64; Chief Justice of Lagos State.

1ST NIGERIAN QUEEN'S COUNSELS (Q.C.)

Chief Frederick Rotimi Adegboyega Williams and Chief H .O. Davies, who were so sworn in at the Federal Supreme Court, Lagos, on Monday,

January 12, 1959. The QC entitled the beneficiary to wear the 'silk', and was the highest status a legal practitioner could attain.

The General Council of the Nigerian Bar abolished the title 'Queen's Counsel', replacing it with Senior Advocate of Nigeria (SAN), the first of which was Rotimi Williams in 1975.

Chief Rotimi Williams, the *Apesin* of Itoku in Abeokuta, is a celebrated legal luminary and constitutional expert. He was involved, on several occasions, with formulating Nigeria's constitutions.

Chief Davies, the *Otun* of Efon Alaye, was founder of *Daily Service* Press; Secretary of the Nigerian Youth Movement (NYM), 1937. Also involved in formulation of Nigeria's constitutions.

1ST SENIOR ADVOCATES OF NIGERIA (S.A.N.)

Chief Frederick Rotimi Alade Williams and Chief (Dr) Nabo B. Graham-Douglas, who were conferred the title on April 3, 1975. SAN, the Nigerian version of the colonial investiture of Queen's Counsel (QC), was instituted in 1972.

1ST FEMALE SENIOR ADVOCATE OF NIGERIA (S.A.N.)

Chief (Mrs) Olufolake Solanke, so conferred on March 5, 1981 (with four male lawyers: Chief Festus Adebayo Kehinde, Chief Sobo Sowemimo, Chief Macaulay O. Akpofure and Dr Arthur Nylander).

A legal luminary, Chief (Mrs) Solanke enrolled at the Supreme Court, Lagos on May 31, 1963, and holds the title of *Yeyemofin* of Ile-Ife,

1ST NIGERIAN NON-ADVOCATE SENIOR ADVOCATE OF NIGERIA (S.A.N.)

Prof. Benjamin Obi Nwabueze, conferred SAN on January 12, 1978. Born in Atani, Anambra State, on December 22, 1932; attended London School of Economics and Political Science, University of London, 1956-61; School of Oriental and African Studies, University of London, 1961-62. Went into teaching career, as Lecturer, later, Senior Lecturer, University of Lagos, 1962-65; Senior Lecturer, University of Nigeria, Nsukka, 1965-67; Acting Dean, University of Nigeria, 1967-70; Professor, School of Law, University of Zambia, 1970-76.

1ST NIGERIAN APPOINTED JUDGE OF INTERNATIONAL COURT OF JUSTICE AT THE HAGUE

Mr Justice Charles Daddy Onyeama of the Supreme Court, Lagos, appointed November 2, 1966, and held the position until 1976.

A jurist from Eke, Enugu State, born on August 5, 1917, and educated at King's College, Lagos; Achimota College, Ghana; University of London, 1937-40. Called to the Bar (Lincoln's Inn), London, 1940. On return, joined the civil service, 1944-46; becoming Member, Eastern Nigeria House of Assembly, 1946-51; Member, Legislative Council of Nigeria, 1947-51; Member, Constitution Drafting Committee, Lagos, 1948-50. Held several positions at the Bench, including Chief Magistrate, 1952-56; Acting Judge, High Court, Western Nigeria, 1956-57; Judge, High Court, Lagos, 1957-64; Judge, Supreme Court of Nigeria, Lagos, 1964-66, before his appointment as Judge of the International Court of Justice at the Hague. Conferred Order of the Federal Republic (OFR), 1980.

1ST NIGERIAN PRESIDENT OF INTERNATIONAL COURT OF JUSTICE AT THE HAGUE

Dr Taslim Olawale Ellas in June 1972. On November 9, 1984, he was re-elected for another nine-year term.

Born on November 11, 1914, he attended CMS Grammar School, Lagos, and Igbobi College, Yaba; University College, London; Council of Legal Education, Institute of Advanced Legal Studies, University of London. Called to Bar (Inner Temple) in 1947. Was Federal Attorney-General/ Minister of Justice 1966-72; Professor and Dean, Faculty of Law, University of Lagos. Later appointed a Judge of International Court of Justice at The Hague. Rose to Vice-President of the Court in 1979 before his elevation to the Presidency.

Also: *1st Chairman, Nigerian Institute of International Affairs (NIIA), Lagos.*

1ST NIGERIAN DIRECTOR, NIGERIAN INSTITUTE OF ADVANCED LEGAL STUDIES

Dr Timothy Akinola Aguda, so appointed 1978 to February 1988; when he retired.

From Akure, Ondo State, born on June 10, 1923, he attended Government College, Ibadan; Higher College, Yaba, Lagos; London School of Economics and Political Science. One-time legal draftsman and Administrator-General of Western Nigeria. Served as Chief Justice of Botswana; Dean, Faculty of Law, University of Ife, 1965-66; Federal Director of Public Prosecutions, 1967-68; Solicitor-General and Permanent Secretary, Western Nigeria Ministry of Justice, 1968; Judge, High Court, Western States, 1968-72; Chief Judge, Ondo State, 1972, until his appointment as Director. Was also President, Nigerian Society of Criminology; Chancellor, Anglican Diocese of Botswana. A prolific writer, his works include *Principles of Criminal Liability in Nigerian Law* and *Law of Evidence in Nigeria.*

1ST NIGERIAN SECRETARY-GENERAL, INTERNATIONAL BAR ASSOCIATION (I.B.A.)

Mr Idowu Sofola, SAN, so appointed in October 1986 at the 21st Biennial Conference of the IBA in New York, USA. The IBA was formed out of the Federation of National Bar Associations worldwide in 1947. It is a non-political organisation having a consultative status with the United Nations. It is a private body of lawyers, basically of national bar associations and law societies of individual countries. Since its inception, none of its four key offices – President, Vice-President, Secretary General and Treasurer – had had a non-White occupant before Sofola's appointment.

Mr Sofola was born in Ikenne, Ogun State, on September 29, 1934; attended Eko Boys' High School, Lagos. Read Law in England and was called to the Bar (Middle Temple) on July 17, 1962. Enrolled at Supreme Court of Nigeria on July 30, 1962, and was in active private legal pratice thereafter. Before this appointment, he was Secretary-General of the IBA (1980-82) and Deputy Secretary-General, IBA (1982-86).

1ST NIGERIAN UNIVERSITY TO MOUNT A DEGREE PROGRAMME IN LAW

University of Nigeria, Nsukka, whose law faculty commenced the training of law students at its Enugu Campus in 1961.

1ST TIME LAWYERS WHOLLY TRAINED IN NIGERIA WERE CALLED TO THE BAR

On July 22, 1966, at the Supreme Court, Lagos.

1ST BATCH OF LAWYERS FROM NIGERIAN LAW SCHOOL ENROLLED BY THE SUPREME COURT OF NIGERIA

A batch of eight lawyers who were so enrolled on March 21, 1963.

NIGERIA'S 1ST PUBLIC EXECUTION

Involved three condemned armed robbers executed at the Bar Beach, Lagos, on Saturday, April 24, 1971.

For details see entry under: *MISCELLANEOUS.*

10 LIBRARY SCIENCE

1ST NIGERIAN CHARTERED LIBRARIAN

Mazi Kalu Chima Okorie. Obtained the professional qualification of Associateship of the Library Association (London) (ALA) in 1951. Later also bagged the Association's Fellowship (FLA), the highest qualification for professional library science practice in the United Kingdom. He had trained on a Federal Government scholarship at the School of Librarianship, Loughborough, and North-Western Polytechnic, London (both in England), 1949-51.

Born on February 25, 1923 in Abam, Abia State, Okorie attended Methodist College, Uzuakoli before proceeding to the UK for further studies. On return to Nigeria, he enjoyed a lengthy professional career during which he held important positions including Director of Library Services, (defunct) Eastern Region, (defunct) East Central State, and Imo State, from where he retired in 1979. Conferred Member of the Order of the British Empire (MBE), 1961, and Officer of the Order of the Niger (OON), 1964.

Also: *1st President, Nigerian Library Association, 1962-64.*

1ST NIGERIAN FEMALE CHARTERED LIBRARIAN

Mrs Ekei Essien Oku, who obtained her professional library science qualification of Associate (ALA) in 1953.

Born on January 22, 1924, in Calabar, Cross River State; educated at Hope Waddell Training Institution, Calabar, 1935-38; St George's School, Opobo, 1936-38; Ovim Girls' School, 1939-41; Queen's College, Lagos, 1942-46; North Western Polytechnic, London. On return to Nigeria was appointed Librarian, Lagos Town Council, in 1955, and rose to Chief Librarian (Director), Cross River State Library Service in 1975.

1ST PRESIDENT, NIGERIAN LIBRARY ASSOCIATION (N.L.A.)

Mazi Kalu Chima Okorie, from 1962 to 1964. The NLA was birthed by the former West African Library Association (WALA) which had been in existence since 1954 as the professional body for librarians in English-speaking West Africa. Prior to his appointment as 1st President of the NLA, Kalu Okorie was the (last) President of WALA, 1961-62.

For biodata, see: *1st Nigerian Chartered Librarian.*

1ST FEMALE PRESIDENT, NIGERIAN LIBRARY ASSOCIATION (N.L.A.)

Mrs Felicia Adetoun Ogunsheye (née Banjo), from 1967 to 1970. Mrs Ogunsheye became the fifth NLA President after Messrs K. C. Okorie, W. J. Plumbe (expatriate), E. B. Bankole and S. C. Nwoye.

For biodata, see: *1st Nigerian female Professor,* ***entry under:*** *EDUCATION – ACADEMIC DISTINCTIONS/HONOURS.*

1ST DIRECTOR/C.E.O. OF THE NATIONAL LIBRARY OF NIGERIA (N.L.N.)

Simeon Babasanya Aje, appointed Director in 1971 and retired from the post in 1986. The NLN was initially established through an Act in 1964 but it was not until Decree 29 of 1970 was promulgated that the 1st Director was appointed. Prior to that date three expatriate Library Advisers – Dr Carl White, 1962-64, Miss Priscilla Taylor (later Mrs. P. Harris), 1964-66, and Mr Phillip Rappaport, 1966-71 – oversaw the management and growth of the Library.

A renowned librarian, Aje was born on June 11, 1927, in Ilara-Ekiti; attended Methodist School, Ijuniti-Ekiti, 1939-41; Christ Church School, Ado-Ekiti, 1942-45; Loughborough College, Leicestershire, England, 1951-60; and University of Chicago, Illinois, USA, 1962-64. Piror to his appointment as Director, National Library of Nigeria, Aje was Regional Librarian, Western Region, 1956-67. Joined the National Library in 1967.

NIGERIA'S 1ST UNIVERSITY LIBRARIAN

Mr (later Prof.) John William Harris, librarian of the University of Ibadan (formerly University College, Ibadan), from the institution's inception in 1948 to 1968.

From New Zealand, Harris was Librarian at Otago University, New Zealand, prior to his appointment at Ibadan. Was later Acting Vice-Chancellor, University of Ibadan, 1967-68. Also set up Nigeria's first library school at the same university.

1ST NIGERIAN UNIVERSITY LIBRARIAN

Mr Samuel Chikwuemeke Nwoye, appointed University Librarian, University of Nigeria, Nsukka, in 1963.

Born on April 19, 1929, in Amawbia, Anambra State; educated at DMGS, Onitsha, 1943-47; University College, Ibadan, 1948-52; University of London, England, 1956-1960, bagging a first degree in history and postgraduate Diploma in Librarianship (1960). Practised as Librarian at the University of Ibadan and rose to Sub-Librarian (1957-61) before leaving in 1961 to become Deputy University Librarian at the newly-established University of Nigeria, Nsukka. Appointed University Librarian in 1963 following the exit of the expatriate librarian. One-time Chairman, Anambra State Library Board, 1986-88.

Also: *1st Nigerian graduate librarian, 1954.*

1ST NIGERIAN FEMALE UNIVERSITY LIBRARIAN

Mrs Tinuade Olabisi Odeinde, appointed University Librarian, University of Ibadan, in 1972, retiring in October 1987.

Born on December 3, 1933 in Lagos, Lagos State; educated at Yaba Methodist School, Lagos, 1940-50; Norwich City College, England, 1952-54; University of Hull, England, 1954-57. Taught briefly before joining then University College Ibadan Library as Assistant Librarian in 1959, rising steadily to the post of University Librarian in 1972.

The Nnamdi Azikiiwe Library at the University of Nigeria, Nsukka. The first Nigerian university librarian worked at this university, in 1963 (see page 116). The library is now named after Dr Nnamdi Azikiwe, the first President of Nigeria (see page 76).

PHOTOGRAPH: UDEAGBALA (2017,).

1ST NIGERIAN PROFESSOR OF LIBRARY SCIENCE

Prof. (Mrs) Felicia Adetoun Ogusheye (née Banjo), appointed Professor of Library Studies, University of Ibadan, on October 1, 1973.

For biodata, see: *1st Nigerian female Professor,* ***entry under:*** *EDUCATION – ACADEMIC DISTINCTIONS/HONOURS.*

1ST NIGERIAN TO BAG A DOCTORATE DEGREE (Ph.D.) IN LIBRARY SCIENCE

Dr Wilson O. Aiyepeku, who obtained his PhD degree from the University of Ibadan in 1973, His doctoral thesis was entitled 'Bibliometric and Documentation Characteristics of Geographical Literature on Nigeria, 1901-1970'. Postgraduate studies was introduced into the Department of Library Studies, University of Ibadan, in the 1969-70 session.

Born in lyara-Ijumu, Kwara State, he graduated in geography (BSc) from Ahmadu Bello University, Zaria, from where he joined the Department of Library Studies, University of Ibadan, as lecturer, rising to Professor and Head of Department.

1ST NIGERIAN UNIVERSITY TO MOUNT A DEGREE PROGRAMME IN LIBRARY SCIENCE

Ahmadu Bello University, Zaria, which pioneered the Bachelor of Library Science (BLS) degree programme (BLS) in Nigeria in 1968.

1ST NIGERIAN POLYTECHNIC TO MOUNT A LIBRARY SCIENCE PROGRAMME

Federal Polytechnic, Nekede Owerri, Imo State (formerly College of Technology, Owerri), whose Department of Library and Information Sciences introduced diploma programmes in Library/Information, Science in September/October 1979, producing 18 pioneer HND graduates in 1983. The Polytechnic was established via the Imo State government Edict 16 of 1978.

1ST NIGERIAN UNIVERSITY TO MOUNT LIBRARY SCIENCE PROGRAMME

University of Ibadan (formerly University College, Ibadan), where its Institute of Librarianship was established in 1959 with an initial grant of US $88,000 from the Carnegie Corporation of America. Mr John Harris, then University Librarian, Ibadan, was its 1st Director up to 1965. In the first three sessions students were prepared for the (London) Library Association Registration examinations, leading to the professional qualification of Associateship (ALA). The 1st batch of Ibadan diploma students (23) were admitted in the 1963-64 session.

11 MASS MEDIA

11.1 BROADCASTING

IST RADIO/T.V. BROADCAST IN NIGERIA

The Radio Distribution Service (RDS), introduced into Nigeria in 1932. At the beginning of the service it consisted simply of re-transmitting British Broadcasting Corporation (BBC) programmes on a relay system similar to the radio relay exchange system operating in Britain since the 1920s. Began as part of the Department of Posts and Telegraphs (P&T) under Mr T. N. Chalmers, seconded from the BBC, London, as 1st Director of Broadcasting in Nigeria April, 1951.

Following the removal of broadcasting from the exclusive Federal Government list to the concurrent in 1953, regional governments introduced broadcasting thus: Western Nigeria – WNBS/TV, October 1959; Eastern Nigeria – ENBC/TV, October 1960; Northern Nigeria – Radio/TV Kaduna, March 1962.

NIGERIA'S 1ST EXTERNAL RADIO BROADCAST

On January 1, 1962, when 'Voice of Nigeria', the external arm of Radio Nigeria (now FRCN) commenced external broadcast. Its first announcer was Emmanuel Omatsola, one of NBC's ace announcers at the time. Prime Minister Sir Abubakar Tafawa Balewa launched the service.

Initially the service (supposed to last few months only but ultimately spanning two years until December 24, 1963) ran for two hours daily from 1700 hours GMT on 31 and 41 metres band, the 1st hour being for English, the second for French programmes. From February 1, 1963, the broadcast period was increased to six hours, from 1400 hours GMT. Arabic was then added to the existing two languages, making three hours of English, two of French and one of Arabic.

1ST RADIO TRANSMISSION FROM NIGERIA'S (NEW) FEDERAL CAPITAL – ABUJA

On October 1, 1980, on the occasion of Nigeria's independence anniversary celebrations. Its programmes were broadcast from Gwagwalada mainly in Hausa, Gwari, Gade, Egbira, Ganagana and English, and covered the entire Federal Capital Territory of Abuja.

Abuja was formally pronounced Nigeria's capital by then Head of State, General Murtala Muhammed, on February 3, 1976.

1ST NIGERIAN RADIO STATION TO TRANSMIT IN FREQUENCY MODULATION (F.M.) MODE

WNBS (Radio O-Y-O; present-day Broadcasting Organisation of Oyo State), Ibadan, in 1978.

Also: *1st (State) radio station to offer a 24-hour broadcast service.*

1ST FREQUENCY MODULATION (F.M.) RADIO STATION IN NORTHERN NIGERIA

Bauchi State FM Radio Station, established in 1981 under the tenure of Mrs Hanatu Ibrahim Tejuoso, then Bauchi State Commissioner for Home Affairs and Information, 1979-83.

1ST BROADCAST ON 'RADIO NIGERIA III'

On September 21, 1987. The station, popularly referred to as the *WAZOBIA* station, caters for educational broadcasts only.

1ST TELEVISION STATION IN NIGERIA

Western Nigeria Television (WNTV), Ibadan, Oyo State. Began commercial operation (transmission) on October 31, 1959 on channels 3 and 4. Originally an associate of Overseas Rediffusion Ltd of England.

Transmission was sequel to the signing of a fifteen-year contract between the Western Nigeria government and Overseas Rediffusion Ltd. for the operation of a two-transmitter commercial TV network in the region. Also 1st in entire Black Africa.

1ST TO APPEAR ON NIGERIAN T.V. SCREEN

Anike Kuforiji, later Mrs Anike Agbaje-Williams. As announcer, hers was the very first face to appear and talk on the night of October 31, 1959, when television transmission formally began in Nigeria courtesy of then WNBS/WNTV, Ibadan, Oyo State.

Born on October 23, 1936, Mrs Agbaje-Williams rose to be Director of Programmes before retiring on July 31, 1986.

NIGERIA'S 1ST T.V. COLOUR TRANSMISSION

In September 1975, when the NBC-TV, Lagos, started transmitting colour signals. The decision for the station to go colour was taken in 1973.

1ST TELEVISION TRANSMISSION IN LAGOS AREA

On April 1,1962, the then Nigerian Television Service (Channel 10) began to transmit in the Lagos area, thus becoming the next such television service after the Western Nigeria Television Service (WNTV), established in 1959. Commenced service as an arm of the Nigerian Broadcasting Corporation (NBC).

Initially it transmitted for only 1½ hours daily (made up of 45 minutes of live show and news, and 30 minutes of foreign films). Duration of transmission was gradually extended to two hours, later to five hours every evening. By February 28, 1963, 'Television House' (comprising the permanent studios and offices) was formally opened.

1ST STATE-OWNED TELEVISION STATION IN NIGERIA

Anambra Television (ATV; now ABC-TV), Enugu, established and began transmission in May 1980 as a State television station on Ultra-High

Frequency (UHF) Channel 50. The bill to establish the television authority was passed into law on December 22, 1981, and assented to the next day. The official opening was performed on March 27, 1982, by Governor Jim Nwobodo of old Anambra State. Cost N24 million, with booster stations at Nsukka and Onitsha.

Also: *1st ultra-high frequency (UHF) station in Nigeria (Black Africa).*

1ST TIME SINCE THE INTRODUCTION OF TELEVISION IN NIGERIA THAT T.V. SCREENS NATION-WIDE WENT BLANK

On June 11, 1980, when employees of Nigerian Television Authority (NTA), belonging to the Radio TV and Theatre Arts Workers Union (RATTAU), embarked on a nation-wide industrial action, following a trade dispute – their first in the history of television broadcasting in Nigeria. The strikers were demanding harmonisation of their salaries with those of their counterparts in radio.

NIGERIA'S 1ST TELEVISION DRAMA SERIES (SOAP OPERA)

Village Headmaster, created in 1968 by Segun Olusola. Conceived as a social drama set in a village. The language of the series was Pidgin English, popularised in *Safe Journey*, a similar drama serialisation which had then been running on Radio Nigeria during the previous nine years.

Born on March 18, 1935, Olusola attended Remo Secondary School, after which he joined the Nigerian Broadcasting Corporation (NBC) Ibadan (now FRCN), rising to Executive Producer and, later, Controller of Programmes, NBC-TV Lagos. Later appointed General Manager, NTA, 1977; Managing Director, NTA Zone A, Ibadan; then Nigeria's Ambassador to Ethiopia, 1986.

1ST CHAIRMAN, NIGERIAN TELEVISION AUTHORITY (N.T.A.)

Alhaji Ismail Babatunde Jose, appointed Chairman, 1977 to 1980. Later re-appointed by General Buhari in June 1984, retiring in October 1986.

NTA was established by Decree 24 of April 1, 1977. Earlier, on April 1, 1976 (as prelude to the establishment of the NTA), the Federal Government took over all television stations then existing in the country, including the Federal Government-owned NBC-TV, established since April 1, 1962.

A renowned Nigerian pioneer journalist, Jose was born on December 13, 1925; attended St Saviour's Boys' High School, Lagos, after which he joined *Daily Times* of Nigeria Ltd in 1941 as technical trainee, rising to Editor, *Daily Times* (1957); Chairman/Managing Director (1968-75). Other posts held include Chairman, National Commission on Change-Over to Right Drive, 1971-73.

1ST DIRECTOR GENERAL/C.E.O., NIGERIAN TELEVISION AUTHORITY (N.T.A.)

Mr Vincent Ifeanyi Dele Maduka, Director-General/Chief Executive from NTA's inception in 1977 to January 1, 1983, when he was removed by then President Shehu Shagari. Was reappointed as Director-General in 1984 by Head of State Major-General Buhari, a post he held until his voluntary retirement in May 1986.

Born on October 5, 1935, in Asaba, Delta State, Maduka attended King's College, Lagos; University of Leeds, England; and National University of Ireland, Dublin. Once served as Senior Engineer with then Western Nigeria Broadcasting Service Television (WNBS-WNTV), Ibadan; later, Chief Engineer, then General Manager, before his appointment in 1977, following the establishment of the NTA.

1ST NIGERIAN TO HEAD NIGERIAN TELEVISION SERVICE (N.T.S.) NEWS DEPARTMENT

Boniface Offokaja, from June 1963, when the NTS began to produce its own new bulletins (and ceased its erstwhile dependence on the newsroom of the NBC at Broadcasting House, Lagos).

From Anambra State, Offokaja later joined (defunct) Eastern Nigeria Broadcasting Service (ENBC), Enugu, 1966.

1ST DIRECTOR, 'VOICE OF NIGERIA' (V.O.N.)

Professor Chinua Achebe, from 1961 to 1966. The VON commenced external broadcasting on January 1, 1962.

A renowned writer, Achebe was born on November 16, 1930, in Ogidi, Anambra State. Attended Government College, Umuahia, 1944-48; University College, Ibadan, 1949-53, before joining the Nigerian Broadcasting Corporation (NBC), in 1954, rising to Regional Controller, Enugu, 1959-61, prior to his appointment as (1st) Director, VON, Lagos. He later entered full academic life as Research Professor with the Universities of Nigeria, Nsukka, and Massachusetts, USA. Also, Founding Editor of *Okike* magazine. Awarded Nigeria's National Trophy, 1961; Commonwealth Poetry Prize, 1972.

See also: *1st winner(s) of Nigeria's National Merit Award,* **entry under:** *AWARDS.*

Chinua Achebe in 2008.

1ST FEMALE MANAGEMENT STAFF OF NIGERIAN BROADCASTING CORPORATION (N.B.C.)

Mrs Eno Irukwu, by virtue of her appointment as Controller, NBC, in December, 1972. Was later promoted to Director. One-time Member, National Electoral Commission (NEC), 1987.

Born in Etinan, Akwa-Ibom State, Mrs Irukwu was brought up in Delta State and later married to Chief Joe Irukwu of Abia State. She attended Queen's College, Lagos.

1ST SIMULTANEOUS NATION-WIDE EVENT COVERAGE BY ALL NIGERIAN RADIO/T.V. STATIONS

The nation-wide radio and television coverage of the 2nd All-Africa Games, held in Lagos, Nigeria, in January 1973. The transmission marked the first major achievement of the Broadcasting Organisation of Nigeria (BON) which had then just been established (1972) in order to pool the resources of all radio and television stations in the country for the coverage of certain national and international events.

11.2 NEWSPAPERS

NIGERIA'S 1ST NEWSPAPER

Iwe Irohin (fun awon ara Egba ati Yoruba). Started publication in December 1859 by Rev. Henry Townsend of the CMS Mission in Abeokuta, Ogun State. Appeared as a Yoruba-language religious fortnightly but later became bilingual when an English-language supplement (translating the Yoruba language) was added from March 8, 1860.

From January 1860 the paper started publishing two separate editions in Yoruba and English. Although it started as a religious paper, its news coverage later expanded to include non-religious activities.

NIGERIA'S 1ST VERNACULAR NEWSPAPER

Iwe Irohin (fun awon ara Egba ati Yoruba), which started in December 1859 as a Yoruba-language religious fortnightly newspaper.

For details see: *Nigeria's 1st Newspaper.*

NIGERIA'S 1ST RELIGIOUS NEWSPAPER

Iwe Irohin (fun awon ara Egba ati Yoruba) (**see above**).

1ST RELIGIOUS NEWSPAPER IN EASTERN NIGERIA

The Leader, which started on August 15, 1956. Originally a monthly, now weekly religious newspaper.

See also entry under: *RELIGION.*

1ST PRESIDENT, NEWSPAPER PROPRIETORS ASSOCIATION OF NIGERIA (N.P.A.N.)

Alhaji Lateef Jakande, journalist and politician from Lagos State.

Born on July 23, 1929; attended Banham Memorial Methodist School, Port Harcourt; King's College, Lagos; Ilesha Grammar School. Entered journalism as a reporter in 1949, serving in the *Daily Service* and *Nigerian Tribune*, and rising to Editor-in-Chief, Amalgamated Press of Nigeria, 1956-60; Managing Director, Allied Newspapers of Nigeria, 1960-66; Managing Director and Editor-in-Chief, African Newspapers of Nigeria.

Elected 1st Executive Governor of Lagos State, 1979 to 1983, on the platform of the Unity Party of Nigeria (UPN). Other positions held include: President, International Press Institute; Patron, Nigerian Guild of Editors.

Also: *1st Civilian (Executive) Governor of Lagos State.*

1ST NIGERIAN FEMALE M.D./C.E.O. OF A NEWSPAPER ORGANISATION

Dr (Mrs) Hamidat Doyinsola Abiola (née Aboaba), through her appointment as Managing Director, Concord Press of Nigeria Ltd, on October 6, 1985.

Born on February 1, 1946, she attended Queen's College, Yaba, Lagos, 1958-63; Universities of Ibadan, 1966-69, and Wisconsin, Madison, 1970-77; State University of New York, USA, 1975-79. Married to Chief M. K. O. Abiola, Chairman/Proprietor, Concord Group of Newspapers. Former Women's Page Editor, *Daily Sketch* (1969); Features Editor, *Daily Times*, 1973-75. Joined *National Concord* as editor in March 1980. Later Editor-in-Chief before her appointment as Managing Director.

Also: *1st Nigerian female to edit a national daily newspaper* – National Concord, *from March 1981*.

1ST NIGERIAN NEWSPAPER EDITOR

Ernest Sesei Ikoli, from Brass in Rivers State. He established his own newspaper on March 10, 1921, which he edited, but the paper collapsed in 1925. Later, together with Messrs Adeyemo Alakija and Richard Barrow, Ikoli established the *Nigerian Daily Times* in 1926 and became its very first editor. The paper was launched on June 1, 1926.

For bio-data see: *1st Editor,* Daily Times.

1ST CHAIRMAN, *DAILY TIMES* BOARD OF DIRECTORS

Sir Adeyemo Alakija, who, as one of the Founding Fathers of the NNPC, (publishers of the *Daily Times)* became its 1st Chairman of Board, June 1, 1926.

A Nigerian lawyer and newspaper entrepreneur, Alakija was son of one of the 'Brazilian' families of Lagos, i.e. Black people repatriated from Brazil and believed to be of Egba descent.

Born on May 25, 1884, he attended CMS Grammar School, Lagos. Later read Law in England, 1910 to 1915, and called to the Bar (Middle Temple), London. Entered private legal practice and politics (on return). In 1926 he made his most notable contribution to history by co-founding (with Ernest Ikoli) the *Daily Times*, with the reputation of being Nigeria's leading newspaper. Was Chairman of its Board until 1948 when the International Publishing Corporation of London took over the paper. Died on May 10, 1952.

Also: *1st Nigerian Grandmaster of Freemasons Nigeria; 1st President of the Egbe Omo Oduduwa, 1945.*

1ST EDITOR, *DAILY TIMES*

Ernest Sesei Ikoli, appointed first editor of the newly-founded *Daily Times*, whose 1st editorial he wrote on June 1, 1926. He left the paper in 1928 to found the *Nigerian Daily Mail*, later *Daily Telegraph*, which he edited for its owner (J. A. Doherty) until 1931 when it ceased publication.
Born on March 25, 1893, in Brass, Rivers State, Ikoli attended Bonny Primary School; King's College, Lagos (a foundation student), and later taught there (1913-19). Joined journalism as Editorial Assistant for the *Lagos Weekly Record*, and after two years founded his own paper – the *African Messenger* – in 1921. Appointed 1st Editor, *Daily Times*, in 1926. His *African Messenger* had in 1925 been taken over by the *Daily Times.* Generally referred to as the 'Elder Statesman of the Nigerian Press', Ikoli was awarded the MBE. Died on October 21, 1960. From 1979 an Ernest Ikoli Memorial Lecture was instituted in his memory.

Also: *1st Nigerian (African) to teach at King's College Lagos; 1st Nigerian newspaper editor.*

1ST FEMALE FEATURES EDITOR OF *DAILY TIMES*

Miss Audrey Ajose, also one-time Editor, *Woman's World,* a *Daily Times* publication.

A lawyer and journalist, Miss Ajose received primary education at CMS Girls' School, Lagos, before proceeding to the United Kingdom, where she had her secondary education and later read for a law degree and a Diploma in Journalism. Was called to the Bar in 1964, following which she went into legal practice, rising to Legal Adviser and Deputy Company Secretary, Lever Brothers Nig. Ltd.

One-time Nigeria's Ambassador to Sweden, accredited to Finland, June 1987.

1ST EDITOR, *SUNDAY TIMES*

Mr Theophilus Adetola Awobokun, so appointed on August 2, 1953 (when the paper was created by Mr Percy Roberts as the 1st Nigerian Sunday newspaper). Awobokun was additionally assigned responsibilities as Assistant Editor (Production) of the *Daily Times* from September to December 1953.

1ST FEMALE EDITOR, *SUNDAY TIMES*

Adaora Lily Ulasi, appointed Editor on November 7, 1954, following the decision to include a page edited by a woman for women in the *Sunday Times*, titled 'Women's Page'. Her 1st article on the 'Women's Page', titled: 'This Thing Called Man', was an explosive and controversial feature on the vices of man. She quit the newspaper early in 1958 to become a prolific novelist whose works include *Many Thing You No Understand* and *Many Thing Begin For Change.*

A US journalism graduate, she hails from Nnewi, Anambra State; attended Ovim Girls' School, Abia State, 1940-45; Reagan Memorial Girls' Secondary School, Yaba, Lagos, 1946-49; George Pepperdine College, USA, 1949-53; University of Southern California, Los Angeles, USA, 1954.

1ST EDITOR, *NEW NIGERIAN NEWSPAPER* (N.N.N.)

Alhaji Adamu Ciroma, from 1969. Subsequently appointed Managing Director, NNN, from 1969 to 1974. NNN was started by the (defunct) Northern Nigeria Government in 1966, and taken over by the Federal Government in April 1975 under Murtala Muhammed.

Born in 1934 in Potiskum, Borno State, Ciroma was educated at Barewa College, Zaria, 1950-55; University College, Ibadan, 1958-61. Was in Northern Nigeria Civil Service, 1961-65; Senior Assistant Secretary, Federal Ministry of Mines & Power, 1965-66, before his appointment as Editor, *New Nigerian Newspaper*. Later appointed: Governor, Central Bank of Nigeria (CBN), 1975-77; Member, Constituent Assembly, 1977-78; Federal Minister of Industries, October 1979.

1ST EDITOR, *SUNDAY NEW NIGERIAN*

Abba Mohammed Dabo, appointed August 14, 1981. Although the *New Nigerian Newspaper* began publishing in 1969, the weekly Sunday edition did not commence until 1981. Dabo, from Kano State, was born on March 21, 1952.

IST FEMALE EDITOR OF *NEW NIGERIAN NEWSPAPER*

Hajia Bilkisu Yusuf, appointed on September 9, 1987. Before her appointment, she was Editor, *Sunday Triumph,* a Kano State government-owned weekly newspaper, 1982-87.

From Sokoto State, born in 1952, she graduated in Political Science from Ahmadu Bello University, Zaira, 1975, with a Masters in Political Science, University of Wisconsin, USA, 1981.

1ST NIGERIAN RECIPIENT OF 'INTERNATIONAL EDITOR-OF-THE-YEAR' AWARD

Raymond Ekpu, voted the 'International Editor-of-the-Year', 1987, by the World Press Review.

See also entry under: *AWARDS.*

1ST RECIPIENT OF 'JOSE AWARD' FOR JOURNALISM

Isaac Akinkunmi in 1984.

See also entry under: *AWARDS.*

12 MEDICINE

1ST NIGERIAN MEDICAL DOCTOR

Dr Nathaniel King, who was the first Nigerian to practise modern medicine in Nigeria after obtaining the Membership of the Royal College of Surgeons (MRCS) qualification in 1874. He later obtained an MB degree from Edinburgh University, Scotland, before returning to Nigeria in 1878, where he served the CMS Mission until his premature death on June 12, 1884.

Born in Hastings, Sierra Leone, in 1847, he received his early education in Nigeria, joining his father, the Rev. Thomas King, when he moved from Sierra Leone to the Yoruba Mission in 1850. Was selected for training in the CMS medical school of the CMS Theological Institute, Abeokuta, in 1861. Later studied medicine at King's College, London, from 1871.

1ST IGBO MAN TO QUALIFY AS MEDICAL DOCTOR

Dr Simon Ezicvuo Onwu, who obtained his medical degree (MBChB) from Edinburgh University, Scotland, in July 1932.

From Affa, Enugu State, he was born on December 28, 1908, and attended King's College, Lagos; Edinburgh University Medical School. Also obtained the Diploma in Tropical Medicine and Hygiene from Liverpool University in 1932. On return to Nigeria, he joined the colonial civil service and practised for 27 years in various parts of Nigeria, rising to Director of Medical Services, Eastern Region, and Permanent Secretary, Ministry of Health, retiring in 1963. One-time Chairman, Eastern Nigeria Housing Corporation; 1st African Vice-President, International Congress of the International Union of Building Societies. Was awarded the Coronation Medal (1953); OBE (1956). Died in London, June 4, 1969.

Also: *1st Nigerian (African) Director of Medical Services, (defunct) Eastern Nigeria (1957); 1st Nigerian (African) Vice President, International Congress of the International Union of Building Societies (1965).*

1ST NORTHERN NIGERIAN MEDICAL DOCTOR

Dr Russell Aliyu Barau Dikko, who graduated in medicine from the University of Birmingham, England, in 1939.

Born on June 15, 1912 in Zaria, he received primary education at CMS School, Wusasa, 1922-29, secondary at King's College, Lagos, 1929-31, before proceeding to the United Kingdom for medical training. On return, he joined government medical service as a Junior Medical Officer in 1940, rising to Medical Officer, 1953; Principal Medical Officer, 1957; Permanent Secretary, (defunct) Northern Nigeria Ministry of Health, 1962-67. In June 1967, he joined the Federal Executive Council as Commissioner (Minister), Health, Mines and Power, and Transport, from where he quit Federal government service in January 1975. Died in April, 1977.

1ST NIGERIAN OPTHALMOLOGIST

Sir Kofoworola Adekunle Abayomi, who completed his specialist course in ophthalmology at Moorfields Eye Hospital, London, obtaining the MB and ChB of Edinburgh University in 1928 and the MD in 1936.

Born in Lagos on July 10, 1896, Sir Abayomi attended Wesleyan College (now Methodist Boys' High School), Lagos, 1909-12, before proceeding to Edinburgh University, Scotland, in 1922. Having graduated in Medicine, he returned to Nigeria in 1930, joined private medical practice as well as politics. Served on Yaba Higher College Advisory Board; Board of Medical Examiners Council, University College, Ibadan, 1947-61; Chairman, Lagos Executive Development Board; President, Nigerian Society for the Blind. Died January 1, 1979.

1ST NIGERIAN OTO-RHINO-LARYNGOLOGIST AND OTOLOGIST

Dr Frederick Oritseatseghan Esiri, a physician. Obtained his specialisation in 1951 from the Institute of Laryngology and Otology of the University of London, British Postgraduate Medical Federation.

Born on December 15, 1912, in Abraka, Delta State, he attended King's College, Lagos, 1928-31, and Yaba School of Medicine, 1931-37, before proceeding abroad on a specialist course. Has been mainly in private medical practice. Was awarded Member of the Order of the British Empire (MBE), 1957; Officer of the Federal Republic (OFR), 1946.

Also: 1st Chancellor, Federal University of Technology, Owerri (FUTO).

1ST NIGERIAN FEMALE OPTHALMOLOGIST

Dr (Mrs) Oyinade Olurin (née Odutola) who completed her specialist course in ophthalmology at Moorfields Eye Hospital & Institute of Ophthalmology, London; Bristol Eye Hospital, 1963-65, bagging MBChB as well as a Masters (ChM) degree, 1975.

For biodata, see: *1st Nigerian female Professor of Medicine.*

1ST NIGERIAN FEMALE MEDICAL DOCTOR

Dr (Mrs) Elizabeth Abimbola Awoliyi (née Akerele), who graduated with 1st-class Honours in 1937 from the University of Dublin, Cefrey's College, then the College of Surgeons.

Born in 1910; conferred Member of the Order of the British Empire (MBE); Chieftaincy titles: *Iya Alaje* of Oyo and *Iya Ibiye* of Lagos. Died September 14, 1971.

1ST IGBO FEMALE MEDICAL DOCTOR

Dr (Mrs) Veronica Obiamaka Ofili (née Egbuna), who obtained the medical qualifications of LRCP, LRCS, LAH, LM from the Royal College of Surgeons and Physicians, Dublin, Ireland, in 1952.

Born in Onitsha, Anambra State, in 1924; educated at St Agnes Training College, 1937-39; Convent School, Sapele, 1943-46; before proceeding to medical school in Dublin, Ireland, in 1946. Positions held on return include: Medical Officer, Ministry of Health, (defunct) Eastern Nigeria, 1954; Medical Officer Grade I, 1963; Senior Medical Officer, 1970; Consultant, 1972; Senior Consultant, 1975. Died on Saturday, January 29, 1977.

1ST FEMALE MEDICAL DOCTOR FROM BAUCHI STATE

Dr Mrs Zaure Sabe, graduated in Medicine from the University of Jos in June 1984.

1ST NIGERIAN MEDICAL DOCTOR EMPLOYED IN NIGERIA'S PUBLIC SERVICE

Dr Obadiah Johnson, who in June 1888 was appointed to the colonial medical service as Assistant Colonial Surgeon. Before then, African doctors were, as a matter of colonial policy, barred from public employment in Nigeria.

Son of a Nigerian freed slave, Erugun (later christened Henry Johnson), believed to have descended from the Oyo royal family, Dr Johnson was born in Hastings, Sierra Leone, in 1849. Schooled partly in Sierra Leone and at Kudeti School, Ibadan, and Faji Day School, Lagos; CMS Grammar School, Lagos; Fourah Bay College, Freetown, Sierra Leone; King's College, London; University of Edinburgh. Returned to Nigeria in 1886 and went into private medical practice before his appointment into public service. Died September 1920 in London.

1ST FEMALE DIRECTOR OF HEALTH SERVICES, (OLD) BENDEL STATE

Dr (Mrs) Clara Akele (née Qkotie-Eboh), appointed Director of Health Services and Chief Executive in old Bendel State Health Management Board on June 6, 1985. Was Chief Consultant Anaesthesist, General Hospital, Benin-City. Graduated in Medicine in June 1966 from the Catholic National University of Ireland, Dublin.

Born on December 15, 1939, in Warri, Delta State, she attended National University of Ireland, 1960-66 (MB BCh); Mater Hospital, Dublin; University College Hospital, Lagos, 1967-68; Johns Hopkins University Hospital, Baltimore, USA. Prior to her appointment as Director of Health Services, she had served as: Senior House Officer, Lagos University Teaching Hospital (LUTH); Medical Officer, Specialist Hospital, Benin-City, 1969-71; Registrar (Anaesthetist); Senior Registrar; Head, Department of

Anaesthesia, in same hospital. Was Consultant Anaesthetist, 1975-78; Senior Consultant Anaesthetist, 1978-81; and Chief Consultant Anaethetist, 1981-June 1985.

1ST NIGERIAN DEPUTY DIRECTOR-GENERAL, WORLD HEALTH ORGANIZATION (W.H.O.)

Prof. Thomas Adeoye Lambo, from November 1973 to July 1988, when he retired. Prior to the appointment, he was for many years Consultant to WHO, rising to Assistant Director-General in 1971.

A psychiatrist and educationist, he was born on March 29, 1923, in Abeokuta, Ogun State. Appointed Vice-Chancellor, University of Ibadan, 1968-71; Chairman, West African Examinations Council (WAEC), 1969-71. Conferred Officer of the Order of the British Empire (OBE); Commander of the Order of the Niger (CON), 1979; and three honorary doctorate degrees.

1ST NIGERIAN CHAIRMAN, GLOBAL ADVISORY COMMITTEE ON HEALTH RESEARCH, WORLD HEALTH ORGANIZATION (W.H.O.)

Prof. Babatunde Olusiji Osuntokun, with effect from January 1, 1987.

A renowned physician from Lagos State, Osuntokun was born on October 26, 1934; educated at University College, Ibadan, 1954-61. After a brief spell of medical practice with the (then) Western Nigeria Government, he joined the University of Ibadan as a Research Fellow in 1964 and rose to Professor of Immunology/Head of Medicine (1973), Dean, College of Medicine and Chief Medical Director.

1ST NIGERIAN UNIVERSITY TO MOUNT A DEGREE COURSE IN MEDICINE

University of Ibadan, Oyo State, from the institution's inception (then University College, Ibadan) in 1948.

See also entry under: *EDUCATION – GENERAL.*

NIGERIA'S 1ST (RECORDED) QUINTUPLETS

Delivered by a 31-year old housewife, Mrs Monica Eze, at the University of Nigeria Teaching Hospital (UNTH), Enugu, on Wednesday, August 19, 1987. The delivery of the babies (three males and two females) took about one hour of Caesarean operation by a team led by Dr Obinna. According to the case record, the weights were as follows:

1st – male – 2.1 kg
2nd – female – 1.8 kg
3rd – female – 1.9 kg
4th – male – 1.85 kg
5th – male – 2.5 kg

They were born at 35 weeks of pregnancy.

NIGERIA'S 1ST (SUCCESSFUL) SEPARATION OF SIAMESE TWINS

Performed at the University of Nigeria Teaching Hospital (UNTH), Enugu, by a team of surgeons led by Prof. Festus Nwako and Dr (Mrs) Obianyo. It involved the successful separation of Siamese twins joined at the buttocks in an operation conducted on January 8, 1988.

NIGERIA'S 1ST (SUCCESSFUL) OPEN HEART SURGERY

Performed at the University of Nigeria Teaching Hospital (UNTH), Enugu, on February 1, 1974, by a team of surgeons led by Prof. Udekwu and Mr Maghi Yacoub.

NIGERIA'S 1ST UNIVERSITY TEACHING HOSPITAL

University College Hospital (UCH), Ibadan, Oyo State, established in November 1957 as the teaching hospital arm of University of Ibadan (formerly University College, Ibadan) Medical School.

See also entry under: *EDUCATION – GENERAL.*

1ST COMPUTERISED TOMOGRAPHY SCANNER IN NIGERIA

Commissioned at the University College Hospital (UCH), Ibadan, Oyo State, on Thursday, November 19, 1987 by President Ibrahim Babangida, as one of the activities marking thirty years of existence of the premier teaching hospital in Nigeria.

The scanner, then valued at over N8.5 million, could literally see through human beings, diagnosing various ailments with ease. The acquisition quest started as far back as 1977.

NIGERIA'S 1ST NATION-WIDE ENVIRONMENTAL SANITATION (CLEAN-UP) EXERCISE

Conducted on Saturday, August 3, 1985. Now institutionalised as a nation-wide event, it stipulates every last Saturday of the month as clean-up day, on which all citizens should tidy homes, offices/workplaces and their environment.

13 POLITICS AND GOVERNMENT

13.1 GENERAL

NIGERIA'S 1ST POLITICAL PARTY LEADER

Herbert Macaulay, founder and leader of the Nigerian National Democratic Party (NNDP), founded in 1922. Born on November 14, 1864, in Lagos, Macaulay was a surveyor and frontline politician who had a series of confrontations with the colonial government during his days. In the elections to the Legislative Council in 1923, 1938, 1943 and 1948, his NNDP won all the seats for Lagos. On formation of the National Council of Nigeria and the Cameroons (NCNC) in 1945, he became its 1st National President. Died in Kano on May 7, 1946, while on a political campaign tour.

NIGERIA'S 1ST FEMALE NATIONAL CIVIL/POLITICAL ACTIVIST

Mrs Funmilayo Ransome-Kuti, whose activities date back to the 1940s. She founded the 'Nigerian Women's Union' in 1949 which, although not a registered political party, pressured and crusaded for the rights of women. She engineered the struggle for women to be given voting rights and to be exempted from taxation. She fearlessly challenged then traditional ruler of Egba-land, the *Alake*, forcing him into exile. Owing to her dynamism, she was the only female member of the delegation of NCNC members sent to England in 1957 to demand independence from Britain. Mother of Nigeria's former Health Minister, Prof. Olikoye Ransome-Kuti, and Afro-beat music star, Fela Anikulapo Kuti. Died on April 13, 1978.

NIGERIA'S 1ST FEMALE POLITICAL PARTY LEADER

Madam Adunni Oluwole, who in the 1940s founded a political party known as the Commoners Liberal People's Party (CLPP). The party was, however, short-lived.

NIGERIA'S 1ST NATION-WIDE POLITICAL ELECTION

Conducted in 1959. The Electoral Commission, charged with the task of conducting the election, had been formed earlier on August 7, 1958, headed by Mr R. R. Wraith, an expatriate lecturer at the University College, Ibadan (University of Ibadan).

Three tribal-based parties – the Northern Peoples Congress (NPC), National Council of Nigeria and the Cameroons (NCNC) and Action Group (AG) of the North, East and West respectively – contested. Alhaji Abubakar Tafawa Balewa of the NPC emerged as the nation's 1st indigenous Prime Minister, while Dr Nnamdi Azikiwe became the 1st Indigenous Governor-General as a result of the coalition between the NCNC and the *Sardauna*-led NPC. Awolowo (AG) became Leader of Opposition in the Federal House of Representatives.

1ST PRESIDENT OF NIGERIA'S SENATE

Dr Nnamdi Benjamin Azikiwe ('Zik'), who was so sworn in January 1960 and occupied the post until November 16, 1960, when, following Nigeria's independence and the exit of the last British Governor-General, Sir James Robertson, Zik became 1st indigenous Governor-General.

For biodata, see: *Nigeria's 1st President,* ***entry under:*** *POLITICS AND GOVERNMENT – HEADS OF STATE/GOVERNMENT.*

NIGERIA'S 1ST SPEAKER OF THE FEDERAL HOUSE (PARLIAMENT)

Chief Jaja Anucha Wachuku, so sworn in May 1960; held the post briefly (until October 1960, when he was appointed a Federal Minister).

A barrister-at-law, politician and businessman, Chief Wachuku was born in 1918. From Mbawsi-Ngwa in Abia State, he was educated at Government College, Umuahia; Higher College, Yaba; New Africa University College, Ghana; Trinity College, Dublin. Bagged the LLB degree and was called to the Bar. Elected into the Eastern House of Representatives, 1952. Resigned from the NCNC, 1955, and became Deputy Leader of Opposition in the Federal House. Rejoined NCNC, 1957. Was later appointed Federal

Minister in charge of Economic Development, October 1960; Foreign Affairs, 1962-65; Aviation, 1965-66. In Nigeria's 2nd Republic he was elected Senator of the Federal Republic for Abia State under the Nigeria People's Party (NPP).

NIGERIA'S 1ST FEMALE SENATOR

Mrs Wuraola Esan, elected into the Senate of the 1st Republic in October 1960, was the only female Senator in that era. On March 11, 1964, she resigned from her party, the Action Group (AG), in protest against the new pact between it and the NCNC.

1ST FEMALE NIGERIAN LEGISLATOR

Mrs Oyinkan Morenike Abayomi, by virtue of her election into the Lagos City Council in 1940.

Born on March 6, 1897, in Lagos, she attended CMS Girls' Secondary School, Lagos; Ryefor Hall College, Gloucester, England, obtaining a degree in music. Founder of Queen's College, Lagos. Was special member of the Western House of Assembly. Also 1st Captain of the Nigerian Girl Guides and one-time President, All-Nigeria Women Association. Was conferred Member of the Order of the British Empire (MBE) and Officer of the Federal Republic (OFR).

1ST FEMALE NIGERIAN DEPUTY MAYOR IN BRITAIN

Councillor (Mrs) Janet Olufunmilayo Adegoke (née Akinkunmi), elected Deputy Mayor of the Boroughs of Hammersmith and Fulham (London) on Wednesday May 20, 1987. As Deputy Mayor, she was also Chairperson, House and Means Committee of the Boroughs. Born in Ibadan, Oyo State, Mrs Adegoke was educated at St Stephen's School, Inalende, Oritamefa, Ibadan, before proceeding to Britain in 1961 to train as a nurse. During her long sojourn in Britain, she worked in various capacities, especially in welfare services. Was also a member of the Labour Party (Britain) for nine years. Died of cancer in November, 1987, barely four months after her election victory.

1ST NIGERIAN ELECTED INTO TWO LEGISLATIVE HOUSES SIMULTANEOUSLY

Chief Dennis Chukwudebe Osadebey, who was elected into the (defunct) Western Nigeria House of Assembly in 1951 and into Nigeria's Federal House of Representatives in 1952, holding both positions simultaneously until 1954, when the country's new Constitution forbade dual membership of any two legislative houses.

Born in Asaba, Delta State, on June 29, 1911, Chief Osadebey was educated at Hope Waddell Training Institution, Calabar, 1929; University of London, 1946-49, where he read Law and was called to the Bar (Lincoln's Inn), London, in 1948.

Practised law on return to Nigeria before his election into the two legislatures. Was Leader of Opposition, Western House of Assembly, 1954-56; President, Nigeria's Senate, 1960; Acting Governor-General of the Federation, 1961. Appointed Administrator, (defunct) Mid-Western Nigeria in 1963, and later became its 1st Premier, 1964 to January 1966. Awarded LLD degree, University of Nigeria, Nsukka, 1964; conferred Grand Commander of the Order of the Niger (GCON), 1964.

1ST PRESIDENT, MID-WEST HOUSE OF CHIEFS

Oba Akenzua II, *Oba* of Benin, appointed in 1964 (following the creation of the Mid-West Region from old Western Region). Served until 1978 when he died.

Born Edokparhogbuyunmun in Benin in 1899 of royal blood, he attended King's College, Lagos, 1918-21. Was installed *Oba* of Benin, with the title *Akenzua* II, in 1933 following his father's death. Between 1946 and 1966 he was a member of the Legislative Council of Nigeria; member, Western House of Assembly; member, Western House of Chiefs. Was instrumental in the creation of Mid-West Region through his formation in October 1953 of the Benin-Delta People's Party to campaign for the unification of both provinces. One-time Chancellor, Ahmadu Bello University, Zaria, 1966-72. Died late 1978.

DAY INDEPENDENT NIGERIA HELD ITS 1ST PARLIAMENTARY SITTING

On Monday, October 3, 1960. Princess Alexandria, Queen Elizabeth II's representative at Nigeria's independence celebrations formally opened the Independence Parliament in Lagos in the presence of a large and distinguished assembly of world statesmen and diplomats.

1ST PRIVATE MEMBER'S BILL TO BE PASSED BY THE SENATE OF THE 2ND (CIVILIAN) REPUBLIC

The Private Member's Bill presenting the National Order of Precedence of Public Officers on State Ocassions Organised by Federal or State governments, sponsored by Chief Jonathan Odebiyi, Unity Party of Nigeria (UPN) Senate Leader. Was approved by the Senate on January 13, 1983. That Senate had been in existence since October 1979.

1ST TIME NIGERIA SENATE WAS PREVENTED FROM TRANSACTING BUSINESS

On January 26, 1980, when it failed to form a quorum. Only 17 of the 96 members were in attendance.

1ST TIME NIGERIA'S MILITARY GOVERNMENT HELD ITS MEETING (S.M.C./A.F.R.C.) OUTSIDE LAGOS

On Tuesday June 16, 1987, when Nigeria's Armed Forces Ruling Council (AFRC) held a formal meeting at Abuja, the nation's new capital. Presided over by then Major-General Babangida, 26 of the 28 AFRC members were present, except Chief of Army Staff Major-General Sani Abacha (on an official trip to Holland) and Air Vice-Marshall Ibrahim Alfa, Chief of Air Staff (on vacation).

Topics deliberated upon centred on plans for a return to civil rule.

13.2 HEADS OF STATE/GOVERNMENT

NIGERIA'S 1ST GOVERNOR-GENERAL

Sir Frederick J. D. Luggard, a Briton. When in January 1914 the two formerly separate administrations of Northern and Southern Nigeria were amalgamated into the Colony and Protectorate of Nigeria, with its capital in Lagos, Lord Luggard became the first overall leader (Governor-General). He ruled until 1919. Prior to his appointment, Luggard was High Commissioner of the then Protectorate of Northern Nigeria. Later, on October 1, 1954, Nigeria became a federation with Sir J. S. Macpherson as Governor-General.

1ST GOVERNOR-GENERAL OF INDEPENDENT NIGERIA

Sir James Robertson, a British colonial administrator, who was so sworn in on Nigeria's independence day October 1, 1960, and occupied the post until November 16, 1960 when Dr Nnamdi Azikiwe, then President of Nigeria's Senate, took over as Governor-General.

Born in Broughty Ferry, Scotland, in October 1899, Sir James was educated at Merchiston Castle School, Edinburgh, and Balliol College, Oxford, England. He had a long and varied colonial public service before his posting to Nigeria as Governor-General.

NIGERIA'S 1ST INDIGENOUS GOVERNOR-GENERAL

Rt Hon. Dr Nnamdi Azikiwe, appointed Governor-General in October 1960 at Nigeria's independence, following the exit of the last British Governor-General, Sir James Robertson. Was sworn in on his 56th birthday (November 16, 1960), at the racecourse, Lagos.

For biodata, see: *Nigeria's 1st President.*

NIGERIA'S 1ST (ONLY) PRIME MINISTER

Alhaji Abubakar Tafawa Balewa, who as Parliamentary Leader of the Northern People's Congress (NPC), the biggest party in the Federal Parliament, was, on September 2, 1957, appointed Prime Minister. Following his party's 1959 election victory, he became the 1st Prime Minister of independent Nigeria on October 1, 1960, a post he held until his death in Nigeria's first military coup d'etat on January 15, 1966.

Born in 1912 in Tafawa Balewa Town, Bauchi Emirate, Bauchi State; attended Bauchi Provincial School; Katsina College. Taught for a while at Bauchi before proceeding to the United Kingdom on a one-year course at the Institute of Education, University of London. Was Vice-President of the newly-formed Northern People's Congress (NPC); member, Council of Ministers, 1953- 57; Federal Minister of Transport and Works, 1953-57.

NIGERIA'S 1ST PRESIDENT

Rt Hon. Dr Nnamdi Benjamin Azikiwe. Became President of Nigeria on October 1, 1963, when Nigeria attained the status of a Republic. Prior to that, he was 1st Nigerian Governor-General of the Federation, from November 16, 1960.

A political scientist, author, journalist and eduationist from Onitsha, Anambra State, Dr Azikiwe was born in Zungeru, Niger State, on November 16, 1904, and educated at CMS Central School, Onitsha; Hope Waddell Training Institution, Calabar; Methodist Boys' High School, Lagos; Storer College, West Virginia, USA; Howard and Lincoln Universities, USA. He started his career as a journalist in 1934 as editor of the *African Morning Post,* Accra, Ghana. Was founder and Editor-in-Chief of the *West African Pilot*, 1934-40.

Conferred Nigeria's highest national honour of GCON, 1980; and installed the *Owelle* of Onitsha.

Also: *1st Premier, (defunct) Eastern Nigeria; 1st President of Nigeria's Senate, January 1960; 1st indigenous Governor-General, November 16, 1960; 1st Nigerian appointed Queen's Privy Councillor, 1963; 1st Chancellor and*

Chairman of Council, University of Nigeria, Nsukka, January 1972 to October, 1975; Founder and Governing Director, African Continental Bank (ACB) Ltd.

NIGERIA'S 1ST EXECUTIVE PRESIDENT

Alhaji Shehu Aliyu Usman Shagari, elected Nigeria's Executive President, August 1979, and sworn in on October 1, 1979, following the disengagement of the Obasanjo-led military regime from Nigerian politics, thus ushering the 2nd civilian Republic. Was removed through a military coup on December 31, 1983.

Shehu Shagari was born in May 1924 in Shagari Village, Sokoto State. Studied advanced administration in the United Kingdom. Founder and 1st Secretary, Sokoto Branch of Northern People's Congress (NPC), 1951-56.

Elected into the Federal House of Representatives (for Sokoto-West), 1954-66. Was Federal Minister of Commerce and Industry, October 1959; Pensions, Establishments and Training in 1960; Federal Commissioner (Minister) for Economic Development, Rehabilitation and Reconstruction, October 1971 to July 1975.

NIGERIA'S 1ST MILITARY HEAD OF STATE

Major-General Johnson Thomas Umunnakwe Aguiyi-Ironsi, who took over headship of the country on January 17, 1966, following the 1st military coup of January 15, 1966, led by Major Nzeogwu. Served until July 29, 1966, when he was killed in a counter-coup.

Born in Umuahia Ibeku, Abia State, in March 1924, he enlisted as a Private in the 7th Battalion, Nigeria Regiment, West African Frontier Force, in 1942 at the age of 17. In 1948 he was selected for officer training in Britain's Camberley Staff College. Was appointed ADC to (then) Governor, Sir John Macpherson, in 1953. Promoted to Captain in 1955; Major in 1956; appointed an Extra Equerry to Her Majesty, Queen Elizabeth II, on the Queen's tour of Nigeria in 1956; Promoted to Lt-Col., 1957, in charge of 5th Battalion, Kano; Brigadier, 1959; sent to London as Military Attaché to the Nigerian High Commission. In 1960, commanded the Nigerian Contingent of the United Nations (UN) Force in the Congo crisis. Promoted to Major-

General in 1964. Killed in the July 29, 1966 counter-coup, buried on January 20, 1967.

1ST NIGERIAN MILITARY HEAD OF STATE TO BE ASSASSINATED

Major-General J. T. U. Aguiyi-Ironsi, Nigeria's 1st Military Head of State, killed in the counter-coup of July 29, 1966, which saw Lt-Col. Yakubu Gowon come to power as Nigeria's 2nd Military Head of State.

For biodata, see: *Nigeria's 1st Military Head of State.*

1ST NIGERIAN MILITARY HEAD OF STATE TO ADOPT THE TITLE 'PRESIDENT'

General Ibrahim Badamasi Babangida. Following his ascent to Nigeria's No. 1 position after the August 27, 1985 coup, which toppled the military regime of Major-General Muhammadu Buhari, he opted for the title 'President'.

Born on August 17, 1941, in Minna, Niger State; attended Provincial Secondary School, Bida, 1957-62. Joined the Nigerian Army in 1963 as Officer Cadet. Attended Indian Military Academy, 1963-64; was commissioned 2nd Lt. in September 1963. Promoted to Lt, 1966; Captain, 1968; Major, April 1970; Lt-Col., 1974; Brigadier, March 1979; Major-General, 1983; General, October 1987. Held several army positions including Chief of Army Staff, January 1984 to August 1985, when he became Head of State.

1ST NIGERIAN HEAD OF STATE TO VOLUNTARILY RELINQUISH POWER

General Olusegun Obasanjo, Nigeria's 5th Head of State, who voluntarily handed over power to a democratically elected civilian government led by Alhaji Shehu Shagari on October 1, 1979.

A soldier/engineer from Abeokuta, Ogun State, General Obasanjo was born on May 5, 1937; attended Baptist High School, Abeokuta; Mons Officer Cadets' School, Aldershot, England; Royal Engineers Young Officers

Course, Shrivenham, England; Indian Staff College; Royal College of Defence Studies, London, 1973-74. Had joined the Nigerian Army in 1958; commissioned in April 1959. Promoted full Lieutenant in 1960, and posted to serve with the UN Peace Forces, Congo (now Zaire). Promoted to Captain, April 1963; Major, January 1965; Lt-Col., 1967; Colonel, 1969; Brigadier, October 1972; Lt-General, January 1976; General, 1979. Served principally in army engineering units and played a major part in prosecuting the Nigerian Civil War, as Commander, 2nd Area Command, Nigerian Army, 1967; Commander of the famous 3rd Marine Commando Division of the Nigerian Army.

Later appointed Federal Commissioner (Minister) for Works and Housing, January to July 1975; Chief of Staff, Supreme Headquarters, 1975-76, before becoming Nigeria's Head of State and Commander-in-Chief of its Armed Forces, following the assassination of former Head of State General Murtala Muhammed on February 13, 1976.

On retirement, General Obasanjo went into big-time farming as well as politics. Member of the four-man Commonwealth Eminent Persons Group that fought against Apartheid in Southern Africa.

Returned later as Nigeria's civilian President under the People's Democratic Party (PDP) for two consecutive four-year terms, 1979-88.

See also: *1st Nigerian awarded Grand Commander of the Federal Republic (of Nigeria), (GCFR, in 1980),* ***entry under:*** *AWARDS.*

NIGERIA'S 1ST 'STATE WEDDING'

That between Head of State Major-General Yakubu Gowon and former Miss Victoria Zakari, which took place at the Cathedral Church of Christ, Lagos, on April 19, 1969. Chief officiating priest was the Very Rev. Festus O. Segun, then Provost of the Cathedral.

See also: *1st Nigerian Chairman of the OAU,* ***entry under:*** *POLITICS AND GOVERNMENT – DIPLOMATIC/EXTERNAL AFFAIRS; 1st Nigerian full Army General,* ***entry under:*** *ARMED FORCES.*

1ST NIGERIAN HEAD OF STATE TO ADDRESS THE GENERAL ASSEMBLY OF THE U.N.

Sir Abubakar Tafawa Balewa, on October 7, 1960. The address followed the formal admittance of Nigeria as the 99th member of the UN body, barely one week after the country's independence.

For biodata, see: *Nigeria's 1st (only) Prime Minister.*

PRESIDENT SHEHU SHAGARI'S 1ST ADDRESS TO THE GENERAL ASSEMBLY OF THE U.N.

He addressed the 35th ordinary session of the world body in New York (USA) on October 7, 1980, where he called on the UN to launch a decade of 'reparation and restitution for Africa', as a master-plan for the economic recovery of the continent. He also called for an oil embargo against South Africa.

1ST NIGERIAN (SITTING) HEAD OF STATE TO PAY OFFICIAL VISIT TO BRITAIN

General Yakubu Gowon, who paid a four-day historic state visit to Britain from June 12 to 15, 1973, as guest of Queen Elizabeth II of England. Was accompanied by his wife, Victoria. They returned to Nigeria on June 17, 1973, spending two extra days in a private capacity.

PRESIDENT SHEHU SHAGARI'S 1ST OFFICIAL TOUR OUTSIDE NIGERIA (ON ASSUMPTION OF OFFICE)

A one-night official visit to the Republic of Benin, February 27-28, 1980.

PRESIDENT SHEHU SHAGARI'S 1ST OFFICIAL ENGAGEMENT OUTSIDE LAGOS (CAPITAL) ON ASSUMPTION OF PRESIDENCY

A two-day official trip to Abuja, the new federal capital, on Thursday 25 and Friday 26 October, 1979. He was accompanied by then Minister of the Federal Capital Development Authority (FCDA), Mr John Jatau Kadiya, the Senate President, Dr Joseph Wayas, and Speaker, House of

Representatives, Mr Edwin Ume-Ezeoke. The mission was to facititate the speedy delivery of Abuja as the new capital.

1ST STATE VISITED BY HEAD OF STATE, GENERAL BUHARI

Rivers State, where he paid a three-day official visit from Monday 13 to Wednesday 15 August, 1985.

NIGERIA'S 1ST (EXECUTIVE) VICE-PRESIDENT

Dr Ifeanyichukwu Alex Ekwueme, elected Vice-President of Nigeria and sworn in October 1, 1979. Removed in the December 31, 1983 military coup.

Born in Oko, Anambra State, on October 21, 1932, Dr Ekwueme attended King's College, Lagos, 1945-50; University of Washington, Seattle, USA, 1952-57, graduating BA Sociology, 1955, Bachelor of Architecture, 1956, and MA Urban Planning, 1957. He later studied for an LLB degree (London), and a PhD, University of Strathclyde, Glasgow (1976-78).

Mostly in private architectural practice (Ekwueme Associates), Dr Ekwueme had been Vice-President, later President, Nigerian Institute of Architects, 1963-64, 1965-68; Fellow, Nigerian Institute of Architects, from 1970; President, Architects' Registration Council of Nigeria, 1976-79. A very successful architect and businessman.

13.3 GOVERNORS/PREMIERS

1ST PREMIER OF (DEFUNCT) EASTERN NIGERIA

Rt Hon. Dr Nnamdi Azikiwe, from 1954 to 1959.

For biodata, see: *Nigeria's 1st President,* ***entry under:*** *POLITICS AND GOVERNMENT – HEADS OF STATE/GOVERNMENT.*

1ST NIGERIAN GOVERNOR OF (DEFUNCT) EASTERN NIGERIA

Sir Dr Francis Akanu Ibiam, installed Governor of Eastern Nigeria on December 15, 1960, in succession to Sir Robert Stapledon, and exited following January 15, 1966 military coup led by Major Nzeogwu. Dr Ibiam renounced his knighthood on September 5, 1967, and chose to be known and addressed simply as Dr Akanu Ibiam.

For biodata, see: *1st Chancellor, Imo State University,* ***entry under:*** *EDUCATION – UNIVERSITIES*.

1ST MILITARY GOVERNOR, (DEFUNCT) EASTERN NIGERIA

Lt-Col. Chukwuemeka Odumegwu Ojukwu, from January 8, 1966, following Nigeria's 1st military coup and installation of Major-General Aguiyi-Ironsi as Head of State.

From Nnewi, Anambra State, Ojukwu was born on November 4, 1936, and educated at CMS Grammar, Lagos; King's College, Lagos; Epsom College, Surrey, England; Oxford University, England. Also attended military courses at Hythe and Warminster, England and Joint Services Staff College, Camberley. Was member of the UN Peace-Force in the Congo (Zaire). On return, he became Quarter-Master-General of the Nigerian Army. Was Commander, 5th Battalion, Kano, when Nzeogwu's coup took place in January I966, after which he was appointed (1st) Military Governor of then Eastern Region, 1966. With the outbreak of the Civil War in July 1967, Ojukwu was proclaimed Head of State and Commander-in-Chief, Republic of Biafra. He fled to Cote d'lvoire on the collapse of Biafra in January 1970. Was granted amnesty and returned to Nigeria to join politics. Honoured with the chieftaincy title of *Ikemba.*

1ST PREMIER, (DEFUNCT) MID-WESTERN NIGERIA

Chief Dennis Chukwudebe Osadebey, first appointed Administrator of the Mid-West when it was created out of the old Western Region on August 9, 1963, and later sworn in as Premier on February 7, 1964. Served until January 1966.

Born on June 29, 1921 in Asaba, Delta State; attended Hope Waddell Training Institution, Calabar; University of London. Was called to the Bar (Lincoln's Inn), London, 1948. Went into private legal practice before he entered politics under the NCNC party. Became Opposition Leader and later Deputy Speaker in the Western House of Assembly. Conferred honorary doctorate degree in Law (LLD) by the University of Nigeria, Nsukka. Was installed *Ojiba* of Asaba.

1ST INDIGENOUS GOVERNOR OF (DEFUNCT) MID-WESTERN NIGERIA

Chief Samuel Jereton Mariere, sworn in on February 7, 1964, and held the post until removed following Nigeria's 1st military coup of January 15, 1966. Thereafter he was appointed Adviser to the Military Governor of Mid-West State, 1966-68.

Born in 1907 at Evwreni, Delta State; educated at St Andrew's School, Warri. Entered politics and elected NCNC Member of the House of Representatives for Urhobo East (1954), and later Urhobo Central (1959). On creation of the Mid-Western Region, of which he was a prominent advocate, he was appointed Deputy Administrator and Commissioner for Chieftaincy Affairs on February 7, 1964. Other positions held include Chancellor, University of Lagos (from July 1967); Chairman, Mid-West State Schools Board; President, Christian Council of Nigeria. Was awarded honorary LLD degrees (Nsukka, 1964, and Ibadan, 1964. Died May 9, 1971, in a road accident.

1ST MILITARY GOVERNOR OF (DEFUNCT) MID-WESTERN NIGERIA

Brigadier David Akpode Ejoor, from January 18, 1966 to 1967.

Born on January 10, 1934 in Ovu, Delta State; attended Government College, Ughelli; Royal Military Academy, Sandhurst, England. Commissioned in 1956. Promoted to Major, 1960; Lieutenant-Colonel, 1964; Brigadier, 1966. Later was Commandant, Nigerian Defence Academy, 1969-70; Commandant, Royal College of Defence Studies, 1971; Chief of Staff, Nigerian Army, 1972-75. Retired in 1975.

1ST PREMIER, (DEFUNCT) NORTHERN NIGERIA

Sir Ahmadu Bello, *Sardauna* of Sokoto, from 1954 to January 15, 1966, when he was killed in Nigeria's 1st military coup.

Born on June 12, 1909 in Kabbah, near Sokoto, Sokoto State, his father was grandson of Usman dan Fodio, the founder of the Sokoto Empire. Attended Katsina Higher College, after which he took a local government course in England. A founding father and party leader of the Northern People's Congress (NPC) from 1949 until his death. Before his appointment as Premier, Sir Ahmadu was Northern Region's Minister of Works; Local Government and Community Development.

The traditional title *Sardauna* means 'war leader'.

1ST INDIGENOUS GOVERNOR OF (DEFUNCT) NORTHERN NIGERIA

Sir Kashim Shettima Ibrahim, sworn in as 1st (African) Governor on January 21, 1962, in succession to Sir Gawain Bell. Served until January 15, 1966, when he was swept out in Nzeogwu's coup.

Born 1910 in Maiduguri, Borno State; educated at Borno Provincial School and Katsina Training College. Taught from 1929 until he joined active politics in 1952. Before being appointed Governor he was Central Minister of Social Services, Lagos, 1952-55; Northern Region Minister of Social Development, 1955-56; later, Adviser to the Military Governor, Northern Nigeria, 1966-68. Also: Chancellor, University of Ibadan, 1966-77; Chancellor, University of Lagos, 1977; Chairman, Provisional Council, ABU, Zaria, 1960-62. Conferred Grand Commander, Order of the Niger (GCON); honorary LLDs of the University of Nigeria, Ahmadu Bello University, Zaria (ABU), and University of Lagos.

1ST MILITARY GOVERNOR, (DEFUNCT) NORTHERN NIGERIA

Major Hassan Usman Katsina, from January 18, 1966 to 1967.

Born on March 31, 1933, in Katsina, Katsina State, he attended Kaduna College, 1948-51; Institute of Administration, Zaria, 1952; Nigerian College of Arts, Science and Technology, Zaria, 1953-55. Also attended army training courses in Teshie (Ghana), Aldershot (England) and the USA. Later appointed Army Chief of Staff, 1968-72; Deputy Chief of Staff, Supreme Headquarters; Federal Commissioner (Minister) for Establishments, 1973-75.

1ST PREMIER, (DEFUNCT) WESTERN NIGERIA

Chief Obafemi Jeremiah Awolowo, from 1954 to 1959.

A renowned lawyer and politician, Awolowo was born on March 6, 1909, in Ikenne, Ogun State. He attended Wesley College, Ibadan; University of London, England. Called to the Bar (Inner Temple), London, 1946. On return to Nigeria, Awolowo taught briefly before venturing into active politics. Was co-founder and General Secretary, *Egbe Omo Oduduwa,* 1949-66. Founder and leader of Action Group (AG) party, 1951-66. Before his appointment as Premier in 1954, was also member of Western House of Assembly, Ibadan, 1951-59; Leader of Government Business, Western Nigeria, and Minister of Local Government and Finance, 1951-54. Later became Leader of Opposition in the Federal House of Representatives, Lagos (1960-62); Federal Commissioner (Minister) of Finance; Vice-Chairman, Federal Executive Council of Nigeria (1966-67); founder and leader, Unity Party of Nigeria, (UPN), becoming the party's Presidential candidate in the 1979 and 1983 elections.

Chancellor, University of Ife; Chancellor, Ahmadu Bello University, Zaria, 1975-78. Conferred honorary degrees by University of Nigeria, Nsukka, (LLD); University of Ife (DSc); University of Lagos (DLitt); University of Ibadan (LLD), May 7, 1987.

1ST INDIGENOUS GOVERNOR (DEFUNCT) WESTERN NIGERIA

Sir Adesoji Aderemi I, so appointed on July 8, 1960. At the time of his appointment, he was also the *Ooni* of Ife. Born on November 15, 1889, in Ile-Ife, Oshun State, he ascended the Ile-Ife throne on September 25, 1930, ruling until July 7, 1980, when he died, thus also becoming the longest-ruling *Oba* in Yoruba-land in recent history. After a brief educational spell, he joined the Nigerian Railways, 1909-1921.

Awarded King's Medal for African Chiefs (1936); CMC (1943). Led Nigeria's delegation to Queen Elizabeth II of England's coronation in 1953. Before his governorship was Federal Minister (without portfolio) 1951-60; President, Western House of Chiefs, 1954-60.

1ST MILITARY GOVERNOR, (DEFUNCT) WESTERN NIGERIA

Lt-Col. Francis Adekunle Fajuyi, from January 18, 1966, to July 29, 1966, when he was killed in Nigeria's 2nd military coup and buried (with full military honours) on January 28, 1967.

Born in Ado Ekiti, Ekiti State, on June 26, 1926. Enlisted in the Nigeria Army in 1943; trained at Command Training School, Teshie, Ghana; Officer Cadets' School, Chester, England. Commissioned in 1954. Participated in the UN Congo operations, 1960-64, and won the Military Cross for his gallantry. Rose rapidly and by the January 1966 coup had risen to Lt-Col.

1ST NIGERIAN TRADITIONAL RULER APPOINTED GOVERNOR

Sir Adesoji Aderemi, the *Ooni* of Ife (1930 to 1980). Appointed Governor of (defunct) Western Nigeria on July 8, 1960.

For biodata, see: *1st Governor, (defunct) Western Nigeria*

1ST GOVERNOR, (DEFUNCT) BENUE-PLATEAU STATE

Police Commissioner Joseph Deshi Gomwalk, from May 27, 1967 to July 30, 1975.

Born on April 13, 1935 in Anper, Pankshin Division of Plateau State, he attended Sudan United; Nigerian College of Arts, Science and Technology, Zaria, 1956-58; University College, Ibadan, 1958-61, bagging a BSc (Zoology) degree. Worked for a while at the Kaduna Veterinary School as Research Officer before he joined the Nigeria Police Force in February

1966, rising quickly, until appointed Military Governor of Benue-Plateau State following Gowon's creation of the 12-state structure on May 27, 1967. Later charged with complicity in the assassination of General Murtala Muhammed, pronounced guilty and executed by firing squad on May 14, 1976.

1ST GOVERNOR (ADMINISTRATOR), (DEFUNCT) EAST CENTRAL STATE

Dr Ukpabi Anthony Asika, appointed civilian Administrator (Governor) on October 28, 1967, and served until July 1975.

Born on June 2, 1936, in Onitsha, Anambra State, Asika was a political science lecturer at the University of Ibadan, 1966-67, at time of his appointment. He attended St Patrick's College, Calabar, 1949; Edo College, Benin, 1951; University College, Ibadan, 1951-61; University of California, Los Angeles, California, USA, 1961-65. A foremost traditional chief in the cabinet of the *Obi* of Onitsha, with the title *Ajie*.

1ST GOVERNOR, (DEFUNCT) NORTH-CENTRAL STATE

Brigadier Abba Kyari, appointed Governor, North-Central State, following the creation of the 12-state structure on May 27, 1967. Was retired on July 30, 1975.

Born on November 7, 1938, in Dewa, Niger State, Kyari attended Government College, Zaria, 1953-58; Military Training Course, Teshie, Ghana, 1959; Mons Officers' Cadet School, Aldershot, England, 1959-60; and many other military courses in England and the USA.

Prior to his appointment as Governor, he had served as Transport Officer, Nigeria Army Supply & Transport Co., Kaduna, 1961-63; Commanding Officer, 5th Battalion, Nigerian Army, 1966-67. Promoted to Brigadier in 1972.

1ST GOVERNOR, (DEFUNCT) NORTH-EASTERN STATE

Brigadier Musa Usman, from May 1967 to July 1975 (retired). Born on February 3, 1940, in Enugu, he hails from Gongola State, and attended Nigerian Military School, Zaria, 1954-58; Mons Officer Cadet School, Aldershot, England, 1959; Military Academy, Sandhurst, England, 1959.

Prior to the appointment, he served in the Congo UN Peace-Keeping Forces, 1961; Nigerian Air Force, Kaduna, 1964. From his first commission as 2nd Lieutenant in 1961, he rose to Brigadier in October 1972, from which post he was retired in 1975.

1ST GOVERNOR, (DEFUNCT) NORTH-WESTERN STATE

Police Superintendent Usman Faruk, from May 1967 to July 1975.
Born on January 1, 1935, in Pindiga, Bauchi State, he attended Government School, Zaria; Agricultural School, Zaria; Police College, Ikeja; and other Police training courses. Joined Nigeria Police Force in 1958, rising to Chief Superintendent of Police in 1967, a post he held at the time of his appointment as Military Governor. Was retired in 1975.

1ST GOVERNOR, (DEFUNCT) SOUTH-EASTERN STATE (CROSS RIVER)

Brigadier Udoakaha Jacob Esuene, appointed Governor, South Eastern State, following the creation of that State on May 27, 1967. Was retired on July 30, 1975 by new Head of State General Murtala Muhammed. In the February 3, 1976 state creation exercise by General Murtala Muhammed, South-Eastern was one of seven existing states essentially unaffected except for minor boundary adjustments and change of name to Cross River.

Born on October 17, 1936, in Afaha-Eket, Akwa Ibom, he attended Mons Officer Cadet School, Aldershot, England, 1958; Military Academy, Sandhurst, England, 1961; and other military courses.

Prior to the appointment, he served as Army Officer, 1958-63, and Air-Force Officer, 1963-67. Later was gubernatorial candidate for the Unity Party of Nigeria (UPN) in Cross River State in the 1979 civilian elections.

1ST GOVERNOR, (DEFUNCT) WESTERN STATE

Brigadier Robert Adeyinka Adebayo, from May 1967 to April 1971.

Born on March 9, 1928 in Ile-Ife, Oshun State, he attended Eko Boys' High School, Lagos. Joined the Army in 1948; commissioned in England in 1953, after which he returned to Nigeria, 1954. Promoted to Captain, 1957; Major, 1960; Lieutenant-Colonel, 1962; Colonel, 1964; Brigadier, 1966.

Prior to his appointment, he served in the Congo UN Peace-Keeping Force, 1961-63; was Army Chief of Staff, 1964-65; Commandant, Nigerian Defence Academy, 1971-75; promoted to Major-General before his retirement in 1975.

1ST GOVERNOR, AKWA IBOM STATE

Col. Tunde Ogbeha, appointed on September 24, 1987, by President Babangida and sworn in next day. Akwa Ibom State (carved out of Cross River State) and Katsina State became Nigeria's newest states. Capital: Uyo.

From Kwara State, Ogbeha was born on September 1, 1947, Until the appointment he was Brigade Commander, 1st Mechanized Brigade, Nigerian Army. Had served as Nigeria's Ambassador to Equatorial Guinea and Defence Adviser in Harare, Zimbabwe. Re-assigned to old Bendel State as Governor in June 1988.

1ST GOVERNOR, ANAMBRA STATE

Lt-Col. John Atom Kpera, who on creation of Anambra State on February 3, 1976 became its 1st (military) Governor. Col. Kpera was, however, already Governor of former East Central State, from which Anambra and Imo States were carved out under Head of State Murtala Muhammed's regime.

1ST CIVILIAN (EXECUTIVE) GOVERNOR, ANAMBRA STATE

Chief Jim Ifeanyichukwu Nwobodo, from October 1, 1979 to September 1983. He had contested the post under the ticket of the Nigeria People's Party (NPP). Was, however, defeated by Mr C. C. Onoh in his October 1983 re-election bid.

Born in Northern Nigeria on May 9, 1940, Jim Nwobodo hails from Amechi-Awkunanaw, Enugu State; attended College of Arts, Science & Technology, Enugu, and University College, Ibadan, where he bagged a BA (Hons) degree in English in 1964. He taught briefly thereafter at King's College, Lagos, and then joined the then Shell-BP, serving until the outbreak of the Nigerian Civil War in 1967. Before joining politics, Jim Nwobodo was Chairman/Executive Director, Link Group Ltd. a successful multi-branch company. Was also Patron of several student organisations and Chairman, Universal Insurance Co. Ltd.

NIGERIA'S 1ST FEMALE STATE GOVERNOR

Dame Virginia Ngozi Etiaba, sworn in as governor of Anambra State on November 3, 2006, replacing then Governor Peter Obi, who was impeached. Served for only three months until February 9, 2007, when Peter Obi was re-instated following his appeal up to the Court of Appeal.

Born on November 11, 1942, Etiaba had primary and secondary education in Kano State, then proceeded to Gombe State for teacher training, obtaining NCE; BEd Certificate in Information Technology.

Thereafter, she served as teacher and Headmistress in the Anambra school system until her retirement, whereupon she entered politics, rising in 2006 to Deputy Governor before her appointment as Governor. Despite her very brief term, she recorded landmark achievements including road construction; promulgation of Anambra State Child Rights Bill into law; enforcement of *Suba kwa Igbo* for Anambrarians to elevate the status of the spoken Igbo language.

See also entry under: *WOMEN.*

1ST GOVERNOR, BAUCHI STATE

Lt-Col. B. Kaliel, appointed to take charge of the State, created out of former North-Eastern State on February 3, 1976, by General Murtala Muhammed.

1ST CIVILIAN (EXECUTIVE) GOVERNOR OF BAUCHI STATE

Alhaji Abubakar Tatari Ali, elected with effect from October 1, 1979. Re-elected for a second term of four years from October 1, 1983. Was, however, removed from office following the December 31, 1983 military coup. Contested and won on both occasions on the platform of National Party of Nigeria (NPN).

Born in 1929 in Katagun, Bauchi State, Alhaji Abubakar attended Bauchi Middle School, 1941-46. His career includes: Accountant, Katagun Native Authority Treasury, 1946-49; 1st Nigerian Staff Officer, Ministry of Agriculture, 1960-61; Senior Assistant Secretary, Establishments Division, Premier's Office, 1961-63; Deputy Permanent Secretary, Ministry of Establishments, 1964-65; Permanent Secretary, Federal Ministry of Works and Internal Affairs, 1965-66.; Chairman, Broadcasting Corporation; Permanent Secretary, Ministry of Health Headquarters. Retired from civil service in 1975. Later appointed Chairman, Bauchi State Development Board, 1978.

1ST GOVERNOR, (OLD) BENDEL STATE

Brigadier George A. Innih, Military Governor from creation of Bendel State on February 3, 1976. Bendel was mere a re-naming of what used to be Mid-West State (former Mid-Western Region), created from the defunct Western Region on August 9, 1963.

From Edo State, Innih was born on September 25, 1938. Received secondary education at Edo College, Benin-City, before joining the Nigerian Army. Innih was also one-time Governor of Kwara State as well as General Officer Commanding (GOC), 1st Infantry Division, Nigerian Army. Voluntarily retired as Major-General in April 1980.

1ST CIVILIAN (EXECUTIVE) GOVERNOR, OLD BENDEL STATE

Prof. Ambrose Folorunsho Alli, elected with effect from October 1, 1979 on the banner of Unity Party of Nigeria (UPN). Lost to Dr Samuel O. Ogbemudia in his 1983 re-election bid.

Born in 1929 at Ekpoma, Edo State, Prof. Alii attended Immaculate Conception College, Benin-City; St Patrick's College, Asaba, where he graduated in 1960. He proceeded to England in 1961 for a specialist course in pathology and forensic medicine. On his return in 1966, he took up a job with the University of Ibadan and later Ahmadu Bello University, Zaria, from 1969 to 1971. Died Friday September 22, 1989.

1ST NIGERIAN TO SERVE AS GOVERNOR OF SAME STATE TWICE

Dr Samuel Osaighovo Ogbemudia, two-time Governor of old Bendel State (former Mid-West State).

1st: As Administrator and later Military Governor, Col. (later Brig.) Ogbemudia governed (old) Mid-West State from September 21, 1967 to July 30, 1975.

2nd: As elected civilian Executive Governor, Dr Ogbemudia governed old Bendel State briefly from October 1, 1983 to December 31, 1983, when his tenure was terminated by the Buhari military coup. Elected on the platform of the National Party of Nigeria (NPN).

Born in Benin, Edo State, September 17, 1932, he attended Western Boys' High School, Benin-City, before joining the army in 1953. Trained at Teshie, Ghana, and Nevheron, Zimbabwe. Later attended Officer Cadet School, Aldershot, England; Army Special Warfare School, Fort Bragg, South Carolina, USA. Served on the United Nations Peace-Keeping Force in the Congo (Zaire) and Tanzania. Promoted to Brigade-Major, 1966; Lt-Col., 1967; Colonel, 1969; Brigadier, 1971. Retired from the army in 1975. Conferred honorary doctorate degree of University of Benin. One-time Chairman, National Sports Commission.

1ST GOVERNOR, BENUE STATE

Maj-Gen. Abdullahi K. Shelleng, Military Governor, from February 3, 1976 to 1978. Benue State, carved out of former Benue-Piateau State, was one of seven new states created by Murtala Muhammed on February 3, 1976.

A soldier, Shelleng was born on January 20, 1942, and educated at Barewa College, Zaria, 1957-61; Military Academy, Pakistan, 1962-65. Held various positions in the Nigerian Army before his appointment as Governor. Returned to regular military duties in 1978, after which he was appointed Provost-Marshall, Army Corps of Military Police, 1978-79; Adjutant General, 1979.

1ST CIVILIAN (EXECUTIVE) GOVERNOR, BENUE STATE

Mr Aper Aku, first elected with effect from October 1, 1979; re-elected for another four-year term with effect from October 1, 1983. Was, however, swept out of office in the December 31, 1983 coup. Won on both occasions on the platform of the National Party of Nigeria (NPN).

Mr Aku was born in 1938 in Ikobo, Benue State. After his early education in Aku and Nkarin Gboko and Kwande between 1943 and 1945, he atttended Keffi College and Nigerian College of Arts, Science and Technology, Zaria, before proceeding to Fourah Bay College, Freetown, Sierra Leone, in 1961, where he obtained a combined honours degree in Arts in 1964. Taught briefly, before joining Federal Public Service in 1968. In 1978, he went into politics, rising to governor of Benue State in 1979. Died on November 14, 1987, while jogging.

1ST GOVERNOR, BORNO STATE

Lt-Col. Muhammadu Buhari, Military Governor from February 3, 1976, when Borno State was created out of the former North-Eastern State over which he (Buhari) was already Governor, 1975 to February 1976. Served as Borno State Governor for months only.

Born on December 17, 1942, in Daura, Katsina State; educated at Katsina Provincial Secondary School, 1956-62; Nigerian Military Training College,

Muhammadu Buhari, photographed in 2015. Buhari was, briefly, the first Governor of Borno State (see page 162), and later President of Nigeria.

Kaduna, and military training courses in England and India, 1972-73. Was Director, Supply and Transport, Nigerian Army (1974-75), prior to his appointment as Military Governor of North-Eastern State in 1975. Later appointed Federal Commissioner (Minister) for Petroleum Resources, 1976-78; Chairman, Nigerian National Petroleum Corporation (NNPC), 1976-79; General Officer Commanding (GOC), 4th Division, Nigerian Army, 1980; Head of State, Federal Republic of Nigeria and Commander-in-Chief of the Armed Forces, December 31, 1983 to August 27, 1985, when he was ousted in a military coup which ushered in military President Ibrahim Babangida. Went into politics and after four unsuccessful attempts was elected as (civilian) president in 2015, with re-election for a second term in 2019, on All Progressive Congress (APC) ticket.

1ST CIVILIAN (EXECUTIVE) GOVERNOR, BORNO STATE

Alhaji Mohammed Goni, sworn in on October 1, 1979 and following re-election in 1983 served until December 31, 1983, when a military coup swept him out of power. Was elected on the platform of the Great Nigeria People's Party (GNPP).

Alhaji Mohammed was born in 1941 at Kareto, Damasak, Borno State, and attended Kano Government College, 1963- 64; Ahmadu Bello University, Zaria, 1964-67, obtaining a Bachelor's degree in Public Administration, July 1967.

Alhaji Mohammed Goni first took up appointment with the Northern Nigeria government, and upon creation of states in 1967 was deployed to North-Eastern State Public Service as Divisional Officer-in-Charge of Katagun and Gombe Divisions, 1968 to 1970. Later, in 1972, he became the General Manager of North-East Line Corporation. In 1977, he transfered his services to the Nigerian National Supply Company (NNSC) as Company Secretary and Administrative Manager, a post he held until he opted for active partisan politics. Represented Kukawa Local Government Area at the Constituent Assembly, 1977-78.

1ST GOVERNOR, CROSS RIVER STATE

Brigadier Udoakaha Jacob Esuene, appointed Governor, South-Eastern State on May 27, 1967, and served until July 30, 1975. In the February 3, 1976 state creation exercise which ushered in Lt-Col. Paul Omu, South-Eastern State was one of seven existing States essentially unaffected except for minor boundary adjustments and a change of name to Cross River State.

For biodata, see: *1st Governor, (defunct) South-Eastern State.*

1ST CIVILIAN (EXECUTIVE) GOVERNOR, CROSS RIVER STATE

Dr Clement Isong, elected in July 1979 and sworn in on October 1, 1979, under the platform of the National Party of Nigeria (NPN). Served until September 1983, having failed to secure a re-election for a second four-year term.

Born on April 20, 1920, at Ikot Udo Esan in Eket Local Government Area of Akwa Ibom State, he was educated at Western College, USA, 1949-50; Harvard University, USA, 1954-57, obtaining BA, MA (Econs) and honorary LLD degrees.

1ST GOVERNOR, (OLD) GONGOLA STATE

Col. M. D. Jega, appointed Governor following the creation of the State from former North-Eastern State by General Murtala Muhammed on February 3, 1976. Served until 1978.

Born on April 23, 1942, in Jega, Sokoto State, he attended Sokoto Secondary School, 1956-61; Nigerian Military Training College, 1962; Pakistan Military Academy, 1962-65; Staff College, Kansas, USA, 1973-74. Promoted to 2nd Lt, 1965; Lt, 1966; Captain, 1967; Major, 1968; Lt-Col., 1969 and Col., 1974.

Prior to his appointment as Governor, Col. Jega had served as Platoon Commander, 1st Infantry Battalion, Bonny, 1967-68; Commander, 26th Infantry Brigade Onitsha, 1968-69; Commander, 26th Infantry Brigade, Lokoja, 1970-74; General Staff, 1st Infantry Division, Kaduna, 1974-76.

1ST CIVILIAN (EXECUTIVE) GOVERNOR, OLD GONGOLA STATE

Alhaji Abubakar A. Barde, elected in July 1979 and sworn in on October 1, 1979, under the platform of Unity Party of Nigeria (UPN). Served until September 1983, having failed to secure re-election in October 1983.

Born in Jalingo, Taraba State in 1938; attended Provincial Secondary School, Yola, 1956-61; Advanced Teachers' College, Zaria, 1962-65; Ahmadu Bello University, 1965-66. Later posted to Lokoja as Provincial Education Secretary, Kabba Province; later transferred to Kaduna as Planning Officer in charge of Technical Assistance in Education, 1967; Secretary, (defunct) North-Eastern State Scholarship Board, Maiduguri 1968-73. In July 1974, was Chief Education Officer, Secondary Schools, until January 1979 when he resigned to join politics.

1ST GOVERNOR, IMO STATE

Navy Commander Ndubuisi Godwin Kanu, appointed February 3, 1976, following the creation of Imo and Anambra States from former East Central State. Left office in August 1977.

From Isiukwuato, Abia State, Kanu was born on November 3, 1943; attended Metropolitan College, Onitsha; National Defence Academy, London; Naval Engineering and Electrical College, India. One-time Command Operations Officer, Kanu was Member, Supreme Military Council (SMC) before his appointment as Governor of Imo State. One-time Chief of Naval Operations; Member, Armed Forces Ruling Council (AFRC).

1ST CIVILIAN (EXECUTIVE) GOVERNOR, IMO STATE

Chief Samuel Onunaka Mbakwe, elected July 1979 and sworn in October 1, 1979, under the banner of the Nigeria People's Party (NPP), and served until December 1983, failing to secure re-election in October 1983.

Born in Avutu, Etiti Local Government Area of Imo State; educated at Awka College for Higher Elementary Certificate in 1950, where he also obtained his Senior Cambridge certificate. Proceeded to Fourah Bay College, Sierra Leone; University of Manchester, England, 1953-56, where he obtained a combined BA degree in Law and Public Administration. Between 1956 and 1958, Chief Mbakwe did postgraduate studies at Hull University, England, and earned an LLB degree. Was called to the Bar (Lincoln's Inn), 1959.

Past positions held include Director, Nigerian Broadcasting Corporation, 1962-66; Chairman, Star Printing and Publishing Company; Chairman, Monier Construction Company (MCC).

1ST GOVERNOR, KADUNA STATE

Brigadier Abba Kyari, appointed Governor, North-Central State, on May 27, 1967, and served until July 30, 1975. In the February 3, 1976 state creation exercise by Murtala Muhammed, North-Central State was essentially merely re-named Kaduna State; barring minor boundary adjustments, the State remained intact.

For biodata, see: *1st Governor, (defunct) North-Central State.*

1ST CIVILIAN (EXECUTIVE) GOVERNOR, KADUNA STATE

Alhaji Abdulkadir Balarabe Musa, elected for a four-year term with effect from October 1, 1979, under the People's Redemption Party (PRP).

However, he was impeached from office following a series of allegations levelled against him. Thereafter his deputy, Alhaji Abba Musa Rimi, took over as governor.

For biodata, see: *1st Nigerian Governor to be impeached (**below**).*

1ST NIGERIAN GOVERNOR TO BE IMPEACHED

Alhaji Abdulkadir Balarabe Musa, Governor of Kaduna State, impeached on Tuesday June 23, 1981 by the Kaduna State legislative. Was sworn in as Kaduna State Governor on October 1, 1979, on the People's Redemption Party's (PRP) platform. However, the State House of Assembly, with a National Party of Nigeria (NPN) majority membership, rendered his efforts at forming a cabinet impossible until he was finally impeached from office.

A politician and chartered accountant, he was born in Kaya, Kaduna State, August 21, 1936. Balarabe attended the Institute of Administration, Zaria, 1962-69, and various colleges in London. Before his election as Governor, he had occupied several accounting posts, including Accountant, Defence Industries Corporation (DIC) Kaduna; Company Secretary/Chief Accountant, Broadcasting Corporation of Northern Nigeria, 1970-74.

1ST GOVERNOR, KANO STATE

Police Commissioner Alhaji Audu Bako, Military Governor from May 27, 1967 (when the State was created) to July 30, 1975.

Born in Kaduna (of Sokoto State origin) on November 24, 1924, Bako was himself the son of a policeman. He was educated at Kaduna Government School; Zaria Middle School. He joined the Nigeria Police Force (NPF) on June 24, 1942, and received training at the Metropolitan Police School and later underwent a Senior Police Officer's training course at Ryton-on-Dunsmore, England. One-time Assistant Commissioner in charge, Kano and Katsina Provinces 1963; Deputy Commissioner of Police, (defunct) Northern Region. Dismissed from the Force in February 1976. Died in 1980.

1ST CIVILIAN (EXECUTIVE) GOVERNOR, KANO STATE

Alhaji Abubakar Mohammed Rimi, elected July 1979, under the People's Redemption Party (PRP), sworn in October 1, 1979. Served until September 1983 having lost to Alhaji Barkin Zuwo in his re-election bid.

Born 1940 in Rimi, Kano State; attended Institute of Administration, Zaria, 1961-62; University of London, 1972-74; University of Sussex, Brighton, 1975, obtaining a Diploma in International Relations and Master of Arts. Career includes: Instructor, Institute of Administration, Zaria, and Clerical Training Centre, Sokoto, 1962-64; Federal Ministry of Information, Lagos, 1966-70; Information and Cultural Attaché, Nigerian Embassy, Cairo, 1970-72; Admin. Secretary, Nigerian Institute of International Affairs, Lagos, 1976-77; Member, Constituent Assembly, 1977-78.

1ST GOVERNOR, KATSINA STATE

Lt-Col. Abdullahi Sarki Moukhtar, appointed September 24, 1987 and sworn in the next day. Katsina State, one of Nigeria's newest States, was created by the Babangida administration out of the former Kaduna State on September 23, 1987, with Katsina as capital.

From Kano State, Lt-Col. Moukhtar was born on July 5, 1949. Prior to his appointment as Governor, he was Cadet Brigade Commander, Nigerian Defence Academy, Kaduna. Later (June 1988) re-assigned to Kaduna State as Governor.

1ST GOVERNOR, KWARA STATE

Col. David Lasisi Bamigboye, appointed Military Governor from the State's creation on May 27, 1967 to July 1975.

Born on December 7, 1940 in Omu-Aran, Ilorin, Kwara State, he was educated at Government College, Zaria; Milility Academy, Kaduna; Mons Officer Cadet Training School, Aldershot, England, 1960-61. Commissioned 2nd Lieutenant, 1962; Served in then Congo (Zaire) UN Peace Force.

Was serving in 2 HQ Area Command, Ibadan, at time of his appointment as Governor. Retired from the Army in 1975.

1ST CIVILIAN (EXECUTIVE) GOVERNOR, KWARA STATE

Alhaji Adamu Atta, elected in July 1979. Sworn in for a four-year term on October 1, 1979, on the platform of the National Party of Nigeria (NPN), and served until September 1983.

Born in Okene, Kwara State, in 1928; educated in Achimota College, Accra, Ghana, where he read law and was called to the Bar (Lincoln's Inn), London.

1ST GOVERNOR, LAGOS STATE

Brigadier Mobolaji Olafunke Johnson, appointed first as Military Administrator of Lagos State in 1966, and later Military Governor from May 27, 1967 to July 30, 1975, when he was retired. Died in 2019.

From Lagos State, Johnson was born on February 9, 1935; educated at Hussey College, Warri; Methodist Boys' High School, Lagos; Officers' Cadet Training School, Teshie, Ghana; Royal Military Academy, Sandhurst, England. Joined the Army in 1958. Positions held include Deputy Adjutant-General; 2 i/c, 4th Battalion, Ibadan; Station Master, Benin-City.

1ST CIVILIAN (EXECUTIVE) GOVERNOR, LAGOS STATE

Alhaji Lateef Kayode Jakande, elected in July 1979 and sworn in on October 1, 1979. Re-elected for another four-year term with effect from October 1, 1983, but served only until December 31, 1983, when a military coup swept the regime out of power. Had contested on both occasions under the banner of the Unity Party of Nigeria (UPN).

A renowned journalist, Alhaji Jakande was born on July 23, 1929, in Lagos. His work career included: Managing Editor, African Press Limited, 1954; General Manager, Amalgamated Press (Publishers of the *Daily Service* and *Sunday Express*), 1956; Editor-in-Chief, Amalgamated Press, 1956-60; Chairman and Managing Director, John West Publications Limited; Lagos Book and Stationery Company Limited; Chairman/Editor-in-Chief, African News Service; Chairman, Board of Governors, Nigerian Institute of Journalism, 1970; Consultant, University of Nairobi School of Journalism, 1974; Co-Founder, Nigeria Institute of Journalism; Co-Founder and 1st President, Newspaper Proprietors' Association of Nigeria; Vice-President, International Press Institute, 1972-74.

1ST (AND ONLY) MAYOR OF LAGOS

Dr Abubakar Ibiyinka Olorun-Nimbe, appointed Mayor of Lagos following his victory in the 1st Lagos Joint Council election held on October 16, 1950. Served until 1953, when the introduction of a new system dispensed with the Mayorship for Lagos.

Mobolaji Olafunke Johnson (1936-2019), first Governor of Lagos State (see page 170). Pictured here in 1966.

PHOTOGRAPH: DEPARTMENT OF TOURISM AND INFORMATION, LAGOS STATE (IN THE PUBLIC DOMAIN).

A medical doctor and politician, Olorun-Nimbe was born in 1908 and attended Tinubu Methodist School, Lagos; Aroloya Government Muslim School, Lagos; CMS Grammar School, Lagos; King's College, Lagos. Graduated in medicine, University of Glasgow, Scotland, in 1937; returned to Nigeria in 1938 to join government medical service; resigned in 1941 and joined Macaulay's Nigerian National Democratic Party (NNDP), then an affiliate of the National Council of Nigeria and the Cameroons (NCNC), on whose ticket (NNDP-NCNC) he was in December 1945 elected to the Legislative Council for one of the Lagos seats. Was re-elected in 1947. Following the Lagos Town Council election held on October 16, 1950, Olorun-Nimbe won as Mayor of Lagos. Died in Lagos on February 5, 1975.

1ST NIGERIAN RESIDENT (COMMISSIONER) OF LAGOS COLONY

Henry Rawlingson Carr. Retired from service on August 1, 1924.

A civil servant, he was born on August 15, 1863, in Lagos. Son of a Sierra Leonean emigrant of Egba origin (Amuwo Carr and Rebecca Carr), he attended St Paul's (Breadfruit) School, 1869-70; Olowogbowo Wesleyan Primary School, 1871-73; Wesleyan Boys' High School, Freetown, Sierra Leone. 1874; Fourah Bay College, Freetown, Sierra Leone, 1877-82, obtaining the BA degree in Mathematics and Physics. Then proceeded to England to read law. Later called to the Bar, Lincoln's Inn.

Returned to Nigeria in June 1885; appointed Senior Assistant Master, CMS Grammar School, Lagos. Joined the colonial civil service in 1889 as Chief Clerk and Sub-Inspector of Schools for Lagos, rising to become 1st African Resident Commissioner of the Colony of Lagos. Later served in several other public offices particularly in education and the church, as Chancellor of the Diocese of Lagos (Anglican Church), 1906-45. Conferred Officer of the Order of the British Empire (OBE) and honorary Doctor of Civil Law degree. Died March 6, 1945.

1ST GOVERNOR, NIGER STATE

Navy Commander Murtala Nyako, appointed February 3, 1976, following the creation of the State out of former North-Western State by General Murtala Muhammed. Served until 1978.

Born at Mayo Belwa, on August 27, 1942, Nyako attended Government Secondary School, Yola (1958-62), before joining the Navy on June 6, 1963. Received military training at Britannia Royal Naval College, Dartmouth, UK, 1963-66; Navigation and Direction course, in India, 1969-70; Maritime, Tactical course, UK, 1974; Naval Staff course, USA 1975; Royal College of Defence Studies, UK, 1983. Had been Chief of Operations, Naval Headquarters; Flag Officer Commanding, Western Naval Command. Member, Armed Farces Ruling Council (AFRC), 1985.

1ST CIVILIAN (EXECUTIVE) GOVERNOR, NIGER STATE

Alhaji Muhammed Anwal Ibrahim, first elected with effect from October 1, 1979, and re-elected for another four-year term from October 1, 1983, on the platform of the National Party of Nigeria (NPN). Served only until December 31, 1983 when a military coup swept him out of power.

Born in September 1941, in Suleija in present-day Federal Capital Territory; attended School of Arabic Studies, Abdullahi Bayero College, Kano, where he obtained the Bachelor of Arts degree, 1967; postgraduate studies at the University of Lancaster, England. In 1967, he joined ABU as a lecturer. Between 1967 and 1973, he was Acting Registrar, Bayero College, before being seconded to the Niger State Government in 1976.

1ST GOVERNOR, OGUN STATE

Lt-Col. Saidu Ayodele Balogun, following the creation of the new state out of the former Western States on February 3, 1976, by General Murtala Muhammed. Removed and reassigned to regular army duties in 1978.

From Idoani, Owo Division of Ondo State, he was born on April 29, 1941; attended Ansar-Ud-Deen School, Idoani, 1947-54; Olu- Iwa College, Ijebu - Ode, 1957-61. Joined the Nigerian Army as Officer-Cadet in 1963 and rose to Lt-Col. in 1972. Positions held include Commander, Supply and Transport, 1964-75; Acting Brigade Commander, 9th Infantry Brigade, Abeokuta, May-November 1976, before his appointment as Military Governor. Later appointed Commander, Army School of Supplies and Transport.

1ST CIVILIAN (EXECUTIVE) GOVERNOR, OGUN STATE

Chief Victor Olabisi Onabanjo, first elected with effect from October 1, 1979, and re-elected for a second four-year term from October 1, 1983, both times on the platform of the Unity Party of Nigeria (UPN). Was, however, removed as a result of the December 1983 military coup.

From Ijebu-Ode, Ogun State, Chief Onabanjo was born in Lagos on February 12, 1927, and attended Baptist Academy, Lagos, where he distinguished himself as the best student, for which his name was put on the Dux Board for the year (1945). Chief Onabanjo later proceeded to the Regent Street Polytechnic School of Modern Languages (later Central London Polytechnic, now the University of Westminster), where he studied journalism and obtained a diploma. He also attended a six-month British Broadcasting Corporation (BBC) course in 1956. A versatile journalist, Chief Onabanjo had been Editor, *Nigerian Citizen,* Zaria; Editor, *Daily Service;* Editor, *Radio Times of Nigeria;* Deputy Editor-in-Chief, Nigerian Broadcasting Service; Editorial Director, *Express* Group of Newspapers; Director, WNBS/WNTW, Ibadan. Also Commissioner in the former Western State, 1966-69, serving in the Ministries of Home Affairs and Information, Health, Lands and Economic Planning; Member, Constituent Assembly, 1977-78.

1ST GOVERNOR, ONDO STATE

Major Ita David Ikpeme, following the creation of the new State out of the former Western States on February 3, 1976, by General Murtala Muhammed. Served until 1978.

1ST CIVILIAN (EXECUTIVE) GOVERNOR, ONDO STATE

Chief Michael Adekunle Ajasin, elected July 1979 and sworn in on October 1, 1979, for a four-year term under the Unity Party of Nigeria (UPN). Re-elected for another term with effect from October 1, 1983, but swept out ofoffice following the military coup of December 31, 1983.

Born in Owo on November 28, 1908, Chief Ajasin had his early education at St Andrew's College, Oyo, 1924-1927. Later proceeded to Fourah Bay

College, Sierra Leone; University of Durham, England, 1943-46 for his postgraduate Diploma in Education, which he obtained in June 1947. Chief Ajasin then attended the Institute of Education, University of London, having earlier obtained Bachelor of Arts degree in English, Modern History and Economics, June 1946.

An accomplished educationist, Chief Ajasin entered the teaching profession and rose to be 1st Principal of Imade College, Owo (September 1947 to December 1962). He was also Founder, Proprietor and 1st Principal, Owo High School, Owo (January 1963 to August 1975).

Before his election as Governor, he was Chairman, Owo District Council, 1954-59; Member, House of Representatives, 1954-66.

1ST STATE TO HAVE THREE MICHAELS AS GOVERNOR

Ondo State: Michael Adekunle Ajasin, October 1979 to December 1983; Michael Otiko, January 1984 to August 1985; Michael Akhigbe, September 1985 to August 1986. The three governors served sequentially.

Ajasin. For biodata, see: *1st civilian Executive Governor, Ondo State.*

Akhigbe. From Bendel State, born on October 1, 1946. After Ondo State, Akhigbe was appointed Governor of Lagos State, August 1986 to July 1988. One-time Director of Planning, Naval Headquarters.

1ST GOVERNOR, OYO STATE

Brigadier (later Major-General) David Jemibewon, following the creation of the State out of the former Western States on February 3, 1976. Served until 1978. Born on July 20, 1940, in Kabba, Kwara State, Jemibewon attended Offa Grammar School, 1955-59; School of Radiography, Lagos, 1960; Nigerian Military College, Kaduna, 1961; Mons Officer Cadet School, Aldershot, England, 1962; Commandant Staff College, Kansas, USA, 1971-72.

Prior to his appointment as Military Governor, he served in several military positions as Platoon, Battalion and Brigade Commander, Adjutant and

Quartermaster-General; General Staff Officer and Director of Military Manuals and Command Duties, Army Headquarters. Later Commandant, Army School of Infantry, Jaji. Retired from the Army as Major-General.

1ST CIVILIAN (EXECUTIVE) GOVERNOR, OYO STATE

Chief Bola Ige, elected in July 1979 on the platform of Unity Party of Nigeria (UPN) and sworn in on October 1, 1979. Served until September 1983, having failed in his re-election bid.

Born at Esa Oke near Ilesha, Osun State, in 1930, Chief Ige had his early education at Ibadan Grammar School, before going to read classics at University College, Ibadan (University of Ibadan), graduating in 1955. Proceeded to the United Kingdom in 1956 to read Law, graduating LLB and called to the Bar in 1958. Returned to Nigeria to set up private legal practice in 1961. Chief Ige's political activities started while he was still at University College Ibadan, where he was Publicity Secretary of the Action Group Youth Club. Later Nigeria's Minister of Power under President Obasanjo.

1ST GOVERNOR, PLATEAU STATE

Col. A. Muhammed, from its creation out of former Benue-Plateau State on February 3, 1976. Served until 1978.

1ST CIVILIAN (EXECUTIVE) GOVERNOR, PLATEAU STATE

Solomon Daushep Lar, elected in July 1979 and sworn in on October 1, 1979 for a four-year term under the banner of the Nigeria People's Party (NPP). Re-elected for another term with effect from October 1, 1983, but removed as a result of the military coup of December 31, 1983.

Born in April 1933 in Langtang, Lar attended Gindiri Teachers' College (obtaining his Teachers' Grade II Certificate in 1957); Ahmadu Bello University, Zaria, where he obtained a Bachelor of Law degree (LLB) in 1970. Lar entered politics in 1959 under United Middle Belt Congress/Action Group Alliance; contested and won elections in the same year (1959) into the Federal Parliament. Was re-elected during the 1964 elections. Appointed Parliamentary Secretary, Federal Ministry of Establishments, 1965-66. Between 1971 and 1979, Mr Lar was in private legal practice in Jos. Launched, in conjunction with Mr Chimezie Ikeazor, the now-popular Nigerian Legal Aid Association, becoming its 1st National Secretary.

Member, Nigerian delegation to the Parliamentary Union Conference in Brazil, 1962; Chairman, panel to examine the manpower needs of Plateau State, 1976; Member, Irikefe Panel on the Creation of New States, 1976; Member, Nigerian Council of Legal Education; Chairman, Board of Directors, African Continental Bank (ACB), 1976-79; Member, Constituent Assembly, 1977-78.

1ST GOVERNOR, RIVERS STATE

Commander Alfred Papapreye Diete-Spiff, appointed Military Governor following the creation of Rivers State on May 27, 1967, by then Head of State Yakubu Gowon. Served until July 1975, when he was retired from the Army. Rivers State was carved out of the former Eastern Region.

From Nembe, Rivers State, Diete-Spiff was born on July 30, 1942; educated at St Joseph's College, Sasse-Buea, Cameroon; Britannia Royal Naval College, Dartmouth, England, 1962-66. Was Lieutenant Commander at time of his appointment, as Governor. Promoted to Navy Commander in 1973.

1ST CIVILIAN (EXECUTIVE) GOVERNOR, RIVERS STATE

Chief Melford Okilo. elected for a four-year term with effect from October 1, 1979, under the banner of the National Party of Nigeria (NPN). Re-elected for a second term starting October 1, 1983, but removed from office following the December 31, 1983 coup.

Born on November 30, 1933, in Emakaoakala near Oloibiri, he attended Teachers' Training College, Diobu, Port Harcourt. Through private studies he passed his GCE examinations and became an interpreter in the Magistrate's and High Courts of Eastern Nigeria, 1956-59. Although by 1960 he was already an elected Member of Parliament (MP), Okilo nevertheless continued his private studies as an external student of London University and passed the LLB and BD degree exams

1ST GOVERNOR, SOKOTO STATE

Lt-Col. U. A. Muhammed, from the creation of the state in February 1976, to 1978.

1ST CIVILIAN (EXECUTIVE) GOVERNOR, SOKOTO STATE

Alhaji Shehu Mohammed Kangiwa, elected for a four-year term with effect from October 1, 1979, under the National Party of Nigeria (NPN). Died in office on November 17, 1981, while playing polo. Thereafter, his deputy, Dr Garba Nadama, was sworn in as Governor on November 27, 1981.

13.4 MINISTERS

NIGERIA'S 1ST FEDERAL ATTORNEY-GENERAL AND MINISTER OF JUSTICE

Dr Taslim Olawole Elias, Federal Attorney-General and Minister of Justice from 1960 to 1366. Was also Attorney-General, 1966-71, and Commissioner for Justice, 1967-72. A jurist, born on November 11, 1914; attended CMS Grammar School, Lagos; Igbobi College, Yaba; University College, London; Council of Legal Education, Institute of Advanced Legal Studies, University of London. Called to the Bar (Inner Temple), London, 1947. Appointed Visiting Professor, University of Delhi, India, 1956; Professor and Dean, Faculty of Law, University of Lagos, 1966-72; Chief Justice of the Federation, 1972-75; Judge, International Court of Justice at The Hague, 1979; Chairman, Nigerian Institute of International Affairs, 1972-75. Awarded honorary LLD degrees of Universities of Dakar, Senegal and Hull, England, and DLitt., Ibadan, 1969. Author of numerous books and treatises on law.

NIGERIA'S 1ST MINISTER OF COMMERCE

Raymond Amanze Njoku, Federal Minister of Commerce and Industry from 1951 to 1955 whence he was assigned to the Federal Ministry of Trade and Industry up to September 1956.

From Emekuku, Owerri, Imo State, he was born in August 1915, and attended St Charles' College, Onitsha; University of London, England, where he read law and was called to the Bar (Middle Temple) in 1947. On return he engaged in private legal practice and politics, joining the National Council of Nigeria and the Cameroons (NCNC) party. Was also Federal Minister of Trade and Industry, 1955-56; Transport, September 1956 to 1964; Communication and Aviation, 1964-66. Conferred Commander of the Federal Republic (CFR) of Nigeria. Died September 21, 1977.

NIGERIA'S 1ST MINSTER OF COMMUNICATIONS

Chief Arthur Edward Prest, from 1951 to 1954.

Born on March 10, 1906, in Warri, Delta State, he was educated at Government School, Warri; King's College, Lagos. Joined the Nigerian Police Force and rose to Chief Inspector before resigning in 1943 to pursue a course in law at the University of London. Was called to the Bar (Middle Temple) in 1946. On return to Nigeria, he entered private legal practice and politics rising to the post of 1st Vice-President of his party, Action Group (AG). Following the creation of the Mid-West Region, Chief Prest was appointed its High Court Judge. Died on September 11, 1976.

NIGERIA'S 1ST MINISTER OF DEFENCE

Alhaji Muhammadu U. Ribadu, so appointed September 1960, and served until 1965.

Born in 1910 at Balala, Taraba State, he was educated at Yola Middle School, where he later taught from 1926. Proceeded on local government course to Britain, 1946. On return, entered politics and entered the Northern House of Assembly in 1947. Died in 1965.

NIGERIA'S 1ST EDUCATION MINISTER

Dr Aja Nwachukwu, appointed Federal Minister of Education in September 1957.

Born on November 1, 1918, in Okposi, near Afikpo, Ebonyi State; educated at CMS School, Uburu; Wolsey Hall, Oxford, England; London School of Commerce. Elected into the Eastern House of Assembly and proceeded from there to the Federal House of Representatives. Was Member, Public Accounts Committee, before his appointment as Federal Minister of Education in 1957. Was Acting Minister of Social Services when the Balewa government was toppled in January 1966.

NIGERIA'S 1ST EXTERNAL AFFAIRS MINISTER

Chief Jala Anucha Wachuku, appointed Federal Minister of Foreign Affairs and Commonwealth Relations in 1961.

For biodata, see: *1st Nigerian Speaker of the Federal House.*

NIGERIA'S 1ST MINISTER OF FINANCE

Chief Festus Samuel Okotie-Eboh, appointed by Prime Minister Tafawa Balewa in September 1957, serving the until January 15, 1966 coup. According to Nigeria's Constitution at the time, the Finance Minister was next in rank to the Prime Minister. Okotie-Eboh presented the nation's first budget in March 1958.

From Warri, Delta State, Chief Okotie-Eboh was born in 1912. He contested the 1959 election, won, and was reappointed Finance Minister until killed on January 28, 1967.

NIGERIA'S 1ST HEALTH MINISTER

Dr Ayo Rosiji, from 1959 to 1961.

NIGERIA'S 1ST MINISTER OF INFORMATION

Hon. Victor Esemingsongo Mukete, appointed Federal Minister of Research and Information from 1958 to 1959. A Cameroonian agriculturist, Mukete was born on November 15, 1918, in Kumba, Cameroon; attended Government College, Umuahia, 1933-38; Higher College, Yaba, 1939; University of Manchester, England, 1948-51; Christ's College, Cambridge University, England, 1951-52. Prior to this appointment, Mukete had served as Federal Minister without Portfolio, 1955-57. At that time Nigeria's political boundary encompassed present-day Cameroon.

NIGERIA'S 1ST INTERNAL AFFAIRS MINISTER

Chief Joseph Modupe Johnson, Federal Minister of Internal Affairs, Labour and Welfare from 1957 to 1959, when he resigned from Prime Minister Balewa's government.

Born on March 30, 1912, he attended William Wilberforce Academy, Lagos, 1928-32. After a service period with the Nigerian Army, 1938-46, he entered politics and was elected Councillor, Ibadan District Council, March 1954, and Chairman, 1955. Was conferred the exalted traditional title of *Apesin* of Lagos. Died June 15, 1987.

NIGERIA'S 1ST LABOUR MINISTER

Chief Matthew Tawo Mbu, appointed Federal Minister of Labour from 1953 to 1954.

Born on November 20, 1929, in Okundi, Ogoja, Cross River State, Mbu held the LLB (Hons) 1959; LLM 1964; Diploma in International Affairs, 1959. Called to the Bar (Middle Temple), England, 1960. Member, Eastern House of Assembly; House of Representatives, Lagos, 1952-53, 1954-55; Acting Minister of Transport; Minister of Commerce, 1954-55; Minister of Defence, Navy, 1961-65; Aviation, 1966. Appointed High Commissioner to the UK, 1955-59. Member, Constituent Assembly, 1978; Pro-Chancellor/Chairman of Council, University of Ife (Obafemi Awolowo University), Ile-Ife, 1980.

***Also:** 1st Nigerian High Commissioner to the UK; 1st Nigerian Chief Representative in Washington 1959-60; 1st Nigerian Chief Representative in the United Nations, 1950-60.*

NIGERIA'S 1ST MINISTER OF LANDS AND NATURAL RESOURCES

Dr Kingsley Ozumba Mbadiwe, from 1952 to 1954. Also served as Federal Minister of Communications and Aviation, 1954-56; Trade and Industry, 1957-58, 1961-62, during which period he initiated Nigeria's first Trade Fair. Later (in the Second Republic), he served as President Shagari's Special Adviser on National Assembly Liaison.

Born on March 15, 1917, in Arondizuogu, Imo State, Dr Mbadiwe attended Hope Waddell Training Institution, Calabar, 1933; Aggrey Memorial College, Arochukwu, 1934; Baptist Academy, Lagos; Igbobi College, Lagos, 1935; Lincoln University, USA. 1939; Columbia University Business College, USA, 1940. Obtained BSc (Banking and Finance) and MA (Political Science) degrees.

NIGERIA'S 1ST MINISTER OF NATIONAL PLANNING

Chief (Mrs) Adenike Ebun Oyagbola, so appointed following the creation of the Ministry of National Planning by then President Shehu Shagari in October, 1979. Resigned in July 1981.

Mrs Oyagbola was born in Igan Alade in Egbado, Ogun State in 1931. Initially trained as a teacher but later proceeded to England where she studied at Balham and Tooting College of Commerce. She had served as an accountant in the Federal Civil Service before her entry into a political career.

***See also:** Nigeria's 1st female Federal Cabinet Minister(s).*

NIGERIA'S 1ST MINISTER OF SCIENCE AND TECHNOLOGY

Dr Sylvester Uzor Ugoh, appointed in 1980, following the elevation of the status of the Science and Technology Unit to that of a full Ministry. Served until 1981.

Born on April 20, 1931, at Umuokrika-Ekwerazu, Imo State, Ugoh obtained a bachelors degree in Economics from University of New Hampshire, USA, and a masters and doctorate in the same discipline from Harvard University, USA. Taught at the University of Nigeria, Nsukka, for several years, rising to Director of the University's Economic Development Institute (EDI), 1970. Member of the Constituent Assembly, 1978, Dr Ugoh was one-time Director, Central Bank of Nigeria (CBN).

NIGERIA'S 1ST STEEL MINISTER

Paul Unongo, appointed Federal Minister in charge of Steel Development from October 1979 to 1980. The Ministry was first created in 1979 during President Shehu Shagari's regime.

NIGERIA'S 1ST MINISTER OF TRADE

Raymond Amanze Njoku, Federal Minister of Trade and Industry from 1955 to 1957. Earlier, 1951 to 1955, he was the Federal Minister of Commerce and Industry.

For biodata, see: *Nigeria's 1st Minister of Commerce.*

NIGERIA'S 1ST MINISTER OF TRANSPORT

Alhaji Abubakar Tafawa Balewa, appointed Federal Minister of Works and Transport from 1953 to 1957.

For biodata, see: *Nigeria's 1st (only) Prime Minister.*

NIGERIA'S 1ST MINISTER OF WORKS

Alhaji Muhammadu Inuwa Wada, appointed Federal Minister of Works and Surveys from September 1955 to 1965.

Born in Kano in 1917 and educated at Kano Middle School, 1930-33; Katsina Higher College, 1933-38; taught at Kano Middle School, 1938-47. Prior to his appointment as Federal Minister of Works and Surveys in 1955, he was simultaneously a member of both Northern Nigeria and Federal Houses.

Was Parliamentary Secretary to the Northern Premier, 1952-54; Federal Minister (without Portfolio), 1954; later, Federal Minister of Defence, 1965-66.

NIGERIA'S 1ST FEMALE FEDERAL CABINET MINISTER(S)

Chief (Mrs) Adenike Ebun Oyagbola and Chief (Mrs) Janet Adefenwa Akinrinade, both appointed Federal Ministers into President Shehu Shagari's cabinet in October 1979. Mrs Oyagbola was assigned the portfolio of National Planning, (a post she resigned from in July 1981), while Mrs Akinrinade was Minister of State for Internal Affairs from December 1979 to 1983.

Chief (Mrs) Akinrinade was born on March 13, 1930, in Otu Iseyin, Oyo State; attended Southampton School of Commerce, Southampton, England, 1957. Worked as Caterer, Ibadan Polytechnic, 1973-76; University of Ibadan, 1975-77; before being elected into the Constituent Assembly, 1977-78, from where she was appointed into President Shehu Shagari's cabinet.

Mrs Oyabola. For biodata, see: *Nigeria's 1st Minister of National Planning.*

13.5 DIPLOMATIC/EXTERNAL AFFAIRS

1ST NIGERIAN ELECTED CHAIRMAN OF THE AFRICAN UNION (FORMER O.A.U.)

General Yakubu Gowon, for the 1973-74 year, which commenced on May 25, 1973. Was then Nigeria's Head of State. The OAU was founded on April 27, 1963, with a later name change to the African Union (AU).

For biodata, see: *1st Nigerian full Army General,* ***entry under:*** *ARMED FORCES; Nigeria's 1st State Wedding,* ***entry under:*** *POLITICS AND GOVERNMENT – HEADS OF STATE/GOVERNMENT.*

1ST NIGERIAN SECRETARY-GENERAL OF THE AFRICAN UNION (FORMER O.A.U.)

Dr Peter Onu, from June 2, 1983 to August 1985. This was, however, in an acting capacity, pending the election of a substantive Secretary-General.

1ST BATCH OF NIGERIA'S 'TECHNICAL AID CORPS'

161 (including 16 female) doctors, engineers, teachers and various other young professionals.

Inaugurated on Wednesday October 7, 1987, by then President Ibrahim Babangida, the Technical Aid Scheme was designed to assist poorer African and 'Third World' countries in need of technical/professional manpower. Under the agreement the Nigerian Government paid every corps member US$500 monthly while the host country provided accommodation, health care and other basic facilities.

1ST OFFICIAL VISIT TO NIGERIA BY A BRITISH MONARCH

Visit by Queen Elizabeth II (and husband Prince Philip, Duke of Edinburgh) to then Federal Capital, Lagos, and to the three Regions of Nigeria, in January 1956. Arrived Lagos, Nigeria, on Saturday January 28, 1956.

1ST (SITTING) BRITISH PRIME MINISTER TO VISIT NIGERIA

Mr Maurice Harold Macmillan, who paid a week's official visit from January 11 to 17, 1960, as part of an African tour which also took him to Ghana and Zimbabwe. During the tour, Macmillan, accompanied by his wife, Lady Dorothy, visited Lagos, Enugu, Ibadan and Kaduna (i.e. then Federal and Regional capitals).

Macmillan was born in London on February 10, 1884, of upper-middle-class parents who owned the renowned publishing firm Macmillan; became Britian's Prime Minister in 1957. Died on December 29, 1986.

1ST (SITTING) BRITISH PRIME MINISTER TO VISIT INDEPENDENT NIGERIA

Sir Alec Douglas-Home, who paid an official visit to Nigeria from March 19 to 20, 1964. Held talks with Nigerian leaders (Azikiwe and Balewa), during which Southern Africa and Commonwealth issues were discussed.

NIGERIA 1ST HIGH COMMISSIONER TO THE U.K.

Chief Matthew Tawo Mbu, from 1955 to 1959.

For biodata, see: *Nigeria's 1st Labour Minister,* ***entry under:*** *POLITICS AND GOVERNMENT – MINISTERS.*

INDEPENDENT NIGERIA'S 1ST HIGH COMMISSIONER TO THE U.K.

Alhaji Abdul Maliki, appointed in 1960 following Nigeria's independence. Served until mid-1966, when he was transferred to France as Ambassador.

Born in 1914, son of the *Attah* of Igbirra, traditional ruler of the Igbirra of Kwara State, Alhaji Abdul was educated at Katsina Training College. Taught at Okene Middle School, 1934-35. Appointed Supervisor of Native Authority Works, 1936-39. Member, Northern Region House of Assembly; Federal House of Representatives, 1952-55; Member of the Nigerian People's Congress (NPC). Prior to his appointment as High Commissioner to the UK, he was Commissioner to the UK for Northern Nigeria, 1955-58. Conferred Officer of the Order of the British Empire (OBE). Died in 1969 while on vacation at home from his duty beat in Europe.

1ST NIGERIAN HEAD OF STATE TO VISIT THE U.S.A.

Prime Minister Sir Abubakar Tafawa Balewa, from July 22, 1961, on the invitation of the then U.S. President John F. Kennedy.

For biodata, see: *Nigeria's 1st (only) Prime Minister,* ***entry under:*** *POLITICS AND GOVERNMENT – HEADS OF STATE/GOVERNMENT.*

Nigerian Prime Minister Abubakar Tafawa Balewa and US President John F. Kennedy at the White House, Washington DC, in 1961 (see page 186).

PHOTOGRAPH: ROBERT L. KNUDSEN (IN THE PUBLIC DOMAIN).

1ST UNITED STATES (SITTING) PRESIDENT TO OFFICIALLY VISIT NIGERIA

Jimmy Carter, who paid an official visit to Nigeria in April 1978, accompanied by his wife, Rosalyn, and daughter, Amy. The visit was to reciprocate an earlier one by Nigeria's then Head of State, Lt-Gen. Olusegun Ọbasanjo, to the United States in November 1977.

1ST (SITTING) NIGERIAN HEAD OF STATE TO OFFICIALLY VISIT GERMANY

President Shehu Aliyu Shagari, who paid a four-day visit to Germany from March 17 to 20, 1982.

For biodata, see: *Nigeria's 1st Executive President,* ***entry under:*** *POLITICS AND GOVERNMENT – HEADS OF STATE/GOVERNMENT.*

1ST (SITTING) GERMAN LEADER TO OFFICIALLY VISIT NIGERIA

President Dr Richard Von Weizsäcker, of the Federal Republic of Germany, who paid a six-day official visit to Nigeria from March 5 to 10, 1988. The visit was part of a 16-day four-nation African tour by the German leader, other countries visited being Mali, Zimbabwe and Somalia. His wife, Baroness Marrianne, leading German politicians and 30 journalists accompanied the German President who, apart from Lagos, also visited Enugu, Jos and Abuja, the new federal capital. The visit was also Weizäcker's 1st African tour since assuming duties in May 1984.

President Weizsäcker was born in Stuttgart, Germany, on April 15, 1920; studied law and history at Oxford, Grenoble and Göttingen Universities. Obtained an LLD degree from Göttingen, 1954. Member of the Bundestag (German Parliament), 1969-81; Mayor of Berlin, 1981. Died in 2015.

1ST NIGERIAN AMBASSADOR TO GERMANY

Chief T. O. C. Ojiako, from 1960 to 1961.

1ST GERMAN AMBASSADOR TO NIGERIA

Dr Harald Graf von Posadowsky-Wehner, from 1960 to 1964.

1ST OFFICIAL VISIT TO NIGERIA BY GHANA'S (SITTING) PRESIDENT

Dr Kwame Nkrumah's 12-day official visit to Nigeria, January 26-28, 1959. Ghana attained independence from Britain on March 6, 1957, with Dr Nkrumah as 1st Prime Minister.

Born on September 21, 1909, at Nkroful, South-West Ghana, Nkrumah was a Ghanain Statesman, 1st President of independent Ghana, and a foremost exponent of Pan-Africanism. One of the founding fathers of the Organisation of African Unity (OAU). Died April 27, 1972.

1ST (SITTING) INDIAN PRIME MINISTER TO VISIT NIGERIA

Shri Pandit Jawaharial Nehru, who visited Lagos from September 23 to 26, 1962. Was accompanied by his daughter, Shrimati Indira Ghandi, who later herself became India's Prime Minister.

1ST COUNTRY WITH WHOM NIGERIA BROKE DIPLOMATIC RELATIONS

France, on January 5, 1961, over that country's utter disregard of African protests over her (French) atomic bomb test in the Sahara Desert.

NIGERIA'S 1ST TRADE PACT WITH AN EASTERN EUROPEAN (COMMUNIST) COUNTRY

That signed with Poland on November 14, 1961, under Prime Minister Abubakar Tafawa Bajewa.

1ST NIGERIAN HEAD OF STATE TO ADDRESS THE GENERAL ASSEMBLY OF THE UNITED NATIONS (U.N.)

Sir Abubakar Tafawa Balewa, on October 7, 1960.

For details, see entry under: *POLITICS AND GOVERNMENT – HEADS OF STATE/GOVERNMENT.*

NIGERIA'S 1ST REPRESENTATIVE AT THE UNITED NATIONS (U.N.)

Chief Matthew Tawo Mbu, appointed Nigeria's Chief Representative at the United Nations in Washington from 1959 to 1960.

For biodata, see *Nigeria's 1st High Commissioner to the UK,* ***entry under:*** *POLITICS AND GOVERNMENT – DIPLOMATIC/EXTERNAL AFFAIRS.*

1ST NIGERIAN TO HEAD UNITED NATIONS (U.N.) ECONOMIC COMMISSION FOR AFRICA (E.C.A.)

Prof. Adebayo Adedeji, appointed Executive Secretary of the ECA on June 1, 1975.

An economist from Ijebu-Ode, Ogun State, Prof. Adedeji was born on December 21, 1930; attended Ijebu-Ode Grammar School, 1944-49; University College, Ibadan, 1953-54; University of Leicester, England, 1955-58; Harvard University, Cambridge, Mass., USA, 1960-61. Served the (defunct) Western Region Government from 1958, and rose to Principal Secretary, Revenue, Ministry of Finance in 1960. Joined Institute of Administration, University of Ife (Obafemi Awolowo University), in 1963, and rose to Director in 1967. Appointed Professor of Public Administration, University of Ife, in 1968. Was Federal Commissioner (Minister) for Economic Development and Reconstruction, 1971-75, prior to his appointment as Executive Secretary. Other positions held include President, Nigerian Economic Society, 1970-71; President, African Association of Public Administration and Management (AAPAM), 1974.

1ST NIGERIAN ORGANISATION OF PETROLEUM EXPORTING COUNTRIES (O.P.E.C.) PRESIDENT

Alhaji Yahaya Dikko, appointed on September 9, 1932.

See also entry under: *INDUSTRY, SCIENCE AND TECHNOLOGY.*

1ST COMMONWEALTH HEADS OF GOVERNMENT SUMMIT HOSTED BY NIGERIA

The two-day summit held at the Federal Palace Hotel, Lagos, from December 11 to 13, 1965, with the primary objective of seeking 'speedy and effective ways and means of bringing the [then] rebel regime in Rhodesia [now Zimbabwe] to an end'. Ten Prime Ministers and Heads of Government personally led their countries' delegations. Of the 19 that formally attended, Australia and New Zealand were present only as observers, while two African countries – Ghana and Tanzania – kept away. Host, Nigeria's Prime Minister Alhaji Abubakar Tafawa Balewa, presided. The Commonwealth Secretary-General at the time was Mr Arnold Smith.

1ST BATCH OF U.S. PEACE CORPS SERVICEMEN IN NIGERIA

Landed in Lagos on September 25, 1961.

1ST CHAIRMAN, GOVERNING BOARD, NIGERIAN INSTITUTE OF INTERNATIONAL AFFAIRS , LAGOS

Sir Adetokunbo Adegboyega Ademola, appointed Chairman of the Institute's six-man Board from October 11, 1961 to April 18, 1971, when Decree 35 establishing the Institute as a corporate body also dissolved its first governing body. Ademola's Board, which included Sir Louis Mbanefo, Dr Kenneth O. Dike, Hon. Shettima Kashim, Chief Simeon O. Adebo and Dr R. A. B. Dikko, held its inaugural meeting on December 13, 1961, now acknowledged as the Institute's founding date.

For biodata, see: *1st Nigerian Chief Justice of the Federation,* ***entry under:*** *LAW.*

1ST DIRECTOR-GENERAL, NIGERIAN INSTITUTE OF INTERNATIONAL AFFAIRS (N.I.I.A.), LAGOS

Dr Lawrence Apalara Fabunmi, from June 1963 to January 1972. Seconded from the Ministry of External Affairs.

Born on December 12, 1925, in Ekiti, Ekiti State; educated at Hope College, Holland, Michigan, USA, 1952; London School of Economics and Political Science, England, 1953-57. Before his appointment, had served the Federal Ministry of External Affairs, Lagos, 1958-61; Has also been High Commissioner to Zambia, 1973-76; Ambassador to Holland, 1979.

1ST GUEST SPEAKER AT THE NIGERIAN INSTITUTE OF INTERNATIONAL AFFAIRS (N.I.I.A.) LECTURE SERIES

Hon. Jaja Anucha Wachuku, MP, then Federal Minister of External Affairs, on June 12, 1983. His subject was 'The Achievements and Significance of the Addis Ababa Conference'. The NIIA lecture series, now quite popular, was designed to further the Institute's 'cardinal role of public enlightenment and the dissemination of information on current and world affairs'.

Born in 1918 in Mbawsi, near Aba, Abia State; educated at Government College, Umuahia; Yaba Higher College; Trinity College, University of Dublin, Eire, where he read law and was called to the Bar. On return to Nigeria in 1947, he entered politics and was elected into the Eastern House of Assembly, 1951-53. Later became Member, Federal House of Representatives, 1960. Positions held include: Federal Minister of Economic Development, 1960-61; Acting Permanent Representative to the UN, 1960-61; Federal Minister of Foreign Affairs and Commonwealth Relations, 1961-63; Federal Minister of Foreign Affairs, 1963-65; Federal Minister of Aviation, 1965-66. Elected Senator for Imo State, 1979-83. Awarded honorary LLD of University of Dublin (1961).

***Also:** 1st Nigerian Speaker, Federal House; Nigeria's 1st External Affairs Minister.*

1ST NIGERIAN TO PRESIDE OVER THE UNITED NATIONS (U.N.) GENERAL ASSEMBLY

Major-General Joseph Nanven Garba (Rtd), whose election as President of the 44th Session of the world body was announced on Tuesday September 19, 1989. Also the sixth African to occupy the post. He took over from Argentina's Dante Capute. As President, Joe Garba presided over the 150 member nations of the UN for twelve months. Prior to this appointment, Garba was Nigeria's Permanent Representative at the UN and Chairman of the body's Committee on Apartheid.

Born on July 17, 1943, in Langtang, Plateau State, he had held several top military and political posts including Commander, Brigade of Guards, 1968-75; Federal Commissioner (Minister) for External Affairs, 1975-78.

1ST NIGERIAN SECRETARY-GENERAL OF THE COMMONWEALTH

Chief Chukwuemeka Eleazar Anyaoku, who, on Wednesday October 18, 1989, at the Commonwealth Heads of Government summit held in Kuala Lumpur, Malaysia, was elected Secretary-General, having beaten fellow contestant, Australia's former Prime Minister, Malcolm Fraser, by 39 to 10 votes.

From Obosi, Anambra State, Emeka Anyaoku was born on January 18, 1933; educated at Merchant of Light School, Oba, and University of Ibadan, before joining Nigeria's diplomatic service in 1962. He rose to Deputy Secretary-General in 1977, a post he held until becoming Secretary-General.

13.6 TRADITIONAL RULERS

1ST SULTAN OF SOKOTO

Alhaji Muhammadu Bello, a traditional ruler, warrior, scholar, theologian and writer, who reigned from 1822 to 1837.

Born in 1781 in Sokoto to Usman Dan Fodio, he continued his father's drive to reform government law and society along Islamic lines and to destroy the remnants of paganism, taking a particular interest in the *Sharia* Islamic law and the *Sharia* courts. Died in 1837; buried at Wurno.

1ST NIGERIAN TRADITIONAL RULER TO BE A GOVERNOR

Sir Adesoji Aderemi, the *Ooni* of Ife, from 1930 to 1980. Was appointed Governor of (defunct) Western Nigeria on July 8, 1960.

For biodata, see: *1st Governor, (defunct) Western Nigeria,* ***entry under:*** *POLITICS AND GOVERNMENT – GOVERNORS/PREMIERS.*

1ST NIGERIAN TRADITIONAL RULER EXILED

Oba Kosoko of Lagos, who was exiled by the British colonial administrators in 1851.

Born in Lagos at the peak of the slave trade business on the West Coast of Africa, Oba Kosoko was son of King Idowu Ojulari, who reigned over Lagos from 1819 to 1832. Having failed in his bid to succeed to the vacant throne following his father's death, Kosoko plotted the overthrow of the newly installed king, Oluwole, his brother, for which Kosoko, then prince, was deported to Porto Novo in present-day Benin Republic. Prince Kosoko, however, returned from exile in 1845 to proclaim himself king, and thus reigned until 1851, when the British dethroned him and forced him back into exile, this time to Epe. In 1862 (after Britain declared Lagos a colony in 1861), Kosoko returned to Lagos, but not to the throne. He died in 1872.

1ST NIGERIAN RULER IN NIGER DELTA TO BE EXILED

King William Dappa Pepple of Bonny, who was sent in exile to London by a British consul, Beecroft, in January 1854, for resisting attempts by the British to take over control of the political and commercial affairs of Bonny. Returned from exile on August 18, 1861. King Pepple reigned over Bonny from 1835 to 1866.

Born around 1817, King Pepple is remembered chiefly as one of 'the first Nigerian rulers to wrestle with the whiteman to maintain his independence' (Prof. Allogoa), and also his introduction of Christianity, which he had imbibed while in long exile in England, to Bonny and the Niger Delta region.

1ST *ITSEKIRI* TRADITIONAL CHIEF TO BE BURIED IN A CASKET

Chief Ogbeni Newe Rewane, *Ologbotsere* (traditional prime minister) of Warri. His (deceased) body was interred at 2.10pm in the partially completed Ologbotsere Hall at Ode-Itsekiri on Sunday, November 29, 1987.

Rewane, a lawyer and educationist, was born on September 14, 1914, and had his secondary school education at Government College, Warri, 1926-31, and later entered Government College, Ibadan. Studied Law at the University of Hull, England, and was called to the Bar (Lincoln's Inn), 1956. Was crowned *Ologbotsere* of Warri in 1985, and had the singular honour of crowning the *Olu* of Warri, Ogiame Atunwatse, in April 1987.

1ST EMIR OF KANO TO PERFORM THE HAJJ

Alhaji Abdullahi Bayero, Emir of Kano, who performed the pilgrimage to Mecca twice, in 1937 and 1951.

For further details, see entry under: *RELIGION.*

14 RELIGION

1ST CHURCH IN NIGERIA

The Methodist Mission, led by its Reverend Thomas Birch Freeman, who first landed in Badagry in 1841 and preached Christian sermons under the old Agia tree in Badagry, near Lagos. His team formally established in Badagry in September 1842. Next came the representatives of the Church Missionary Society (CMS) mission, led by Rev. Henry Townsend, who landed in December 1842.

Badagry, once a busy slave post, and fondly referred to as 'the land of coconuts', was once a kingdom and one of the first international ports, and a gateway to Nigeria. The decline of Badagry as a chief port started in 1851, with the abolition of the slave trade.

1ST ANGLICAN (C.M.S.) OUTPOST IN NIGERIA

At Badagry (Agbadaigi), Lagos, established on December 17, 1842, by Rev. Henry Townsend, a (CMS) missionary. From Badagry, he proceeded to Abeokuta in 1843. He then returned to Sierra Leone after reconnoitering 'parts of Yoruba country'. Later, in October 1852, he returned to Badagry, this time with Rev. Gollmer and his wife and Rev. (later Bishop) Samuel Ajayi Crowther, the Nigerian liberated slave/clergyman, and some 'negro catechists' and helpers from Sierra Leone, to form the CMS Yoruba Mission. The CMS Niger Mission arrived at Onitsha on July 27, 1857.

The CMS movement was formed in 1799 for the purpose of carrying the gospel to the 'heathen' as an extension of the Church of England. The West African Mission of the CMS was formed on April 14, 1804.

1ST ROMAN CATHOLIC CHURCH IN NIGERIA

Following the establishment of the Vicariate of the Bight in 1861, with base in Dahomey (Benin), the Society for African Missions in Lyons, France, was assigned the regions between Rivers Volta and the Niger to explore. Thus

Obelisk, erected in 2012, on the site of the Agia tree (see page 196), site of the first Christian sermons preached in Nigeria.

PHOTOGRAPH: SAMUEL TOBBYTEX007 (2012, CC-BY-SA 4.0, CROPPED).

from Dahomey, Rev. Fr Borghers paid the first visit by a Catholic missionary to Nigeria (Lagos). The 1st resident priest in Lagos was, however, Rev. Fr Bouche, who landed in 1868. In the same year, Lagos was established as the headquarters under Rev. Fr Borghero, the Pro-Vicar Apostolic. Lagos, however, remained under the direction of Dahomey until 1883. In 1891, Bishop Chauses was consecrated first Vicar Apostolic.

1ST ROMAN CATHOLIC OUTPOST IN EASTERN NIGERIA

Established at Onitsha, Anambra State, on Saturday December 5, 1885, with the arrival of Fathers Joseph Émile Lutz and Joseph Home on the same date.

Although the Catholic missionaries first set foot in Eastern Nigeria at Akassa (November 20, 1885) and Brass (November 21, 1885), both in present-day Bayelsa State, they chose to settle in Onitsha when they could no longer continue to Lokoja. Their first Holy Mass at Onitsha was celebrated on December 25, 1885.

The pioneer Catholics belonged to the Holy Ghost Congregation, founded in France by Father Francis Claude Poullard des Places in 1703.

NIGERIA'S 1ST INDIGENOUS CHURCH

The United Native African Church (UNA). Later (from 1985) First African Church Mission. Was 1st African Mission in Nigeria and parts of the West African Coast. Founded on August 14, 1891, by a group known as the 'Immortal Nine', comprising: W. E. Colde (Convener), John O. George, C. A. Williams, N. T. Nelson, D. A. Ghoncester, J. A. Thompson, R. Chaseheigh, J. B. Kenny and Rev. C. W. Cole. At its inaugural meeting the body decided that 'a purely native African church be founded for the evangelisation and amelioration of our race to be governed by Africans'. It also adopted the motto 'My presence shall go with thee' (Exodus 33.14).

With headquarters, at 9, Phoenix Lane, Lagos, and parishes and dioceses all over Nigeria, it has a general council headed by a President, with other important title holders like the Chancellor, Registrar, Legal Adviser,

Medical Consultant, etc. Celebrates its Founders Day every August 14. Its 1st clergyman was ordained on December 26, 1913.

1ST NIGERIAN (AFRICAN) BISHOP

Right Rev. Samuel Ajayi Crowther, consecrated Bishop of Western Equatorial Africa by the Archbishop of Canterbury in Canterbury Cathedral, England, on June 29, 1862. He had earlier, in 1844, been ordained priest (the first so to do).

Born around 1806, from Abeokuta, Ogun State. His family was sold into slavery in 1821 but were intercepted en route to America and resettled in Freetown, Sierra Leone, where he went into the care of a CMS schoolmaster. Was converted to Christianity and baptised on December 11, 1825, adopting the new name, Samuel Crowther. In 1826, he travelled overseas and enrolled in a school in Liverpool Street, Islington, London, thus becoming the first Nigerian to school together with English children. After a spell in Fourah Bay University, Freetown, Sierra Leone, he returned to England in 1843 and was ordained Priest the next year. He finally returned to Nigeria in 1845, serving in a parish in Abeokuta, where a Christian mission was then being established. He translated the New Testament of the Holy Bible into the Yoruba language, for which he was honoured with an honorary Doctor of Divinity degree by Oxford University, He died on December 31, 1891.

1ST NIGERIAN ORDAINED PRIEST

Right Rev. Samuel Ajayi Crowther, ordained Priest in 1844.

For biodata, see: *1st Nigerian (African) Bishop.*

1ST TRANSLATION OF THE HOLY BIBLE INTO YORUBA LANGUAGE

By Bishop Samuel Ajayi Crowther, then Anglican Bishop of the Niger. Translated the New Testament only. Printed on Townsend's Printing Press in Abeokuta in 1862.

In recognition of his effort, Crowther was awarded an honorary Doctor of Divinity (DD) degree by Oxford University, England.

1ST TRANSLATION OF THE HOLY BIBLE INTO IGBO LANGUAGE

By Archdeacon Denis, who translated the new Testatment of the Bible into Union Igbo in 1908.

An expatriate missionary of the CMS Mission. Denis had to settle in Egbu, near Owerri, Imo State, in 1906, primarily for the translation exercise.

1ST RELIGIOUS NEWSPAPER IN NIGERIA

Iwe Irohin (fun owon ara Egba ati Yoruba), which started as a Yoruba-language religious fortnightly paper.

For details see: *Nigeria's 1st newspaper,* ***entry under:*** *MASS MEDIA – NEWSPAPERS.*

1ST RELIGIOUS NEWSPAPER IN EASTERN NIGERIA

The Leader, started on August 15, 1956, as a monthly, on mimeograph paper, with the title *Confraternity of Christian Doctrine.* Later changed to a weekly with its present-day title, *The Leader*. The 1st editor was Father George Lahiffe.

1ST ROMAN CATHOLIC SEMINARY IN NIGERIA

St. Paul's Seminary, Igbariam, near Onitsha, Anambra State, started by Bishop Shanahan and officially opened on July 19, 1924, as a combined Junior and Senior Seminary. Commenced with six minor (Junior) seminarians (who included William Obelagu, John Aghanti Idigo and Simon Okoye) and three senior seminarians, of which only one, John Cross Anyogu, was Nigerian.

Its first Rector was Father William O'Donnel, who was soon replaced by Bishop Charles Heerey. The Seminary ended its first phase in 1951, when it was transferred to a permanent site at Enugu and renamed Bigard Memorial Seminary.

1ST ROMAN CATHOLIC PRIMARY SCHOOL IN EASTERN NIGERIA

Holy Trinity School, Onitsha, Anambra State, which was started in 1893 by the Holy Ghost Fathers comprising Father Joseph Lutz, Father Joseph Home, and Brothers Hermas and John Gotto. The nucleus of the school, however, dates back to 1885 when, on first arrival in Onitsha, the missionaries commenced a makeshift school within their mission with about forty children rescued from, slavery. The first head of the school was Brother Davis Doran, who took charge for sixteen years from 1894.

1ST POPE TO VISIT NIGERIA

His Holiness Pope John Paul II, who paid a six-day official (state) visit to Nigeria from February 13 to 18, 1982. Was received by then President Alhaji Shehu Shagari. While in Nigeria, the Pope visited Lagos, Enugu, Onitsha, Kaduna and Ibadan.

Born on May 18, 1920; from Poland; graduated in Moral Law from the State University of Krakow; a multi-linguist, who spoke Polish, German, French, Italian and English. Ordained Priest, November 6, 1946, and Bishop, September 28, 1958; appointed Archbishop of Krakow on June 26, 1967; created Cardinal on June 26, 1967; elected Pope on October 16, 1978.

Also: *1st Non-Italian Pope since 1523; 1st Pope from a Communist country.*

1ST (ANGLICAN) ARCHBISHOP OF CANTERBURY TO VISIT NIGERIA

The Most Rev. Dr Robert Kennedy Runcie, who paid a two-week pastoral visit to Nigeria from April 5 to 18, 1982. Was received in audience by then President, Alhaji Shehu Shagari. Later visited Nigeria a second time in 1984, for the Anglican Consultative Council meeting held at the Administrative Staff College of Nigeria (ASCON), Badagry (received by then Head of State, General Muhammadu Buhari).

1ST NIGERIAN CARDINAL

His Eminence Cardinal Dominic Ekandem, created Cardinal by Pope Paul VI in April 1977.

Born 1917 in Obio-Ibiono, Itu, Akwa Ibom State; attended Christ the King's College, Onitsha; Senior Seminaries at Okpala and Owerri; Bigard Memorial Seminary, Enugu. Ordained Priest, December 7, 1947; consecrated Auxilliary Bishop of Calabar by Pope Pius XII, February 7, 1954; Bishop of Ikot Ekpene, 1963, before his creation as Cardinal. Was President, National Episcopal Conference of Nigeria, comprising all bishops of the 35 Roman Catholic dioceses in Nigeria. Conferred Officer of the Order of the British Empire (OBE), 1960, and Commander of the Order of the Niger (CON), 1963.

By his elevation to Cardinal, he thus became member of the 120-man Sacred College of Cardinals which assists the Pope in the governance of the Roman Catholic Church as well as a possible candidate for the Papacy.

See also: *1st Nigerian Roman Catholic Bishop.*

1ST ANGLICAN ARCHBISHOP OF NIGERIA

The Most Rev. Timothy Omotayo Olufosoye, who became the First Primate of the Church of Nigeria (Anglican Communion) in February 1979, when the Province was carved out of the Province of West Africa (formerly comprising Ghana, Sierra Leone, the Gambia and Nigeria). The Dioceses in Nigeria increased in number from 13 in 1929 to 26 in 1988. Retired in April 1988.

From Ondo, Rev. Olufosoye was born on March 31, 1918, and attended St Stephen's School, Ondo; St Andrew's College, Oyo; University of British Columbia, Vancouver, Canada. Served as Chaplain, Christ Church, Lagos; Vicar, Holy Trinity, Ebutte-Ero, Lagos. Following his consecration, served as Bishop of the Gambia in 1965, and later Bishop of Ibadan Diocese. Member, World Council of Churches; All-Africa Conference of Churches; World Congress of Christian Education; Sunday School Association.

1ST NIGERIAN ROMAN CATHOLIC ARCHBISHOP

His Grace Dr John Kwao Amusu Aggrey, who was enthroned Archbishop of the Holy Cross Cathedral, Lagos on March 8, 1966.

A naturalised Nigerian, born in 1908; appointed member of the Curia, the Roman Catholic Church's central governing body, on January 3, 1968. Died March 14, 1972.

Also: *1st indigenous Catholic Archbishop of Lagos.*

1ST NIGERIAN ANGLICAN BISHOP

Right Rev. Samuel Ajayi Crowther, consecrated Bishop of the just-created 'Diocese of the Nigeria Territories' in 1862.

For biodata, see: *1st Nigerian (African) Bishop.*

1ST NIGERIAN ROMAN CATHOLIC BISHOP

Bishop Dominic Ekandem, ordained Bishop on February 7, 1954. At that time there were 33 Catholic dioceses in Nigeria, each with a bishop. Ekandem was the first West African Catholic bishop.

See also: *1st Nigerian Cardinal.*

1ST NIGERIAN VICAR OF THE PRO-CATHEDRAL CHRIST CHURCH, LAGOS

Bishop Adolphus Williamson Howells, so appointed in 1919.

Born in Abeokuta, Ogun State, on August 9, 1866, he studied at Fourah Bay College, Freetown, Sierra Leone; Durham University, England. Before his appointment he was Deacon (1897); Ordained Priest (1889); Curate of Christ Church Pro-Cathedral, Lagos (1900). Consecrated Bishop at St Paul's Cathedral, London, by the Archbishop of Canterbury on June 24, 1920. Later served in the Niger Diocese before being sent back to Lagos Diocese to succeed Bishop Melville Jones as Bishop of Lagos. Retired on August, 10, 1936. Died December 3, 1938.

Also: *1st Resident Bishop of Abeokuta.*

1ST NIGERIAN BISHOP OF THE DIOCESE OF NORTHERN NIGERIA

Very Rev. Festus O. Segun, appointed by the Anglican Episcopal Synod of West Africa on January 5, 1970. Prior to his appointment, Rev. Segun was Provost, Cathedral Church of Christ, Lagos. His consecration was performed in Lagos by Right Rev. Moses Scott, then Archbishop of West Africa, on April 5, 1970.

1ST IGBO ROMAN CATHOLIC PRIEST ORDAINED

Rev. Father Paul Emechete, ordained in 1921. Hailed from Asaba, Delta State.

1ST IGBO PRIEST (EAST OF THE NIGER) ORDAINED ROMAN CATHOLIC PRIEST

Rev. Father John Cross Anyogu, ordained in 1930. Entered the newly established St Paul's Seminary, Igbariam, near Onitsha, in 1924 as the only indigene among the class of three pioneer senior seminarians. Hailed from Onitsha, Anambra State.

1ST RURAL ROMAN CATHOLIC DIOCESE IN NIGERIA

Ahiara Diocese in Imo State, set up in January 1988 with Right Rev. Dr Victor Chikwe as its 1st Bishop. The Diocese comprises the following five clans: Ahiara, Agbaja, Ekwerazu, Ezinihitte and Oke Uvuru. The choice of the name 'Ahiara Diocese' is in keeping with the Catholic tradition of naming a diocese after the name of the area where the see of that diocese is situated.

Rev. Chikwe was ordained the 1st Bishop of the newly-created diocese of Maria Mater Ecclesiac, Ahiara Mbaise, by His Holiness Pope John Paul II in

Rome, and was formally installed on Sunday January 31, 1938 by His Excellency, Archbishop Paul Tabet, the Papal Nuncio to Nigeria, at Ahiara.

1ST NIGERIAN REVEREND SISTER

Sister Gertrude Nwaturuocha, who made her first religious profession on April 21, 1940, along with three others. From Nguru Mbaise in Imo State; born in 1915, she entered religious life in 1931. Belonged to the Congregation of the Handmaids of the Holy Child Jesus, the 1st Nigerian indigenous congregation established by Sr Mary Charles Walker, Irish Sister Charity, in 1931, with a pioneer set of four aspirants, others being Sisters Mary Ignatia Bassey (Efik), Sister Aloysia Ugoaro (Igbo from Umuahia), and a Cameroonian.

1ST ROMAN CATHOLIC REVEREND FATHER IN NIGERIA

Father (later Bishop) Joseph Shanahan, who first set foot in Onitsha, Anambra State, in 1902.

Born in Ireland in 1871, Shanahan was ordained Priest on April 22, 1900; sent to eastern Nigeria on his personal request, where he joined and later (in 1905) took over from the pioneer French Catholic missionaries. Was Prefect Apostolic, Southern Nigeria, 1905. Established the first Catholic Seminary in Nigeria at Igbariam, near Onitsha, Anambra State, in 1924. Bishop of Eastern Nigeria, 1920. Left Nigeria in 1932. Died in Nairobi, Kenya on December 25, 1943. His remains were exhumed and reburied in Onitsha Cathedral in 1956. Bishop Shanahan College, Orlu, was dedicated to his memory.

1ST NIGERIAN TO BE BEATIFIED

Rev. Father Cyprian Michael Iwenne Tansi, a Roman Catholic Igbo reverend of non-Christian parentage. Sent to Catholic mission school, beatified by Pope John Paul II on 22 March 1998 in Oba, Anambra State

From Aguleri, Anambra State, born in 1904, Father Tansi was ordained Priest in 1937. Proceeded to the monastery of Mount St Bernand in Leicestershire, England, and after 14 years in the abbey, died of thrombosis on January 12, 1964. Later exhumed and re-buried in Onitsha, Anambra State, on Friday October 17, 1986.

1ST NIGERIAN TO WIN THE KING FAISAL MEMORIAL AWARD

Sheik Abubakar Mahmud Gumi, who was one of three recipients of the award for 1987. Presented on January 14, 1987, in Saudi Arabia, for his academic excellence and contribution to Islam.

For further details, see entry under: *AWARDS.*

1ST EMIR OF KANO TO PERFORM THE HAJJ

Alhaji Abdullahi Bayero, Emir of Kano, who went to Mecca to perform the hajj twice: in 1937, when he travelled by car, and the second time in 1951, by air. On return, he opened a new mosque.

Son of Emir Muhammadu Abbas (who ruled from 1903 to 1919), Alhaji Abdullahi was appointed the 10th Fulani Emir of Kano in 1926, and installed in February 1927. Died December 25, 1953. Bayero University, Kano, is dedicated to his memory.

1ST IGBO ALHAJI

Seidi Ibrahim Niass Nwagwu. He left Nigeria on holy pilgrimage to Mecca on April 18, 1963, by virtue of which he became an Alhaji.

15 SPORTS

15.1 GENERAL /ATHLETICS

NIGERIA'S 1ST (MODERN) STADIUM

Liberty Stadium, Ibadan, Oyo State, commissioned in 1959. Built by the (defunct) Western Nigeria Government under the premiership of Chief Obafemi Awolowo, who officially declared it open on September 30, 1960.

NIGERIA'S 1ST NATIONAL SPORTS FESTIVAL

Took place in Lagos in August 1973. (Old) Bendel State (former Mid-Western State), then under the governorship of Brigadier Samuel Ogbemudia, emerged overall winner in the games, in which the twelve States then existing participated. The festival, introduced by Mr Jerry Enyeazu, Nigeria's 1st National Director of Sports, takes place biennially.

NIGERIA'S 1ST OLYMPIC GAMES OUTING

The 12th Olympic Games, held in Helsinki, Finland in 1952. Returned without any medals.

The Olympic Games originated in Greece, and was first staged in 776 BC. Now the world's foremost amateur sports competition. Since its inception, it has grown in number of events competed for and participating countries, e.g. in the 776 BC Games the only event was the 200-yards sprint.

The modern Olympic Games, however, started in 1896 in Athens, Greece, and takes place every four years. Except during the World War years, the periodicity has been kept. Nigeria's participation in the 1952 Games was without her national soccer team.

1ST NIGERIAN PRESIDENT OF THE SUPREME COUNCIL FOR SPORTS IN AFRICA (S.C.S.A.)

Abraham Alegbe Ordia, who occupied the exalted office for seventeen years.

SCSA was formed in 1966 with headquarters in Yaounde, Cameroon, and has to date organised four All-Africa Games. Its first President was André Bombassa of Congo-Brazzaville.

The International Olympic Committee (IOC) in September 1988 conferred on Ordia the 'Olympic Order', its highest honour on an individual.

NIGERIA'S 1ST OLYMPIC GAMES MEDALIST

Nojeem Maiyegun, who won a bronze medal on October 20, 1964 in the light middle-weight boxing category at the 18th (Tokyo) Olympics of 1964.

Obalende Road, Lagos, was renamed after him. The Nojeem Maiyegun boxing cup championship was also (in 1987) instituted in his honour. Later relocated to Vienna, Austria.

NIGERIA'S 1ST OLYMPIC (GAMES) SILVER MEDALIST

Peter Konyegwachie, who captured a silver medal in boxing in the feather-weight class at the 23rd Olympics, held in Los Angeles, USA, in July 1984, having lost in the final to American Meldric Taylor.

22 years old at the time, Konyegwachie had also earlier won featherweight gold at the 1982 Commonwealth Games in Brisbane, Australia.

1ST NIGERIAN OLYMPIC GOLD MEDALIST

Chioma Ajunwa, who on August 2, 1996 won gold at the Atlanta, Georgia, USA, Olympic Games in the long jump event with a record-breaking 7.12 metres jump, the 1st Nigerian gold medallist in an individual sports event.

Nigeria's team, the 'Golden Eaglets', also won the nation's 1st gold in the football event, and 1st in group sports, at the same Olympics.

Born on December 25, 1971, in Ogbe-Ahiazu, Imo State, Chioma graduated with Bachelor's and Master's Degrees from the University of Lagos, 2004-10, 2017, and was awarded an honorary Doctorate (PhD degree) by Gregory University, Uturu, Abia State.

A police officer at time of her feat in Atlanta, Chioma (now Mrs Opara) has risen to Assistant Commissioner of Police.

See also entry under: *WOMEN.*

1ST INDIGENOUS PRESIDENT OF THE NIGERIA OLYMPIC COMMITTEE

Sir Adetokunbo Adegboyega Ademola.

For biodata, see: *Nigeria's 1st indigenous Chief Justice of the Federation,* ***entry under:*** *LAW.*

NIGERIA'S 1ST COMMONWEALTH GAMES GOLD MEDALIST

Emmanuel Ifeajuna, in the high jump at the 1954 Commonwealth Games held in Vancouver, Canada, with a jump of 6'8" (2.05 metres). By that jump he set a Commonwealth and new national record.

At the time Ifeajuna was a science undergraduate at University College, Ibadan (now University of Ibadan). Ifeajuna, from Onitsha, Anambra State, later joined the Nigerian Army, and rose to Major at the outbreak of the Civil War, which he fought on the Biafran side. Sadly, he was executed on allegation of sabotage.

NIGERIA'S 1ST FEMALE COMMONWEALTH GAMES MEDALIST

Violet Odogwu (later Mrs Nwajei), who won a gold medal in the long jump event at the 1966 Commonwealth Games held in Kingston, Jamaica.

1ST NATIONAL DIRECTOR OF SPORTS

Chief (Sir) Jerry Amadi Enyeazu, appointed Director of Sports in the National Commission from 1973 to 1976.

Born on August 1924 in Ngwa, near Aba, Abia State, he attended Government College, Umuahia, 1937-42; Yaba Higher College, 1943-45; University of Wisconsin, USA, 1954-55, where he earned a Master's degree in Physical Education and Sports Administration; Loughborough College, England, 1957-58.

Prior to the appointment, Chief Enyeazu was 1st Director of Sports, (defunct) Eastern Nigeria Sports Commission, 1966-73. On leaving Lagos he became the 1st Director of Sports, Imo State Sports Council, from 1976 to 1982, when he retired.

1ST NIGERIAN UNIVERSITY GAMES ASSOCIATION (N.U.G.A.) COMPETITION

Held March 22 to 29, 1966, at the University of Ibadan, involving participants from the five universities existing then, viz. Ibadan, Zaria, Lagos, Nsukka and Ife. In that maiden edition, only nine events (athletics, badminton, cricket, hockey, lawn tennis, netball, handball, table tennis and volleyball) were competed for. Fourteen events were available at the 1988 edition held, in Port Harcourt, Rivers State, and the number of participating Universities had also grown to 24. NUGA Games are held every four years.

1ST NIGERIAN MEMBER OF THE EXECUTIVE COUNCIL OF THE INTERNATIONAL UNIVERSITY SPORTS FEDERATION (F.I.S.U.)

Dr Michael Oti, appointed in July 1977, at the World Students Games held in Zagreb, Yugoslavia. The Nigerian University Games Association (NUGA) joined FISU (the co-ordinating body for University Games Associations world-wide) in 1970, and has participated in FISU games ever since. Dr Oti was one-time Chairman, NUGA.

NIGERIA'S 1ST MOTOR RALLY

Tagged 'Tour of Nigeria' motor rally, it took place on November 9, 1962. Was flagged off from Victoria Island, Lagos, and covered 1,850 miles (2,960 km) of Nigerian territory, and lasted 24 hours.

1ST NIGERIAN MEDALIST AT THE WORLD ATHLETICS CHAMPIONSHIP

Mr Ajayi Agbebaku, who won a bronze in the triple jump event at the inaugural World Athletics Championship held in Helsinki, Finland, in 1983.

1ST NIGERIAN ATHLETE TO CLOCK A WORLD RECORD TIME

Chidi Imoh, the US-based Nigerian student-athlete, who on August 8, 1987, at the 4th All-Africa Games held in Nairobi, Kenya, ran the 100 metres in a world record time of 9.92 seconds. However, the very next day, (August 9, 1987) two Americans, Raymond Stewart and Calvin Smith, both broke Imoh's record with 9.89 and 9.91 seconds respectively.

1ST CHAMPION OF THE (MILO) NATIONAL MARATHON

Abbas Mohammed from Kaduna State, who won the maiden (1985) Milo Marathon race by doing the 42.195 km race in 2 hours 58 minutes and 23 seconds.

The championship, now an annual event, is sponsored by Food Specialities Nigeria Limited, a beverage company, and organised by the Amateur Athletic Association of Nigeria (AAAN).

The female category of the race was won by Ladi Musa of Plateau State, who later represented Nigeria in Mexico in December 1985, where she was placed 20th overall.

15.2 BOXING

1ST NIGERIAN WORLD BOXING CHAMPION

Okon Bassey Asuquo, popularly known as Hogan 'Kid' Bassey, who on June 24, 1957 captured the world boxing crown in the featherweight class by beating Cherif Hamia of Algeria in a bout staged at the Old Winter Velodorome, Paris, France, before a crowd of over 20,000 fans. Hogan Bassey stopped Hamia in the 10th round due to severe injuries. The crown was, however, captured from him by American Davey Moore on March 18, 1959, after a 21-month reign.

From Creek Town, Calabar, Cross River State, Bassey was born on June 2, 1932. On retirement from professional boxing in 1960, he was appointed National Coach for boxing until 1980, when he retired. Was personally conferred Member of the Order of the British Empire (MBE) by Queen Elizabeth II on July 22, 1958. Died January 26, 1998. Awarded one of Nigeria's highest Federal honours in 1973.

1ST NIGERIAN WORLD MIDDLEWEIGHT BOXING CHAMPION

Richard Ihetu, popularly called Dick Tiger, on October 23, 1962, by beating American Gene Fullmer at Candlestick Stadium, San Francisco, USA, over 15 rounds.

Born on August 14, 1929, in Amaigbo, Imo State, he began his boxing career in 1950, but went professional in 1952. Was Nigerian, and, later, Commonwealth middleweight boxing champion. After his second middleweight defeat by Emile Griffith on April 25, 1966, he moved up to the light-heavyweight class and became world champion until 1968, when he lost to Bob Foster in the USA. on a fourth-round knockout, his first ever. Retired from boxing in 1971, with a record of 64 wins (26 by knockout) and 17 losses. Died December 1, 1971. Was named 'Fighter of the Year' in 1962 and 1965, and in 1974 was elected into the 'Hall of Fame' by the renowned international *Ring* magazine.

Hogan Bassey, Nigeria's first world boxing champion (see page 212).

PHOTOGRAPH IN THE PUBLIC DOMAIN.

1ST NIGERIAN TO WIN WORLD MIDDLEWEIGHT BOXING CHAMPIONSHIP TWICE

Richard Ihetu (Dick Tiger). Won the crown first by beating Gene Fullmer of the USA. in San Francisco, USA, on October 23, 1962, and held the title until December 7, 1963; the second time by beating American Joey Giardello on October 22, 1965. Giardello had earlier wrested the crown from him in a match staged on December 7, 1963 in Atlantic City, New Jersey, USA. Dick Tiger retained the crown until April 25, 1966, when he was defeated by Emile Griffith.

For biodata, see above.

1ST NIGERIAN TO WIN WORLD BOXING CROWNS IN DIFFERENT WEIGHT CATEGORIES

Richard Ihetu (Dick Tiger; ***see above***). First won the world middleweight boxing crown on October 23, 1962, beating American Gene Fullmer in San Francisco, USA; the second time on December 16, 1966, having moved up the weight class, where he challenged and beat defending champion José Torres to win the light-heavyweight crown in a bout staged in New York, USA.

1ST NIGERIAN TO WIN A WORLD BOXING CROWN THREE TIMES

Richard Ihetu (Dick Tiger; ***see above***), who captured a world boxing crown three times: first on October 23, 1962 by beating Gene Fullmer to capture the world middleweight crown; second on August 10, 1963 by recapturing the world middleweight crown from Gene Fullmer; and the third time on December 16, 1966 by beating José Torres to capture the world light heavyweight title.

1ST NIGERIAN WORLD JUNIOR CRUISERWEIGHT BOXING CHAMPION

Bashiru Ali, the US-based Nigerian boxer who captured the title on April 11, 1987, in a fight staged in Jacksonville, Florida, USA, by out-pointing

American Tommy Richardson over 12 rounds for the vacant title. It was a World Boxing Council (WBC) championship fight.

Born in 1956, Ali hails from Agbede in Etsako Local Government Area of Edo State. He has a degree in political science. Boxing record: 66 wins and 46 knockouts to his credit, plus 14 losses. On November 28, 1987, he successfully defended his title against Kevin Wagsta of Australia at the Liberty Stadium, Ibadan, Nigeria.

1ST WORLD BOXING TOURNAMENT STAGED IN NIGERIA

On August 10, 1963, between Dick Tiger of Nigeria and Gene Fullmer of USA at the Liberty Stadium, Ibadan, Oyo State. This was Dick Tiger's defence of his world middleweight boxing crown, which he had won over Gene Fullmer on October 23, 1962, in San Franscisco, USA. Tiger knocked Fullmer out in the seventh out of 15 rounds, to retain the crown.

For biodata, see: *1st Nigerian world middleweight boxing champion.*

1ST NIGERIAN WORLD HEAVYWEIGHT BOXING CHAMPION

Samuel Okon Peter, who beat Oleg Maskaev on March 8, 2008, at the principal bullfighting venue in Cancun, Mexico, in a World Boxing Council (WBC) title bout. Peter won by technical knockout, with the referee stopping the fight with a few seconds remaining in the sixth round.

Samuel Okon Peter, born on September 6, 1980, is a Nigerian/American professional boxer. In his prime, he was known for his rivalry with the Klitschko brothers, having faced Wladimir twice (2005 and 2010) and Vitali once. Peter is known for his punching power and holds a 78.9% knockout-to-win ratio.

1ST NIGERIAN TO HOLD THREE UNIFICATION FIGHT CHAMPIONSHIPS

Anthony Oluwafemi Olaseuni Joshua, a Nigerian-born British professional boxer who is a two-time unified heavyweight champion, having held the WBA (Super), IBF, WBO and IBO titles since December 2019. At regional level, he held the British and Commonwealth heavyweight titles from 2014 to 2016.

Born on October 15, 1989. Conferred Officer of the Order of the British Empire (OBE) in 2012.

1ST NIGERIAN OLYMPIC BOXING MEDALIST

Nojeem Maiyegun, who won a Bronze medal at the Tokyo Olympics on October 20, 1964.

See also: *Nigeria's 1st Olympic boxing medalist,* **entry under:** *SPORTS – GENERAL/ATHLETICS.*

1ST NIGERIAN OLYMPIC BOXING SILVER MEDALIST

Peter Konyegwachie, who bagged a silver medal at the July 1984 Los Angeles (USA) Olympics in the featherweight class.

See also: *1st Nigerian to win a silver medal at the Olympic Games,* ***entry under:*** *SPORTS – GENERAL.*

15.3 FOOTBALL/SOCCER

1ST NIGERIAN FOOTBALL TEAM TO WIN A F.I.F.A. WORLD CUP

Nigeria's Under-17 football team (popularly referred to as the 'Golden Eaglets') at the 16-nation FIFA-organised Kodak-sponsored Junior World Cup finals held in Beijing, China, in August, 1985. Nigeria beat their opponents, Germany, 2–0 in the final match on August 11, 1985 to clinch the trophy which was being competed for in its maiden edition in that year. Head of State Major-General Buhari christened the team, led by skipper Nduka Ugbade, the 'World Golden Eaglets'.

1ST AFRICAN COUNTRY TO PLAY IN THE FINALS OF THE F.I.F.A. COCA-COLA JUNIOR (UNDER-20) WORLD CUP SOCCER COMPETITION

Nigeria's Under-20 national football team, the 'Flying Eagles'. Played against Portugal in the grand finale of the 5th edition of the competition, hosted in Riyadh, by Saudi Arabia from Friday March 3, 1989. The Flying Eagles, however, lost 0–2 to Portugal, thus settling for silver.

In the 1985 (3rd) edition of the same competition, played in the Soviet Union, Nigeria's Flying Eagles secured bronze (third place).

NIGERIA'S 1ST PARTICIPATION IN OLYMPIC GAMES SOCCER

In 1968, at the 16th Olympic Games held in Mexico. Although Nigeria first participated in the 12th Olympics held in Helsinki, Finland in 1952, she then did not field her national soccer team, the 'Green Eagles'. Nigeria played in Zone 'B' along with Brazil, Spain and Japan.

Apart from the 1968 outing, Nigeria's Green Eagles have won the ticket to represent Africa in 1976 and 1980, the latter as stand-in for Ghana who qualified but failed to participate.

1ST TIME NIGERIA WON THE AFRICA CUP OF NATIONS FOOTBALL COMPETITION

In March 1980. At the final played at the National Stadium, Surulere, Lagos, Nigeria's 'Green Eagles' beat Algeria 3–0, under skipper Christian Chukwu.

The Africa Cup of Nations football competition, also referred to as the Unity Cup, is Africa's mini-World Cup, contested biennially. 1980 was also Nigeria's first time of hosting the competition. The maiden edition was held in Addis Ababa, Ethiopia, in 1957.

1ST COUNTRY TO WIN THE TESSEMA FOOTBALL CUP FOR KEEPS

Nigeria. In the Cup's first five-years history, Nigeria's 'Flying Eagles' lifted it thrice consecutively to retain it permanently.

1st time: 1983 – Nigeria 3, Algeria 1
2nd time: 1985 – Nigeria 3, Tunisia 2
3rd time: 1987 – aggregate score: Nigeria 5, Togo 1

The cup is competed for biennially. The donor of the cup is Yduekatchew Tessema, an Ethiopian football administrator and Chairman of the Confederation of African Football (CAF), who died on August 19, 1987 at the age of 66.

NIGERIA'S 1ST NATION-WIDE FEMALE SOCCER COMPETITION

The All-Nigeria Women Soccer Championship for Under-20s, organised by the Youth Sports Federation of Nigeria (YSFON).

The finals of the maiden edition (1986) were played in Ilorin, Kwara State, between old Bendel, Imo, Kano and Kwara States. The grand final match between old Bendel and Imo States ended in a 1–1 draw. Bendel, however, emerged winner by virtue of scoring the highest number of goals overall in the competition. The competition's cup was donated by Alhaja (Chief) Simbiat Abiola, wife of Concord Press proprietor, Basorun Moshood Abiola. Sixteen female clubs nation-wide participated in the 1988 (3rd) edition of the championship scheduled for November 15 to 20, 1988.

1ST NIGERIAN PROFESSIONAL FOOTBALLER

Tesilimi Olawale (Teslim) 'Thunder' Balogun. Entered professional football when he signed on with Queen's Park Rangers, a London-based football club, in the 1950s. The Teslim Balogun Stadium in Lagos is named in his honour.

1ST NIGERIAN FOOTBALLER TO PLAY IN ENGLAND'S F.A. CUP FINAL

John Fashanu, the London-based professional footballer, who played for his team, Wimbledon, in the 1988 FA Cup Final match against Liverpool at Wembley Stadium, London, on Saturday May 14, 1988. The match, which ended 1–0 in favour of Wimbledon, was also the club's first (and only) FA Cup Final appearance.

Also: *1st Nigerian to captain a foreign football club, by virtue of being appointed captain of London-based Wimbledon FC in October 1988.*

1ST NIGERIAN 'AFRICA'S FOOTBALLER OF THE YEAR'

Emmanuel Okala, the renowned Enugu Rangers International Football Club's, and Nigeria's, goalkeeper for several years. Was voted Africa's Footballer of the Year, 1978.

Okala retired from active football in 1980, after ten years of a brilliant footballing career as goalkeeper, which culminated in the 'Green Eagles' (Nigeria's national team) winning the 12th Africa Cup of Nations in March 1980. From Onitsha, Anambra State. Later appointed Coach with Enugu Rangers.

1ST NIGERIAN TO PARTICIPATE IN FIVE CONSECUTIVE AFRICA CUP OF NATIONS FOOTBALL FINALS

Mudasiru Lawal, who took part in the Nations Cup finals of 1976 (Ethiopia), 1978 (Ghana), 1980 (Lagos, Nigeria), 1982 (Libya) and 1984 (Ivory Coast).

Also: *1st Nigerian to bag the Cup of Nations Gold (1980), Silver (1984), and Bronze (1976) medals.*

1ST NIGERIAN CLUB TO WIN THE AFRICA CUP WINNERS' TROPHY

The IICC Shooting Stars of Ibadan, Oyo State, Nigeria's flag-bearers in 1976. In the 1976 finals, IICC beat Tonnerre Kalala of Cameroon by a goal aggregate of 4–2.

Nigeria's representative in the competition is usually the Challenge Cup winner in the previous season.

1ST NIGERIAN DIVISION II CLUB TO PROGRESS TO THE AFRICAN CUP WINNERS' CUP FINAL

Leventis United Football Club of Ibadan, Oyo State, in 1985.

1ST NIGERIAN FOOTBALL CLUB TO WIN THE WEST AFRICAN FOOTBALL UNION (W.A.F.U.) CUP

New Nigeria Bank Football Club of Benin-City, Edo State, in 1983.

1ST NIGERIAN FOOTBALLER TO SCORE A GOAL AT THE NATIONAL STADIUM, SURULERE, LAGOS

Yakubu Mambo on December 4, 1972, in the match between Nigeria's 'Green Eagles' and the Mali national soccer team. The match, which ended 3–0 in favour of Nigeria, marked the formal opening by Head of State General Yakubu Gowon, of the N6 million National Stadium complex at Surulere, Lagos. Yakubu Mambo was then in the Stationery Stores Football Club, Lagos.

1ST NIGERIAN FOOTBALL MATCH PLAYED UNDER FLOODLIGHTS

Took place at the Liberty Stadium, Ibadan, Oyo State, on October 11, 1960. The ultra-modern stadium (the first of its kind in Nigeria) was formally opened on September 30, 1960.

NIGERIA'S 1ST 'CHAMPION OF CHAMPIONS' CLUB

Leventis United Football Club of Ibadan, Oyo State, in 1984. The Champion of Champions contest was designed to produce the country's overall football champion for a given year and is usually played between the National League Division One champions and the winners of the Challenge Cup in the same year.

The National Stadium, Surulere, Lagos (see page 220), pictured in 2019.

PHOTOGRAPH BY TAYVAY, COURTESY OF SHUTTERSTOCK.

1ST NIGERIAN CLUB TO WIN ALL THE NATION'S FOOTBALL TROPHIES SIMULTANEOUSLY

Leventis United Football Club of Ibadan, Oyo State, in the year 1986, when it captured the National League Division One trophy, the Challenge Cup and the Charity (Champions') Cup.

National League Division One: overall winners with 30 points from 22 matches; Challenge Cup: beat Abiola Babes Football Club of Abeokuta 1–0 in the final; Charity Cup: automatic qualifiers by virtue of winning the other two competitions.

1ST NIGERIAN CLUB TO WIN THE TWO COVETED NATIONAL FOOTBALL TROPHIES SIMULTANEOUSLY

Enugu Rangers International Football Club, Enugu, Anambra State, who clinched both the Challenge Cup and League Division One trophy for the year 1981. In the Challenge Cup final encounter, Enugu Rangers defeated Bendel Insurance of Benin-City 2–0 to retain the cup. It also bagged the highest overall points to win that year's Division One league.

1ST NIGERIAN FOOTBALL CLUB TO CONSECUTIVELY WIN DIVISION III, DIVISION II AND DIVISION I NATIONAL LEAGUE TROPHIES

Leventis United Football Club of Ibadan, Oyo State, between 1983 and 1986. It thus became the1st Nigerian football club to climb from Division III to capture the Division I football trophy.

1ST NIGERIAN FOOTBALL CLUB TO WIN THE NATIONAL LEAGUE DIVISION I CUP

Rangers International Football Club of Enugu, Anambra State, in 1972. The winning team qualifies to represent the country in the Africa Champion Clubs competition, which itself commenced in 1975.

Although the National League football championship commenced in 1969, it was initially confined to Lagos clubs, until 1972, when clubs outside Lagos, were admitted and the home and away match system introduced.

By 1979, as a result of its popularity, three Divisions – I, II, and III, with 12 teams each – were created, Division 1 being reserved for the best 12, and so on. A system of down-grading and up-grading teams within Divisions on the basis of performance in the previous year's competition was also introduced. A fourth Division was added in 1987.

1ST CLUB TO WIN THE NATIONAL LEAGUE DIVISION I FOOTBALL COMPETITION IN ITS VERY 1ST SEASON

Leventis United Football Club of Ibadan, Oyo State, in 1986. Emerged overall winner with 30 points from 22 matches. Iwuanyanwu National Football Club of Owerri, Imo State, came 2nd with 27 points. Twelve teams competed.

1ST FOOTBALL CLUB TO WIN THE NATION'S LEAGUE DIVISION I TROPHY FIVE TIMES

Enugu Rangers (International) Club of Enugu, Anambra State, in 1975, 1977, 1981, 1982 and 1984.

1ST NIGERIAN FOOTBALL CLUB TO WIN THE F.A. (CHALLENGE) CUP

Marine XI of Lagos, in the competition's first edition in 1945. In the final, played in Lagos, Marine XI beat Corinthians (also of Lagos) 1–0.

Since its inception, the tournament has been contested every year, except in 1973.

1ST NIGERIAN FOOTBALL CLUB TO LIFT THE F.A. (CHALLENGE) CUP SEVEN TIMES

Railways Football Club of Lagos. Won the following seven times, following the tournament's introduction in 1945:

1946 – Railways 3, Port Harcourt XI 0
1948 – Railways 3, Warri XI 0
1949 – Railways 3, Port Harcourt XI 3
1951 – Railways 3, Plateau XI 2
1956 – Railways 3, Warri XI 1
1957 – Railways 5, Zaria XI 1
1964 – Railways 3, Plateau XI 2

1ST NIGERIAN FOOTBALL CLUB TO LIFT THE F.A. (CHALLENGE) CUP THRICE CONSECUTIVELY

Enugu Rangers (International) Football Club of Enugu, Anambra State, in 1974, 1975 and 1976. Final match results were:

1956 – Rangers 2, Mighty Jets of Jos 1
1957 – Rangers 1, Shooting Stars of Ibadan 0
1964 – Rangers 3, Alyuf Salam Rocks of Ilorin 0

1ST NORTHERN NIGERIAN FOOTBALL CLUB TO LIFT THE F.A. (CHALLENGE) CUP

Kano XI, in 1953. In the final, played in Lagos, Kano XI beat Dynamos of Lagos 2–1.

Was also: *1st time the Challenge Cup moved out of Lagos.*

1ST TIME AN (OLD) BENDEL STATE FOOTBALL CLUB LIFTED THE F.A. (CHALLENGE) CUP

October 21, 1972, when Bendel Insurance Football Club of Benin captured the trophy by beating Mighty Jets of Jos, Plateau State, 3–1 in a replay cup-final at the Liberty Stadium, Ibadan, Oyo State.

1ST DIVISION III LEAGUE CLUB TO LIFT THE CHALLENGE CUP

Leventis United Football Club of Ibadan, Oyo State, in 1984. In the final, played in Lagos, Leventis United Football Club (then in Division III of the

National League) beat Abiola Babes of Abeokuta (then in Division League) by a lone goal.

1ST TEAM TO WIN THE PEPSI-COLA HIGHER INSTITUTIONS CHAMPIONSHIP

University of Calabar football team, which beat University of Ilorin team 2–0 in the final match, played on Saturday, April 11, 1986, in Lagos. The Pepsi-Cola Cup competition was introduced in 1986 to honour the best student football team among the nation's tertiary institutions.

1ST NIGERIAN FOOTBALL COMMENTATOR

Ishola Folorunsho, who started running football commentaries on Radio Nigeria from 1955, taking over from expatriate commentors. One of his earliest was the live commentary from Accra, Ghana, on the international football match between that country and Nigeria.

15.4 HANDBALL, ETC.

NIGERIA'S 1ST-EVER INTER-REGIONAL NETBALL TOURNAMENT

Held at the Enugu Sports Stadium in October 1962, between former Eastern and Western Regions. Eastern Region defeated the West 18–11. Formerly scheduled to be the 1st national netball tournament for then North, East, West and Lagos, but that could not be held due to the financial handicap of Lagos and the North.

1ST ALL-AFRICA JUNIOR HANDBALL CHAMPIONSHIPS

Held at the Sports-City, Lagos, in January 1981. Nigeria won the gold medal as well as the Murtala Muhammed gold cup for the male category. The male team also captured the 'fair play' trophy.

1ST NIGERIAN CLUB TO WIN THE ALL-AFRICA HANDBALL CLUBS CHAMPIONSHIP

Grasshoppers Handball Club of Owerri, Imo State, which won gold at the maiden edition of the championships held in the Republic of Benin in 1978.

Also: *1st club to win handball gold when handball was first introduced at the 3rd National Sports Festival in 1977; 1st Nigerian club to win Mr Shuba Handball trophy during the African Handball Championships, Cairo, Egypt, 1979; 1st Nigerian club to win the All-Africa Champion of Champions cup competition, Cairo, Egypt, 1985.*

1ST MALE NIGERIAN TEAM TO WIN THE ALL-AFRICA HANDBALL CLUBS CHAMPIONSHIP

The Lions handball team of Imo State, which emerged overall winners at the 9th All-Africa Handball Clubs competition held in Owerri, Imo State, from Saturday 19 to Sunday December 27, 1987. In the final encounter, played on December 27, 1987, the Lions defeated Niger United from Minna, Niger State, 22–19.

The Lions and Niger United both represented Nigeria in the eight-nation fiesta, which Imo State hosted for the first time.

NIGERIA'S 1ST PROFESSIONAL BASKETBALL PLAYER

Akeem Abdul Olajuwon, the US-based 7-foot (2.10 metre) millionaire Nigerian basketball player who played for the Houston Rockets in Texas, USA. He went professional in November 1984, when he was signed on for US $1.5m (N6m) by the National Basketball Association (NBA) of America.

From Oyo State, Olajuwon attended Muslim Teachers Training College, Lagos, after primary education at Ansar-Ud-Deen Elementary School, Surulere, Lagos. Although he had shown promising signs and keen interest in basketball, it was not until January 1981, after he gained admission to study Business Technology in the University of Houston (1980), that he took the American basketball scene by storm. He initially played for Houston Cougars, and won the trophy for the most outstanding basketball player at the 1982 National College Amateur Associations Basketball Championships.

1ST NIGERIAN TEAM TO WIN THE WORLD UNDER-12 HANDBALL CHAMPIONSHIPS

Kwara State under-12 handball team, who were Nigeria's flag-bearers at the 1985 World Championships held in Sweden. Beat Locomotive Vrosovige of Yugoslavia in the final 18–12 to win the cup. Altogether, the team played 14 games, winning all with 127 goals in their favour and 22 against. Also won that year's (1985) trophy for the best-behaved team at the competition.

15.5 TENNIS

NIGERIA'S 1ST HARD COURT (INTERNATIONAL) LAWN TENNIS CHAMPIONSHIP

Ogbe Hard Court (International) Lawn Tennis championships, first held in Benin-City, Edo State, in 1973. Declared open on October 31, 1973, by (then) Mid-West Governor, Brigadier Samuel O. Ogbemudia. Has become an annual event ever since.

1ST NIGERIAN (AFRICAN) TO PLAY IN THE WIMBLEDON FINALS

Nduka 'Dada' Odizor, in the 1983 edition where he advanced to the last 16, but eventually lost to Chris Lewis of New Zealand. In the same year he climbed to a World ATP Top 50 ranking.

A US-based professional tennis player, Odizor, nicknamed 'the Duke' at the 1983 Wimbledon championships, was born in 1958, in Asaba, Delta State. He attended Edward Bridden Primary School, Lagos; New Era College, Benin-City. Married to wife, Karen.

1ST NIGERIAN (AND BLACK MAN) TO WIN THE 'LORD RUMENS' LAGOS LAWN TENNIS CLASSIC

Nduka 'Dada' Odizor, on March 4, 1985. 'Lord Rumens' is the popular name of the Lagos Lawn Tennis Club championship, whose sponsorship Chief Olatunji Alabi, a renowned Lagos lawn tennis enthusiast, took over, following the withdrawal of patronage by past sponsors in 1983. Cash prizes worth US $75,000 are won in the one-week competition, with a first prize of US $15,000 cash. Odizor made his debut at Lord Rumens in the same year (1985).

See also: *1st Nigerian (African) to play in the Wimbledon finals.*

1ST NIGERIAN TO PARTICIPATE IN LAWN TENNIS AT THE OLYMPICS

Tony Mmoh, who on Tuesday September 20, 1988 represented Nigeria in its maiden appearance in Olympic tennis tournament when he took on Wotjeck Kowalski of Poland in the opening-round match at the 24th Olympics held in Seoul, South Korea.

Mmoh, ranked no. 2 in Nigeria and no. 306 in the world, beat his better-rated opponent in three straight sets, 6–2, 6–4, 6–4, to move into the second round, in which he lost.

The 24th Seoul Olympiad marked the re-emergence of tennis in the Olympics as a medal-winning event, since its removal in 1924. It also marked Nigeria's 1st appearance in the sport at the Olympics.

1ST NIGERIAN TO WIN THE MEN'S SINGLES TITLE IN THE COMMONWEALTH TABLE TENNIS CHAMPIONSHIP

Atanda Musa, who defeated Zoran Kosanovic of Canada, 21–17, 21–23, 21–19 in the 1982 contest held in Bombay (Mumbai), India.

1ST NIGERIANS TO WIN THE KENYA OPEN LAWN TENNIS CHAMPIONSHIP

Lawrence Awopegba and Thompson Onibokun, who paired to become the doubles champions in the finals played on August 6, 1968 in Nairobi, Kenya.

1ST WINNER OF PRESIDENT IBRAHIM BABANGIDA CUP (FOR TENNIS)

Sadiq Abdullahi, who won the All-Nigeria Tennis competition, introduced in 1988, by beating Yakubu Suleiman 6–3, 2–6, 6–4 in the final played at the Lagos Lawn Tennis Club on Saturday November 5, 1988. The cup carried a cash prize of N20,000 for the singles category.

16 TRANSPORT AND COMMUNICATIONS

NIGERIA'S 1ST DOMESTIC AIRPORT

Bodija Airport in Ibadan, Oyo State, built in 1940 by the (British) Royal Air Force (RAF). The runway is 5 kilometres long and 60 metres wide. The total width of the runway plus the shoulders is 92 metres. The apron is 100 metres long and 60 metres wide. Emergency landing space of 17' x 25' (grass runway) is provided.

NIGERIA'S 1ST PLANE CRASH

Occurred on May 2, 1949, involving a 'Dove' aircraft flying from Port Harcourt, Rivers State, to Benin City, Edo State. The crash occurred at Urhonigbe, about 80 kilometres south-east of Benin. All eight people on board (six passengers and two crew) died. This was barely two years after the formation of the West African Airways Corporation (WAAC), which covered the country's air operation, in 1947.

The country's second recorded air crash occurred on Saturday, February 5, 1955, involving a 'Wayfarer' aircraft flying from Enugu to Calabar, in which all nine passengers and four crew also died.

1ST CHAIRMAN, NIGERIAN AIRPORTS AUTHORITY (N.A.A.) (NOW F.A.A.N.)

Chief Osita Okeke, appointed in June 1977 and served until 1978. The NAA, which came into being through Decree 45 of 1978, has sole responsibility for the provision of the nation's airports and airport facilities and services.

An administrator and broadcaster, Chief Osita Okeke was born on October 9, 1936, in Abagana, Anambra State, and educated at Government College, Ughelli, 1950-55; University College, Ibadan, 1955-56, bagging a

BSc degree in Physics. Also underwent some mass media training courses in England. Prior to this appointment, Osita Okeke had served in various capacities. notably as Production Executive, East-Central State Broadcasting Service, 1966-72; Commissioner for Establishments, 1972-74; Information, Culture and Youth in East Central State. Later appointed again as Commissioner for Education, Anambra State, October 1979.

1ST DIRECTOR-GENERAL/CHIEF EXECUTIVE, NIGERIAN AIRPORTS AUTHORITY (N.A.A.) (F.A.A.N.)

Alhaji Ahmed Tijani, appointed Managing Director in 1978 and served until 1985.

NIGERIA'S 1ST RAILWAY LINE

From Lagos to Ibadan. Construction commenced in 1898, and was completed in 1900.

NIGERIA'S 1ST RAIL/TRAIN DISASTER

The Lalupon train disaster, which occurred at about 02.25 hours on Sunday, September 29, 1957, at Mile 138 between Lalupon and Odo-Ona stations in (then) Western Region. Sixty-six people died, 104 were injured, and several coaches were damaged. The UP to Kano Limited train had left Lagos Terminus on Saturday, September 28, 1957. It was travelling at an estimated 50 kph when the accident, said to have been caused by the washing off of rail tracks, occurred.

Nigeria's 2nd rail disaster was the Langalanga derailment, which occurred at Mile 378 on the Eastern line from Port Harcourt on February 16, 1970, and in which at least 100 people died.

1ST INDIGENOUS CHAIRMAN, NIGERIAN RAILWAY CORPORATION (N.R.C.)

Dr Okechukwu Ikejiani, appointed September 1960, succeeding the 1st Chairman, Sir Clifford Dove, an expatriate who served from April 1955. Although the NRC was established as a statutory body on October 1, 1955, through an Act which thus transferred the business, assets and liabilities of the corporation to the new body, the Nigerian Railways traces its inception to 1898, from which time it was run and managed as a government undertaking.

1ST INDIGENOUS GENERAL MANAGER/CHIEF EXECUTIVE, NIGERIAN RAILWAY CORPORATION (N.R.C.)

Mr Joseph C. Egbuna, who took over from the 1st expatriate General Manager, Sir Clifford Dove, who had served from April 1955 to July 1961.

NIGERIA'S 1ST SWITCH TO RIGHT-HAND DRIVE

On Sunday April 2, 1972. This was in response to a major traffic reform ordered by the Federal Government. It followed 24 months of preparation. The move was aimed at bringing Nigeria in line with other African and world countries, most of which drive on the right. Britain, and many former British colonies, as well as Japan and some other countries, are exceptions.

1ST DAY OF THE LAGOS-CITY TRAFFIC SYSTEM (ODD-AND-EVEN) CHANGE

January 5, 1977. The Lagos State government edict, which placed all car registration numbers into two categories – odd and even – kicked off on that day.

Cars with registration numbers beginning with odd figures plied major designated Lagos streets only on Mondays, Wednesdays and Fridays, while those with registration numbers plied even on Tuesdays and Thursdays. Saturdays and Sundays were free for all. Commercial vehicles (taxi cabs and buses) were exempted from the odd/even rule.

NIGERIA'S 1ST MOTOR-CAR ASSEMBLY PLANT

Volkswagen Assembly Plant at Ojo, Lagos State, commissioned by then Head of State General Yakubu Gowon, on March 21, 1975.

See also *entry under: INDUSTRY, SCIENCE AND TECHNOLOGY*

1ST 'MADE-IN-NIGERIA' MOTOR-CAR PISTONS

Developed and manufactured in December 1986 by research scientists from the Anambra State University of Technology (ASUTECH), Enugu.

See also entry under: *INDUSTRY, SCIENCE AND TECHNOLOGY.*

1ST CHAIRMAN, NIGERIAN NATIONAL SHIPPING LINES (N.N.S.L.)

Sir Louis Odumegwu Ojukwu, appointed in 1960. Then known as Nigerian Shipping Lines, it was incorporated in 1959 to carry a considerable percentage of cargoes generated by the nation's economy.

Sir Louis Ojukwu was born in Nnewi, Anambra State, in 1909. After schooling, he joined the Produce Inspection Service in 1928 as Produce Examiner. Later joined John Holt Company, but resigned in 1934 to start his private transport business. Entered politics in 1951 on the platform of the NCNC. Appointments held included: Chairman, Nigerian Cement Co., Nkalagu; Chairman, Eastern Nigeria Marketing Board; Chairman, African Continental Bank. Was awarded the Queen Elizabeth II Coronation Medal (1953); knighted in 1960; conferred honorary LLD, University of Nigeria, Nsukka, 1963. Died September 13, 1966.

Father of Chief Emeka Odumegwu Ojukwu, *Ikemba* of Nnewi, 1st Military Governor, (defunct) Eastern Nigeria, and Head of State of (defunct) Republic of Biafra.

NIGERIA'S 1ST WARSHIP

NNS Obuma (formerly *NNS Nigeria),* built and acquired in 1965.

See also entry under: *ARMED FORCES.*

NIGERIA'S 1ST EXTERNAL COMMUNICATIONS SERVICE

Began on September 4, 1886, when the African Direct Telegraph (ADT) Co. Ltd opened the first overseas public telegraph service, which linked Lagos by subterranean cable with the outside world. The cables of that company were laid along the west coast of Lagos, linking Lagos to Brass and Bonny eastward and Accra (Ghana), Freetown (Sierra Leone) and Bathurst (the Gambia) westward to Europe.

The Nigerian External Telecommunications Ltd (NET) came into operation on January 1, 1963. By January 1985, NET and the Posts and Telegraphs (P&T) were merged into Nigerian Telecommunications Ltd (NITEL).

NIGERIA'S 1ST SATELLITE COMMUNICATIONS EARTH STATION

At Lanlate in Oyo State. The £1.8m (N14m) contract for the construction of the satellite communications earth station was signed between the Federal Government and General Telephone and Electronics International of America on February 3, 1970.

The 2nd earth station at Kujama, Kaduna State, was commissioned by then President, Alhaji Shehu Shagari on May 24, 1983.

NIGERIA'S 1ST INTERNAL TELEPHONE LINK

Established in 1893 when Lagos became linked to Ilorin and Jebba by telegraphs. The system consisted of a wire-earth-return-telegraphy-circuit, constructed on wooden poles, by the Public Works Department (PWD). By 1903 a network of telegraph system had been set up linking several points of the then Southern and Northern provinces of the country. The Posts and Telegraphs (P&T) took over from the PWD in March 1907.

1ST AFRICAN COUNTRY TO HAVE DIRECT TELEPHONE LINK WITH NIGERIA

Dahomey (now Republic of Benin), from August 7, 1962.

NIGERIA'S 1ST MINISTER OF COMMUNICATIONS

Chief Arthur Edward Prest, from 1951 to 1954.

See also entry under: *POLITICS AND GOVERNMENT – MINISTERS.*

17 WOMEN

1ST WOMEN'S UPRISING (RIOT) IN NIGERIA

The Aba Women's Riot of 1929.

See entry under: *LABOUR.*

1ST NIGERIAN FEMALE TO BAG THE 'INTERNATIONAL RECOGNITION AWARD'

Maryam Babangida, who bagged the prestigious award for 1988.

See also: *1st Nigerian to receive the International Recognition Award,* ***entry under:*** *AWARDS.*

NIGERIA'S 1ST FEMALE LEGISLATOR

Mrs Oyinkan Morenike Abayomi, elected into the Lagos City Council in 1940.

See entry under: *POLITICS AND GOVERNMENT – GENERAL.*

1ST NIGERIAN FEMALE DEPUTY MAYOR IN BRITAIN

Mrs Janet O. Adegoke (née Akinbunmi), elected Deputy Mayor of the Borough of Hammersmith and Fulham in London on May 20, 1987.

See entry under: *POLITICS AND GOVERNMENT – GENERAL.*

NIGERIA'S 1ST FEMALE CIVIL RIGHTS LEADER

Mrs Funmilayo Ransome-Kuti, in the 1940s.

See entry under: *POLITICS AND GOVERNMENT – GENERAL.*

NIGERIA'S 1ST FEMALE POLITICAL PARTY LEADER

Madam Adunni Oluwole, founder and leader of Nigeria's first known political party, Commoners Liberal Peoples Party (CLPP).

See entry under: *POLITICS AND GOVERNMENT – GENERAL.*

NIGERIA'S 1ST FEMALE STATE GOVERNOR

Dame Virginia Ngozi Etiaba, sworn in as governor of Anambra State on November 3, 2006, replacing then Governor Peter Obi, who was impeached. Served for only three months until February 9, 2007, when Peter Obi was re-instated following his appeal up to the Court of Appeal.

For biodata, see: *POLITICS AND GOVERNMENT – GOVERNORS/PREMIERS.*

NIGERIA'S 1ST FEMALE SENATOR

Mrs Wuraola Esan, elected Senator of the Federal Republic with effect from October 1960.

See entry under: *POLITICS AND GOVERNMENT – GENERAL.*

NIGERIA'S 1ST FEMALE FEDERAL CABINET MINISTERS

Chief (Mrs) Adenike Ebun Oyagbola and Chief (Mrs) Janet Adefenwa Akinrinade, both so appointed in October 1979.

See entry under: *POLITICS AND GOVERNMENT – MINISTERS.*

NIGERIA'S 1ST FEMALE CIVIL COMMISSIONER

Dora Mauda Miller, appointed Commissioner for Health and Social Welfare in (defunct) North-Central State from May 1967 to 1973, under Governor Brigadier Abba Kyari.

Born in Zaria in 1933; attended Nigerian College of Arts, Science and Technology, Zaria; Rolle College, England, 1960. Was teacher, at Holy

Trinity School, Kano; later Principal, Girls' Secondary School, Minna, Niger State, at the time of her appointment as Commissioner in 1967.

1ST FEMALE IGBO CIVIL COMMISSIONER

Mrs Flora Nwanzuruahu Nkeiru Nwakuche (née Nwapa), appointed Honourable Commissioner for Health and Social Welfare, (defunct) East Central State from 1970 to 1971. Later assigned Ministry of Lands, Survey and Urban Development, 1971-74; Ministry of Establishments, 1974 to July 1975.

From Oguta, Imo State; attended Archdeacon Crowther Memorial Girls' School, Elelenwa, 1945-46; CMS Girls' School, Lagos, 1949-50; University College, Ibadan, 1953-57; University of Edinburgh, Scotland, 1957-58. Positions held prior to her appointment as Commissioner include: Women's Education Officer, 1958-62; Assistant Registrar (Public Relations), University of Lagos, Lagos, 1962-67; Member, Governing Council, University of Ilorin. Conferred Officer of the Order of the Niger (OON); Merit Award for Authorship and Publishing; Distinguished Alumni Award, University of Ibadan. A prolific and celebrated writer of children's books.

1ST FEMALE CIVIL COMMISIONER, AKWA-IBOM STATE

Mrs Affiong Monday Abasi-Attai, appointed Commissioner for Education in the newly-created Akwa-Ibom State and sworn in October 7, 1987. Prior to the creation of the State, she was Commissioner for Education, Cross River State. Attended Queen's College Yaba, Lagos, 1960-62. Principal, Federal Government Girls' College, Calabar at time of her appointment.

1ST FEMALE CIVII COMMISSIONER , BAUCHI STATE

Hanatu Ibrahim Tejuoso, Bauchi State Commissioner for Home Affairs and Information from 1981 to 1983. Later Commissioner for Social Welfare, Youths, Sports and Culture, October to December 1983.

1ST FEMALE CIVIL COMMISSIONER, BENUE STATE

Elizabeth Afadzwana Ivase, Benue State Commissioner for Special Duties and Parastatals from 1979 to 1981. Thereafter, appointed Federal Minister in Shehu Shagari's government, 1981.

Born on August 8, 1936 in Gboko, Benue State; attended Institute of Education, Ahmadu Bello University, 1973-74; University of Cardiff, Wales, UK, 1975-77. Was Chief Education Officer in Gboko at time of her appointment as Commissioner.

1ST FEMALE CIVIL COMMISSIONER, BORNO STATE

Mrs Hamro Imam, appointed Commissioner in Borno State cabinet by Governor Alhaji Mohammed Goni on November 19, 1979.

Mrs Imam, 32 years old at time of her appointment, hails from Maiduguri, Borno State; graduated Bachelor of Arts from Abdulahi Bayero College (now Bayero University, Kano).

1ST FEMALE CIVIL COMMISSIONER , IMO STATE

Mrs Rose Uregbulam Mezu, appointed Commissioner (Governor's Office, with responsibility for Social Welfare and Special Projects) in October 1979. The Division was later upgraded to the status of a full Ministry, in 1981. She served until 1983.

Born on November 12, 1947, in Lagos, she hails from Emekuku, Imo State; attended Holy Rosary Secondary School, Port Harcourt, 1961-65; Queen of the Rosary College, Onitsha, 1966-67; University de Sorbonne, Paris, France, 1968; State University of New York at Buffalo, USA, 1969-72, acquiring BA (French), 1970, and MA (French), 1972. One-time Principal, Emekuku Girls' Secondary School, 1976-81, before her appointment as Commissioner.

1ST FEMALE CIVIL COMMISSIONER, KWARA STATE

Alice Elsie Folayan, appointed Commissioner for Housing and Environment, October 1979 to 1981, in Governor Adamu Atta's administration. Later assigned the portfolio of Social Welfare Youths, Sports and Culture, 1981 to September 1983.

1ST FEMALE CIVIL COMMISSIONER IN NIGER STATE

Mrs Amina I. Ahmed, appointed Commissioner for Education from March 1984 to August 1987, when she resigned.

1ST FEMALE CIVIL COMMISSIONER, ONDO STATE

Chief (Mrs) Omobolaji Osomo, appointed Commissioner for Trade, Industry and Co-operatives from 1979 to 1983, under Governor Michael Ajasin's administration.

1ST FEMALE CIVIL COMMISSIONER, OYO STATE

Ruth Ogunjimi, appointed Commissioner for Health from 1984 to 1985.

1ST FEMALE CIVIL COMMISSIONER, PLATEAU STATE

Mrs Kathryn H. Hoomkwap, appointed Commissioner for Health from 1979 to 1983, in Governor Solomon Lar's administration.

1ST FEMALE CIVIL COMMISSIONER, RIVERS STATE

Mrs Ingor Ogan, appointed Commissioner for Information, Social Welfare, Youth, Sports and Culture in 1984, Deployed in May 1985 to Health, serving to September 1985.

1ST FEMALE SOLE ADMINISTRATOR, BAUCHI STATE

Mrs Zainab Ibrahim, appointed Sole Administrator and Chairman of Alkaleri Local Government Area of Bauchi State in October 1984.

Born in 1944 in Biliri in Bauchi State, she was School Principal at Kalturigo Women Teachers' College prior to her appointment.

1ST NIGERIAN FEMALE SECRETARY TO GOVERNMENT AND HEAD OF SERVICE

Mrs Tejumade Alakija, appointed Secretary to Government/Head of Service of Oyo State from 1979 to 1983.

NIGERIA'S 1ST FEMALE PERMANENT SECRETARY

Mrs Felicia Ighodalo, whose appointment as Permanent Secretary in (defunct) Western State Civil Service was announced on April 12, 1968.

NIGERIA'S 1ST FEMALE VICE-CHANCELLOR

Prof. (Mrs) Grace Awani Alele-Williams, appointed Vice Chancellor, University of Benin, on October 4, 1985.

***See also entry under:** EDUCATION – GENERAL.*

NIGERIA'S 1ST FEMALE POLYTECHNIC RECTOR

Dr (Mrs) Humulhairi Anjorin, Rector, Lagos State Polytechnic, from October 2, 1985.

***See also entry under:** EDUCATION – GENERAL.*

1ST NIGERIAN FEMALE UNIVERSITY LECTURER

Mrs (later Prof.) Bolanle Alake Awe (née Fajamibola), appointed Lecturer in the Department of History, University College, Ibadan (University of Ibadan), in 1960.

***For further details, see entry under:** EDUCATION – GENERAL.*

1ST NIGERIAN FEMALE PRESIDENT, SCIENCE ASSOCIATION OF NIGERIA

Dr (Mrs) Yejide O. Kehinde Osikanlu, President from 1985 to 1988. She holds a doctorate degree in agricultural sciences and served with the Institute of Agricultural Research and Training, Ibadan.

1ST NIGERIAN FEMALE MEDICAL DOCTOR

Dr (Mrs) Elizabeth Abimbola Awoliyi (née Akerele), who qualified in 1937.

For biodata, see entry under: *MEDICINE.*

1ST NIGERIAN FEMALE DENTAL SURGEON

Dr (Mrs) Grace A. Guobadia (née Pepple) who obtained the qualifying degree of LSD from the University of Durham.

Born in Bonny, Rivers State, but married into Edo State, she attended Queen's College, Lagos; Norwich City College; King's College, University of Durham; Sutherland Dental School, Newcastle-upon-Tyne, England. Holds the Foundation Fellowship of the Nigerian Medical Council (FMCGDS). Had been a government dental surgeon in old Western Nigeria, rising to Senior Dental Surgeon. Member, Governing Council, University of Ilorin, 1978-82, and trustee, Nigerian Dental Association.

1ST NIGERIAN FEMALE PRESIDENT, NIGERIAN MEDICAL ASSOCIATION (N.M.A.)

Dr (Mrs) T. A. Abiola-Oshodi, so elected at the 1988 Annual General Meeting of the NMA held in Owerri on July 9, 1988. NMA has been in existence since 1960.

Aged 55 at time of her appointment, Mrs Abiola Oshodi was Medical Director, Abiola Memorial Hospital, Yemetu, Ibadan. She had been Chairperson, Oyo State chapter of the NMA, 1983-86, and was detained in her official capacity during the 1983 proscription of the NMA by the Buhari/Idiagbon regime.

1ST NIGERIAN FEMALE LAWYER

Mrs Aduke R. Alakija. Enrolled as a lawyer on May 13, 1946, and called to the Bar, July 3, 1946.

See entry under: *LAW.*

1ST FEMALE LAWYER FROM BAUCHI STATE

Hajia Zainab Ali, graduated in law in June 1975 from Ahmadu Bello University, Zaria, and called to the Bar in July, 1976.

From Bauchi State, she was born in 1950 and attended Queen's School, Ilorin; Ahmadu Bello University, Zaria. Was Chief Magistrate, Kaduna State, 1982-85, before her appointment into Bauchi State High Court as Chief Registrar, 1986.

1ST FEMALE HIGH COURT JUDGE, LAGOS STATE

Justice (Mrs) Roseline Ajoke Omotoso, so appointed on March 6, 1978. Served as Chairman, Tribunal on Recovery of Public Property.

1ST FEMALE HIGH COURT JUDGE, OGUN STATE

Mrs Titilola Mabogunje (née Ogunmekan), so appointed on March 15, 1981. Formerly Deputy Registrar of Ogun State High Court.

1ST FEMALE HIGH COURT JUDGE, OYO STATE

Justice (Mrs) Atinuke Omobonike Ige (née Oloko), so appointed on June 1, 1977.

Born on April 4, 1932 in Ibadan, Oyo State, she attended CMS Grammar School, Lagos, 1945-50; University College, Ibadan, 1952-58; Council of Legal Education, London, 1959. Called to the Bar (Lincoln's Inn), London, May 1959. Prior to her appointment as High Court Judge, Mrs Ige had been Magistrate, 1962, Senior Magistrate 1966-69, Chief Magistrate, 1972-75, and Deputy, later Chief, Registrar, High Court, 1976-77. Married to 1st (civilian) Executive Governor of Oyo State, Chief Bola Ige.

1ST FEMALE HIGH COURT JUDGE, SOKOTO STATE

Justice Hajiya Aisha Inuwa Anka, so appointed in September 1987 by State Governor, Col. Mohammadu Daku, Before her appointment, she was Sokoto Chief Magistrate.

Married to Alhaji Muhammadu Inuwa Anka, Sokoto State Commissioner for Commerce, Industries and Cooperatives.

1ST FEMALE ATTORNEY-GENERAL/COMMISSIONER FOR JUSTICE, ANAMBRA STATE

Mrs Victoria Uzoamaka Onejeme, from February to August 1977.

For biodata, see: *Nigeria's 1st Female Attorney-General,* ***entry under:*** *LAW.*

1ST FEMALE ATTORNEY GENERAL AND COMMISSIONER FOR JUSTICE, KADUNA STATE

Mrs (later Justice) Hansine Napwaniyo Donli (née Aleyideino), appointed Attorney-General and Commissioner for Justice of Kaduna State on December 28, 1984.

Born in Numan, Taraba State; educated at Ahaadu Bello University, Zaria, graduated LLB in 1973. Was called to the Bar in 1974. After a brief career as State Counsel, she transferred to the Judiciary in 1977 as Senior Magistrate, rising to Chief Magistrate I, 1982, until her appointment as Attorney-General. Appointed Judge, High Court of Justice, Kaduna State, in 1987.

1ST NIGERIAN FEMALE VICE-PRESIDENT, NIGERIAN BAR ASSOCIATION (N.B.A.)

Mrs Priscilla O. Kuye, so elected in 1987. Before her elevation, Mrs Kuye had served the Lagos Branch of the NBA in various capacities.

From Ikija, Ijebu, in Ogun State; attended St Anne's College and St Theresa's College, both in Ibadan, before proceeding to the University of London, where she bagged a BSc degree in Law in 1966. On her return to Nigeria, she set up her own private practice in 1970.

1ST NIGERIAN FEMALE LAW PROFESSOR

Mrs Jadesola Akande, appointed Professor of Law by the Lagos State University in 1984.

A graduate of the University of London, Mrs Akande was called to the Bar in 1964. After brief service with the Western State Public Service Commission (1964-65), she joined the Faculty of Law, University of Lagos, as Assistant Lecturer, 1965. She later bagged a Master's degree in Law (Unilag, 1967) and a PhD (University of London).

Appointed Professor and Dean, Faculty of Law, Lagos State University; Member, Constitution Review Committee (CRC), 1989; Former President, Female Lawyers' Association of Nigeria (FIDA).

NIGERIA'S 1ST FEMALE PROFESSOR OF MEDICINE

Prof. (Mrs) Oyinade Olurin (née Odutola), appointed professor of Ophtalmology in 1976 by the College of Medicine, University of Ibadan, Ibadan.

Born in Ijebu-Ode, Ogun State, on February 2, 1934, into the well- known millionaire industrialist/philanthropic Odutola family, she had her early education at CMS Girls' School, Lagos, from 1945 before proceeding to the UK for her A-levels and then medical training in the University of Bristol Medical School, 1953-59, bagging MBChB (1959), Master's (ChM), 1975. On return to Nigeria, she took up appointment at the University College Hospital, Ibadan, from where she returned to England for her specialisation in ophthalmology at Moorfields Eye Hospital, Institute of Ophthalmology, London. From Lecturer, she rose to Professor in 1976, becoming the first female so appointed

Also: *Nigeria's 1st female ophthalmologist.*

1ST FEMALE MANAGER OF BOOTS COMPANY (NIG.) LTD

Mrs Bose Coker, whose appointment as Consumer Products Manager was announced in the *National Concord* of Saturday, October 22, 1988. This is the highest post so far occupied by a woman since the company was established.

Mrs Coker holds an MSc degree (Marketing) from the University of Surrey, England. Prior to joining Boots, she had worked at Insight Communications Ltd, Lagos, and also as Sales Executive with Communications Associate (Nig.) Ltd, Lagos.

1ST NIGERIAN FEMALE BANK CHAIRMAN

Chief (Mrs) Bolajoko Kuforiji-Olubi, appointed Chairman, United Bank for Africa (UBA) in November 1984.

See entry under: *FINANCE, BANKING AND INSURANCE.*

NIGERIA'S 1ST FEMALE ACCOUNTANT-GENERAL

Mrs Victoria O. Eronini (née Okeke), appointed Accountant-General of Imo State from 1976 to 1981.

See entry under: *FINANCE, BANKING AND INSURANCE.*

1ST NIGERIAN FEMALE NEWSPAPER MANAGING DIRECTOR (C.E.O.)

Dr (Mrs) Hamidat Doyinsola Abiola (née Aboaba), appointed Managing Director (Chief Executive) of the Concord Press Nigeria Ltd on October 6, 1985.

See entry under: *MASS MEDIA – NEWSPAPERS.*

1ST NIGERIAN FEMALE MANAGING DIRECTOR, WORLD BANK

Dr Ngozi Okonjo-Iweala, appointed Managing Director (Operations) in 2007, number 2 position in the apex global development finance institution.

For biodata, see: *1st Nigerian MD, World Bank,* ***entry under:*** *FINANCE, BANKING AND INSURANCE.*

Ngozi Okonjo-Iweala, Managing Director (Operations) at the World Bank from 2007 (see above and page 88).

PHOTOGRAPH: ASKSIMONRESOURCES (2016, CC-BY-SA 4.0).

1ST NIGERIAN FEMALE (LICENSED) STOCK-BROKER

Dr (Mrs) Ndi Okereke-Onyiuke.

See entry under: *FINANCE, BANKING AND INSURANCE.*

1ST FEMALE EDITOR, *SUNDAY TIMES* NEWSPAPER

Miss Adaora Ulasi, appointed editor from November 7, 1954 to early 1958, when she resigned.

See entry under: *MASS MEDIA – NEWSPAPERS.*

1ST FEMALE EDITOR , *NEW NIGERIAN NEWSPAPER*

Hajia Bilkisu Yusuf, so appointed on September 9, 1987.

See entry under: *MASS MEDIA – NEWSPAPERS.*

1ST NIGERIAN FEMALE FELLOW, NIGERIAN INSTITUTE OF PUBLIC RELATIONS (N.I.P.R.)

Mrs Patricia Love Uloho-Sokoh, whose elevation from the status of Member to that of Fellow of the Institute was announced at the Institute's biennial general meeting held in Horin, Kwara State, effective July 21 1988.

A graduate of English, Mrs Sokoh trained at Watford College of Technology, England. She started her public relations career at the New Nigeria Bank Ltd in 1976, and rose to be Public Relations Manager in 1980, before retiring in 1984. She was recalled early in 1988 to head the newly-created Corporate Affairs Department of New Nigeria Bank Ltd. Has served the NIPR in various capacities including 1st Vice-President; 1st female Chairman.

1ST WOMEN CONFERRED NATIONAL HONOURS

Mrs Winifred Ayodele McEwen and Mrs Lucy Hauwa Saidu, who in 1977 were conferred Member of the Order of the Federal Republic (MFR) and Member of the Order of the Niger (MON) respectively.

1ST FEMALE 'NATIONAL MERIT' AWARD RECIPIENT

Hajiya Ladi Kudi, recipient of the award in 1982 for her outstanding skill in pottery. Hajiya Ladi was a joint recipient for that year with Prof. Solomon Adebayo Oladele Babalola.

1ST NIGERIAN FEMALE 'DISTINGUISHED AUTHOR AWARD' RECIPIENT

Dr (Mrs) Tess Osonye-Akaeke Onwueme, for the year 1987. The presentation ceremony was held on February 2, 1988.

See entry under: *ARTS AND CULTURE.*

1ST FEMALE MANAGEMENT STAFF OF NIGERIAN BROADCASTING CORPORATION (N.B.C.)

Mrs Eno Irukwu, by virtue of her appointment as Controller, NBC, December 1972. Later promoted to Director.

See entry under: *MASS MEDIA – BROADCASTING.*

1ST NIGERIAN FEMALE TELEVISION PRESENTER

Anike Kuforiji (later Mrs Anike Agbaje-Williams), on the inaugural night (October 31, 1959), WNTV, Ibadan transmission as Nigeria's (Black Africa's) 1st television station.

For further details, see entry under: *MASS MEDIA – BROADCASTING.*

1ST NIGERIAN FEMALE LIBRARIAN

Mrs Ekei Essien Oku, who obtained the Associateship of the Library Association (London) (ALA) in 1953, thus qualifying as Chartered Librarian.

See entry under: *LIBRARY SCIENCE.*

1ST NIGERIAN FEMALE UNIVERSITY LIBRARIAN

Mrs Tinuade Olabisi Odeinde, appointed University Librarian, University of Ibadan, in 1972.

See entry under: *LIBRARY SCIENCE.*

1ST NIGERIAN FEMALE COMMERCIAL PILOT

Captain Chinyere Onyelucheya (later Mrs Kalu), who obtained her commercial pilot's licence on May 20, 1981, whereupon she operated her maiden flight into Murtala Muhammed Airport, Ikeja, amid cheers from hundreds of spectators. Prior to that, she had obtained her private pilot's licence on graduation from NCAT, Zaria, in 1978.

From Ukwa, Abia State, Chiyere had attended Anglican Girls' Grammar school, Yaba, Lagos, before going into aviation schools. On qualifying as private pilot, she subsequently undertook several additional aviation and transport courses in the UK and USA, leading to her commercial licence, 1981. Later appointed Rector and Chief Technical Instructor, NCAT, Zaria, under President Goodluck Jonathan, May 2011 to February 2014.

1ST NIGERIAN FEMALE GRADUATE ENGINEER

Grace Chijinwa Ezekoka (later Mrs Ezema), who graduated BSc Electrical Engineering from Ahmadu Bello University (ABU), Zaria, in June 1966.

From Isiokpo, Imo State, Mrs Ezema served in former NEPA (then ECN), 1966-78, before setting up a private construction firm: Guftane Eng. Co., Enugu.

1ST NIGERIAN FEMALE MARINE ENGINEERS

Mrs Yemisi Adedeji and Mrs O. Fasuji. Both graduated in Marine Engineering from the National Nautical College, Oron, Akwa-Ibom State, in September, 1987. Later boarded for the first time a Nigerian ship, *MV Binta Yar'Adua,* on their maiden cruise to serve for 18 months before proceeding to cruise Britain, for a final course on manning ships. All Nigeria's 24 ocean-going vessels were manned and operated by men.

1ST NIGERIAN FEMALE TO ATTAIN THE RANK OF ASSISTANT INSPECTOR-GENERAL OF POLICE (A.I.G.)

Mrs Cecilia Adebisi Ugowe, so appointed on November 1, 1986. Then the highest rank attained by a female indigene in the Nigeria Police Force.

From Ogbomosho, Oyo State, Mrs Ugowe joined the Force on September 1, 1957, as Cadet Sub-Inspector, after her secondary school education at Holy Child College, Ikoyi, Lagos. After a 12-month training at the Southern Police College, Ikeja, she was posted to the Juvenile Welfare Centre, Lagos, in 1958. Later promoted to Assistant Superintendent of Police (ASP), April 1, 1960; Deputy Superintendent of Police (DSP), 1965; Superintendent of Police, 1967; Chief Superintendent, 1969; Assistant Commissioner of Police (ACP), 1974; Deputy Commissioner of Police (DCP), 1980; Assistant Inspector-General (AIG), 1984.

Also: *1st female Nigerian Police Cadet, Assistant Commissioner of Police, Deputy Commissioner of Police and Commissioner of Police.*

1ST NIGERIAN FEMALE DEPUTY DIRECTOR OF PRISONS

Mrs S. U. Omu, appointed Deputy Director (Welfare, Inmate Training and Productivity) in January 1988. This was the highest rank attained by a female indigene in the Nigerian prison service. A Bendelite, she joined the Prisons service on July 1, 1966. Also became 1st female Deputy Controller General, Prisons.

1ST NIGERIAN FEMALE 'GRAMMY' AWARD WINNER

Helen Folasade Adu (Sade), in 1985 in the 'Best New Artist' category.

See: *1st Nigerian (African) 'Grammy' music award recipient,* **entry under:** *AWARDS.*

1ST NATION-WIDE 'MISS NIGERIA' BEAUTY QUEEN

Grace Tinuke Oyelude, crowned 'Miss Nigeria' in its maiden edition in 1957.

See entry under: *ARTS AND CULTURE.*

1ST NIGERIAN (CATHOLIC) REVEREND SISTER

Sister Gertrude Nwaturuocha, who made her first religious profession in 1940, along with three others.

See also entry under: *RELIGION.*

1ST NIGERIAN OLYMPIC GOLD MEDALIST

Chioma Ajunwa (Mrs Opara), who on August 2, 1996 won gold at the Atlanta, Georgia, USA, Olympic Games in the long jump event with a record-breaking 7.12-metre jump. The 1st Nigerian (and African) gold medallist in an individual sports event.

For biodata, see entry under: *SPORTS – GENERAL/ATHLETICS.*

Helen Folasade Adu (Sade; see pages 19 and 251), performing at Mannheim, Germany, in 2016.

PHOTOGRAPH BY THILO PARG (WIKIMEDIA COMMONS, CC-BY-SA 3.0).

18 MISCELLANEOUS

NIGERIA'S 1ST NATIONAL ANTHEM

'Nigeria, we Hail Thee', written by a Briton, Miss Williams, in 1960 to mark Nigeria's attainment of independence. The second (current) anthem came into being in 1978 under the Obasanjo regime, with the opening line 'Arise, O compatriots, Nigeria's call obey'.

1ST (COLONIAL) OCCUPATION OF NIGERIA

On August 6, 1861, when Lagos was first occupied, following the signing of the treaty between the British and Oba Akintoye's son, King Dosunmu, transferring absolute dominion and sovereignty of the port and island of Lagos to the British Government. From Lagos, the British soon spread their influence to lands around the island and into Yoruba-land.

1ST TIME BRITISH SHIPS SAILED UP THE RIVER NIGER TO THE CONFLUENCE OF RIVERS NIGER AND BENUE

In 1832 in two ships – *Quorra* and *Alburkah.*

NIGERIA'S 1ST NATION-WIDE POPULATION CENSUS

Conducted in 1911. However, separate arrangements were made to enumerate the Southern Provinces and the Northern Provinces. The census was organised from Government House, Zungeru, Niger State, then capital of the entire Northern Region.

Total Population: 15,966,380 indigenes, comprising Northern Provinces, 8,110,631 indigenes; Lagos Colony and Southern Protectorate, 7,855,749 Indigenes.

This Census was before the unification of the Northern and Southern Protectorates into Nigeria in 1914.

NIGERIA'S 1ST POST-INDEPENDENCE NATIONAL CENSUS

Was conducted in 1962, commencing on May 13, led by Alhaji Waziri Ibrahim, then Federal Minister of Economic Development. However the census figures were, on February 19, 1963, nullified by the then Prime Minister, Sir Abubakar Tafawa Balewa, following failure of all existing four regional governments to approve them, as stipulated by statutes. (One of the four regions had refused to approve the figures.) Consequently, a new national census was ordered, with Prime Minister Abubakar Balewa taking over direct responsibility, It began on November 5, 1963, and the final census figures were announced on August 29, 1964, with Nigeria's population fixed at 55,620,268.

NIGERIA'S 1ST GIANT

Nwokoro Onwubunta, popularly known as 'Giant Alakuku'. Born in Mballa Isuochi, Abia State in 1907, he grew to be over 10 feet (3.05 metres) tall. At age fifteen, he was already 8 feet (2.44 metres) tall. Served for a while as orderly to Mr James Swaby, then colonial District Officer for Awgu, Enugu State. Died about April 1959.

NIGERIA'S 1ST INTERNATIONAL TRADE FAIR

Held in Lagos from October 27 to November 18, 1962. Forty-one countries were officially represented, and 3,000 commercial firms took stands at the exhibition, declared open by Dr Nnamdi Azikiwe, then Governor-General of the Federation.

NIGERIA'S 1ST 'BETTER LIFE FOR RURAL DWELLERS' FAIR

Held at Tafawa Balewa Square, Lagos, from Wednesday September 14 to Sunday September 18, 1988.

The event was jointly organised by the 'Better Life for Rural Women' Committee and the Directorate for Food, Roads and Rural Infrastructure (DFRRI). The fair itself represented the first-year actualisation of the 'Better Life Workshop for Rural Women', held in Abuja in September 1987 under the initiative of Nigeria's First Lady, Mrs Maryam Babangida. The movement embraced all 304 local government areas of the federation and had as its primary objective the upliftment of working and living conditions of rural dwellers.

Niger State emerged overall winners at the six-day fair, at which all states of the Federation and the Federal Capital Territory, Abuja, displayed different farm products and wares produced by rural citizens.

NIGERIA'S 1ST HYDRO-ELECTRIC POWER STATION

The Kainji Dam, located near New Bussa, and commissioned on Feburary 15, 1969, by then Head of State General Yakubu Gowon.

Built at a cost of over US $200 million (N800m), the Kainji Dam project was to produce 960 megawatts of electricity initially. Feasibility studies and initial construction work began in the nation's first National Development Plan, 1955-60, under Prime Minister Abubakar Tafawa Balewa. Several foreign countries and international bodies subscribed to the project's execution.

DATE NIGERIA 1ST WENT METRIC

January 1, 1973. From that date, all equipment and products calibrated in imperial units also carried the metric conversion of such calibrations and markings. All imperial units of measurement ceased to be legal from one year later, January 1, 1974.

NIGERIA'S 1ST RECORDED ECLIPSE

On Tuesday, May 20, 1947. A total eclipse of the sun, it occurred about 4.00pm and lasted for over one hour in some parts of the country.

1ST BATCH OF NATIONAL YOUTH SERVICE CORPS (N.Y.S.C.) PARTICIPANTS

A group of 2,364 graduates from Nigerian universities throughout the then 12 states of the Federation commenced the NYSC programme on July 2, 1973, when the scheme was officially launched. The scheme came into effect through Decree No. 24 of May 22, 1973, although the announcement of the government's decision to introduce the scheme was made by then Head of State General Gowon on October 1, 1972.

Under the scheme, whose primary objective was to provide the physical, mental and spiritual environment in which the nation's educated youth could grow up to be worthy citizens, the Nigerian graduate (under 30 years of age) of a university or polytechnic, locally or abroad, is required to serve a compulsory 12-month period of quasi-military and public service in whatever part of the country he/she may have been posted to.

1ST DIRECTOR/CHIEF EXECUTIVE, NATIONAL YOUTH SERVICE CORPS (N.Y.S.C.)

Col. (Dr) Ahmadu A. Ali, so appointed on May 18, 1973; served until August 1976. Between January 1975 and August 1976, he combined this position with that of Federal Commissioner (Minister) of Education, which post he held from January 1975 to August 1978.

1ST NATIONAL YOUTH SERVICE CORPS (N.Y.S.C.) POSTHUMOUS AWARD RECIPIENT

Umar Shaaba, who was bestowed the NYSC award posthumously in 1985. Before his death he was a Fine Art graduate of Ahmadu Bello University, (ABU), Zaria.

NIGERIA'S 1ST ONE-STOREY BUILDING

At St Thomas's Anglican Church Vicarage, Badagry, near Lagos, completed on December 19, 1842, by Rev. Henry Townsend. A one-storey (two floors) building, near present-day Marina.

Converted into a tourist centre by the Anglican Diocese of Lagos, and opened at a ceremony performed by then Governor of Lagos State, Navy Captain Mike Akhigbe, on Saturday November 14, 1987. The tourist complex includes a chapel, a craft centre (where Nigerian works of arts and crafts are displayed), a library, a souvenir shop and a guest house.

NIGERIA'S 1ST SKYSCRAPER

'Cocoa House' Ibadan, Oyo State, the 22-storey high-rise building completed in 1960. Property of O'dua Investments (owned by the Oyo, Ogun and Ondo State governments).

NIGERIA'S 1ST PUBLIC EXECUTION

That of three condemned armed robbers, which took place at the Victoria Island Beach (Bar Beach) Lagos, on Saturday April 24, 1971.

Two of them, Sub-Lieutenant William Alders Oyazimo and Joseph Ilobo (trader), were jointly accused of violently robbing Alhaja Taibatu Opene of a record-player and loudspeaker, while the third, Babatunde Folorunsho, was charged with robbing (with arms) one Mr Alfred Marshall of a motor car. In his judgement of April 8 and 13, 1971, the trial judge Mr Ojomo found them guilty and sentenced them to death by firing squad.

The Robbery and Firearms Decree, which stipulated the death penalty for armed robbers, was promulgated in 1970.

1ST NIGERIAN PRESIDENT, WORLD FEDERATION OF THE RED CROSS

Mr Justice Joseph Adetunji Adefarasin, who occupied the seat from 1977 to 1981. The body co-ordinates Red Cross activities the world over.

Born on April 24, 1921, in Lagos, Adefarasin attended Cathedral Church School, Lagos; Igbobi College, Lagos; University of London. In private legal practice 1950-53, before joining the Bench as Magistrate in 1953, rising to Chief Judge of Lagos State, 1964.

NIGERIA'S 1ST PRINTING PRESS

Installed by the Presbyterian Mission on their arrival in Calabar in 1846.

1ST NIGERIAN COMMERCIAL PILOT

Robert Hayes, who obtained his commercial pilot's licence in 1955. He trained at the Air Science Training College, Hamble, Southampton, England. Born in 1935, Hayes started his career as pilot at the age of 20.

1ST NIGERIAN FEMALE COMMERCIAL PILOT

Miss Chinyere Onyelucheya (later Mrs Kalu), who received her commercial pilot's licence on May 20, 1981.

For further details, see entry under: *WOMEN.*

1ST VICTIM OF A LETTER/PARCEL BOMB IN NIGERIA

Mr Dele Giwa, who was blasted to death by a parcel bomb at his residence in Ikeja, Lagos, on Sunday, October 19, 1986, at the age of 39.

Dele was Founding Editor and Chief Executive of *Newswatch* magazine from 1984, when the paper was established, until his death.

Born 1947 in Ile-Ife, he hails from Ugbekpe-Ekperi, Edo State, where he was buried on Saturday, November 8, 1986.

NIGERIA'S 1ST GAME RESERVE

The Yankari Game Reserve in Bauchi State. Opened to the public on December 1, 1962, and covering approx. 207,800 hectares of open woodland, it rises from between 215 and 369 metres above sea level. It houses, in a pure natural setting, wild animals, including elephants (over 200), hippos, antelopes, buffaloes, different species of monkeys and birds, lions (over 50), giraffes and leopards. It has been transformed into a tourist centre by the Bauchi State government. It holds the largest number of wild animals in Africa.

Postage stamp depicting cheetahs in the Yankari Game Reserve (see page 258). The stamp dates from before Nigeria's conversion to decimal currency in 1973 (see page 84).

IMAGE BY YANGCHAO, COURTESY OF SHUTTERSTOCK.

INDEX

Page numbers in *italics* refer to illustrations.